RUNNERS & WALKERS

WESTON'S MARCH TO CHICAGO.

EHRGOTT, FORBRIGER & CO., LITH., CINCINNATI.

CLEVELAND,
Published by S. BRAINARD & SONS, 203 Superior St

4

RUNNERS & WALKERS

A Nineteenth Century Sports Chronicle

By John Cumming

REGNERY GATEWAY
CHICAGO

International Standard Book Number 0-89526-664-4
Library of Congress Catalog Number 80-54683
Manufactured in the United States of America

Preface

For primitive man running and walking were hardly regarded as sports, yet even he from time to time probably tested his speed against another human for recreation or for simply proving that he was the better man. As technology diminished the need for running and walking, these activities grew in popularity as recreational pastimes. Today, when the need for using one's legs is reduced to a minimum, the popularity of running and walking is greater than it has ever been.

Today thousands respond to the starter's pistol in marathon races throughout the land. Although the superior athlete is lionized for his record-breaking feats, the motivation for most participants is good health, both mental and physical, which is supposedly derived from the exercise.

Since the beginnings of organized competition, the motivation for participation in pedestrian competition has varied from generation to generation. Initially, monetary reward prompted the contestants to vie for honors; and the opportunity to wager on the outcome of the contest stimulated the interest of the spectators. Athletic competition, almost entirely, during the first half of the nineteenth century was professional, attracting for the most part, participants from the low income immigrant groups who benefited from the money won and, even more significantly, from the social mobility which recognition of success afforded.

Professionalism was abhorrent to the upper classes in America, not only for the corruption and gambling which were attached to the sport, but also for the rough element of the participants and those who patronized professional races. It was not until the post-Civil War years that successful efforts to provide competition for amateurs materialized. At first the amateur movement was an elitist device which fostered class distinction, but the urge to win soon broke down all barriers as the athletic clubs sought to enlist superior athletes from the lower classes. Inducements used to enlist athletes were often promises of employment in better jobs and career opportunities. Thus the amateur movement served as a vehicle for upward social mobility for many lower class athletes.

In a similar manner the development of inter-collegiate competition toward the close of the century made it possible for many young men from the lower income levels to acquire a college education and move into higher level positions in business and in the professions.

Organized athletic competition first got under way in the United States during the 1820's. Prior to this time competition was usually local and spontaneous in nature. In most respects, from the early professional meets to the amateur and inter-collegiate movements, athletic competition followed the patterns set across the sea in England. As the American athletes developed, heroism was attained in vanquishing an English opponent. Sports became an important facet of the national spirit.

Throughout the first half of the nineteenth century sports were ignored by most newspapers. If they acknowledged the existence of sports at all, it was to condemn them. There were exceptions such as the New York *Post* and the New York *Sun;* but the Detroit *Free Press* in one ten year period carried only three paragraphs about sports. In the 1830's *The American Turf Register* and the *Spirit of the Times*, the principal focus of both of which was on horseracing, nevertheless gave considerable attention to other sports activities. With the establishment of the *New York Clipper* in 1853 sports coverage was expanded substantially.

The Civil War which brought thousands of young men together from all parts of the country spread the interest in organized competition and accelerated the need for attention on the part of the newspapers. Sports columns were first introduced, then the sports page, and by the end of the century the sports section. In the post-war years the *National Police Gazette* turned its attention to sports and enlivened the scene with graphic illustrations. In nearly every section of the country special sports newspapers were published during the last quarter of the century. Sports competition had become an important part of national life.

The importance of sports in the history of the United States is just beginning to be assessed. Classes in sports history have been organized in colleges and universities, and scholarly journals have been started. The North American Society for Sports History annually attracts scholars from not only the United States and Canada for its conference but from Europe as well. Popular sports journals have become more sophisticated, and they are also paying more attention to history.

—

For assistance in locating and collecting illustrations for *Runners & Walkers*, the author is indebted to a number of people. John Kelley, Photoduplication Services, Library of Congress, made a special effort to provide copies of illustrations from the files of the *National Police Gazette*. Mr. Paul Mellon through his curator Mary Ann Thompson provided the excellent portrait of "Jackson, the American Deer." Georgia Bumgardner, Curator of Graphic Arts at the American Antiquarian Society and a long distance runner in her own right, lent enthusiastic assistance and advice. Kenneth Newman, Old Print Shop, provided the picture of Deerfoot and a lithograph of Edward Payson Weston. Patrick J. Noon, Yale Center for British Art, gave valuable advice which led to the procurement of several pictures. To these generous people the author is grateful.

Contents

America's First Champion

The Hoboken ferry shuttled back and forth across the river crowded with passengers en route to the New Jersey side. It was the morning of July 5, 1824, the day of the great running races at the Orchard in Hoboken.

The enterprising proprietors of the Hoboken ferry for some time had been advertising in the newspapers the races which they were sponsoring on their newly constructed track. Two races were scheduled, one at 220 yards and one at a half-mile. The entry fee for the shorter event was set at $3, and for the longer distance, $5. The contestants were to run the distance twice, with a brief rest between heats. The prize for the 220 was $50, and for the half-mile, $100. The winner of the $50 prize would not be eligible to compete for the $100 purse.

This was the beginning of what was promised to be a regular program of foot racing. Up until this time running as a sport in the United States had been essentially a neighborhood affair. Local champions won their laurels in spontaneous competition, often in settlement of a wager. Frequently the city streets or the village road served as a running course and a race around the court house square brought scores of spectators into the community from outlying areas. The contest may have originated in a tavern or the general store where one supporter may have voiced confidence in the athletic prowess of a friend, only to encounter disagreement from somebody else's friend. The dispute could only be settled with a race between the principals, accompanied by wagers and supported by a purse collected for incentive to the participants. From time to time a stranger from the next town appeared to issue a challenge to the local champion. Along the more densely populated East coast an athlete might go on tour from New England as far south as Baltimore, seeking contestants en route. Even so, the races were usually arranged on the spot, or with little advance notice, and seldom with any great fanfare or promotion. Occasionally, the sponsors of horse races, the only developed and organized sport in the country, would include as added attractions foot races, wrestling, cudgeling, and other entertainment. As the distances between towns were shortened by improved transportation, the opportunities for competition increased, and sports activities began to receive attention from the organizers and promoters. Thus the new steam ferry had brought the New Jersey shore closer to New York City.

In 1823 a race between the leading thoroughbred horses of the North and the South attracted 60,000 spectators to the Union Race Course at Long Island. If that many fans would attend a horse race, running races between humans might also be profitable. In England pedestrian contests had been sponsored with considerable success for some years. News of the exploits of the English athletes was being read with interest in this country.

The proprietors of the Hoboken ferry expected that their new track would be a popular attraction. Abram Van Boskerck, who was in charge of the racing program, invited prospective contestants to use the track for training. Constructed at a location known as the Orchard, the track was soft and uneven in spots. In addition, it was not level; in some places there were slight inclines.

On July 5, five men toed the mark in the 220-yard race, which was won by a young fellow from Long Island named Newton, who took both heats and the $50 purse. In the second contest a runner named Lawrence took the first heat, running the half-mile in 2 minutes and 19 seconds. However, he was outdistanced in the second heat by a man named Warren, identified as a "Frenchman," who captured the $100 purse. Because Lawrence had taken the first heat with ease, the betting was 5 to 1 on him to win. There were some heavy winnings that day.

Before the excitement of the races had subsided, challenges were being hurled about. Newton's winning of the fifty dollar prize prevented his running in the half-mile race. Now he demanded a chance to try his speed against either Warren or Lawrence.

Lawrence was anxious to have another crack at Warren; and to hasten that, he issued a challenge in the columns of the *New York Evening Post* on July 8. "Being desirous of testing in a more satisfactory manner, the 'speed' and 'bottom' of Warren, who took the $100 purse at Hoboken on the 5th inst. I offer to run him, two weeks from this date, from 200 yards to half a mile and repeat, for any sum from $100 to $500," he wrote.

At the same time Lawrence offered to race Newton at 150 yards on the following Thursday for $500.

Warren responded to Lawrence's challenge through a friend, who explained that Warren was not particularly anxious to run against Lawrence. The friend maintained in what appeared to be feigned modesty that Lawrence was probably the swifter runner and that he had just had an unlucky day. Warren might, however, face Lawrence if he felt disposed to take recreation at that time and if he was "at leisure at the hour of the race." It was really unimportant, concluded Warren's friend, for

he had no intention of making running his profession.

In the meantime the proprietors of the Hoboken ferry announced that they were offering a prize of $100 for the winner of a foot race which would take place at the Orchard on Monday, July 19, at 5:00 p.m. The distance would be a half-mile and repeat. Entrance fees of $5 would be received by Abram Van Boskerck at Hoboken.

In the *Evening Post* on July 12, Warren published a notice, informing the public that since his lack of enthusiasm for a race with Lawrence had been interpreted by some as an admission that he lacked confidence in his ability to win, he would disclaim any doubt by meeting Lawrence. He would race him in two heats of one mile for $1,000, or in two heats of a half-mile for $500. The race would take place on Monday, July 19, at 5:00 p.m. at Hoboken. With the confirmation of this match race, the proprietors of the ferry postponed their previously scheduled race until the following Thursday. It all had the appearance of a scheme for promoting interest in the contest between the rivals.

On the day of the race Warren and Lawrence ran close together over the course in the first half-mile heat; but Lawrence pulled away at the finish to win by ten yards in 2 minutes and 9 seconds. The length of the rest period between heats which had been agreed upon by the two candidates was thirty minutes. The judges, however, understood that the rest was to be limited to twenty minutes. When Lawrence had not put in an appearance at what the judges thought was post time, they waited several minutes, then gave the signal for Warren to start alone. At this point Lawrence was returning to the track. He protested, arguing that the agreed rest period was thirty minutes. With the consent of the contestants, the judges decided that the race should be re-scheduled for the following week. The contestants subsequently called the race off, however.

In the race sponsored by the proprietors of the Hoboken ferry on Thursday of that week there were five starters, but only two were worthy of notice, Newton and Lawrence. This contest for a $125 purse was to be run in three heats. Lawrence loafed through the first heat, obviously conserving his energy for the second and third heats. Newton won in 2 minutes, 14 seconds. In the second heat Lawrence took the lead at the start and was not headed throughout the race, winning over Newton by six feet. In the third heat Lawrence again jumped into the lead which he maintained for two thirds of the distance. Here Newton passed him and went on to win by fifty or sixty feet. The *Evening News* commented: "There were but few bets made, from the general impression that all was not right, and the knowing ones reaped but a slender harvest — all were shy."

In a postscript to the report on the race, the *Evening News* revealed that the judges, having learned that collusion existed between Lawrence and Newton, awarded the purse to Van Winkle, who had finished third in each of the three heats. The judges declared that all bets made upon the race were void. The *Evening News* concluded: "We are glad to learn that the proprietors of the Ferry have determined to have no more foot racing at Hoboken. We cannot help regretting that so manly a sport should be brought into disrepute by the disgraceful conduct of the competitors."

Thus ended the first attempt at organized athletic competition in the United States. Promotional efforts, though somewhat inept, were employed, and interest was generated. The collusion which brought an abrupt end to the sports promotion by the proprietors of the Hoboken ferry was a signal of the shadow which would be cast over professional competition throughout the century. Since betting was the primary motivating force in generating interest among the racing spectators, the temptation for collusion or throwing a race was too often greater than a human could resist. The professional runners of the period were from the lower income levels to whom a purse of $100 might equal a total year's income. The prospects of winning even more by losing was a temptation; the money was more attractive than the glory of winning. Horse racing was held essentially for improving the breed. Winning meant high fees for stud service and high prices for the offspring of a successful sire or dam. Then, too, the backers of horse racing were very wealthy people who could afford to be content with the win-

ner's purse. The backers of running races were from a less affluent class to whom the lure of winning wagers was paramount. This is not to say that there were not fixed horse races. Indeed, such practices became so common toward the middle of the nineteenth century that the sport fell into general disrepute; but the basic factors of the sport were strong enough to cause the backers to enact rules for supervision which would insure the survival of the sport.

The Hoboken experience did not pull the curtain down on all foot racing, but it was still to remain local and spontaneous for a few years longer. Had there been no collusion at Hoboken, the program might have developed into organized competition such as that which was flourishing in England.

Reports of contests which would hardly attract more than a few smiles of amusement today were reported in the nineteenth century with all seriousness. For example, the *New York Evening Post* related an athletic feat performed by one John Finch at Amity, New Jersey, which the Post presumed equaled or surpassed anything of the kind ever achieved. Finch's task: "One hundred eggs were placed in a direct line, three feet apart — a box was placed at one end of the line, and in forty-seven minutes, Mr. Finch took them up singly, and carried them one by one to the box and placed them carefully in it. He performed the feat with apparent ease, and it was the opinion of several gentlemen present, that he might have performed it in much less time."

A match race for $100 over ten miles was run in 1829 between Owen Atkins and John Boling in Pittsylania County, Virginia. Boling was tall, trim, and about twenty-one years of age. Atkins, thirty-six, enjoyed quite a reputation for speed and tenacity by those who had hunted with him. At the appointed time the runners set out on their long run, followed by thirty persons on horseback. After a few hundred yards, Atkins took the lead and soon left his opponent far behind. "By the best judges, it is believed that no man in Virginia is able to run ten miles with Atkins," wrote the Virginia reporter. The image of thirty horsemen trotting along with a lone runner evokes an interesting picture.

Since professional runners were all from the lower income classes, to go on tour meant walking great distances between cities, unless the athletes could secure backing from someone who would finance travel by stage or horseback. By the 1830's, however, the cities along the coast had grown to considerable size, aided largely by immigration. The crowds were now available for organized athletic entertainment. Furthermore, the various immigrant groups brought with them the interest and enthusiasm for athletic contests.

In June 1835 a running race was held at the Union Race Course on Long Island which decided what should be recognized as the first American champion. The sponsors had offered a large purse of $1,000, later increased to $1,300, for the runner who could cover ten miles within one hour. The size of the purse stimulated great interest among the sporting fans and attracted a stellar field.

On the day of the race as early as nine o'clock in the morning, many hundreds had already crossed the river to witness the great race. From early morning until nearly two o'clock in the afternoon, the road from Brooklyn to the Union Race Course was an unbroken line of carriages of all descriptions "from the humble sand cart to the splendid barouche and four." In many places carriages moved in a double line. By two o'clock the crowd was estimated at somewhere between 16,000 and 20,000 persons.

The day was bright and clear, but a strong wind was blowing, a factor which might impede the runners and prevent their accomplishing the goal of running the ten miles within one hour. Mr. Stevens, in charge of the race, considering the vast amount of money being wagered, decided to postpone the race. The uproar of protest quickly persuaded him to reverse his decision.

Isaac Downes was the general favorite in the betting. He was well known in the community for his running prowess; he had already run eight miles in the good time of forty-eight and a half minutes. He also enjoyed the advantage of having been trained by his father who was quite a runner himself, having at the age of thirty-nine run seventeen miles in one hour and forty-five minutes, doing the first twelve and a half miles in one hour and fifteen minutes.

In the field were nine runners: Charles Wall, 18 years of age, brewer by trade; Henry Sutton, 23, house-painter; George Glauer, 27, ropemaker; Isaac Downes, 27, basket-maker; John Mallard, 33, farmer; William Vermilyea, 22, shoemaker; Patrick Mahoney, 33, porter; Henry

Immigrant groups, particularly the Scots, brought with them to the United States a love for athletic competition which was an important part of their annual picnics and gatherings.

Stannard, 24, farmer; and John McCargy, 26, butcher. A black man, Francis Smith, from Virginia, appeared for the race but was not allowed to compete for the prize, since he had not entered before the deadline.

Attired in colorful running suits, the contestants approached the starting line. The betting was pretty even on whether a runner would cover the ten miles within an hour, but Downes remained the general favorite. He was dressed in a white shirt, white pantaloons with a blue stripe and a blue belt. He wore no shoes or stockings. Mallard, another favorite, came to the line, wearing blue calico, and also bare-footed. He slipped in the betting when it appeared that he was drunk. Stannard, the tallest man in the race at six feet one inch, was wearing a white shirt and black silk pantaloons. Sutton wore a yellow shirt and cap, buff breeches, white stockings and red slippers. Equally colorful was Glauer in white silk with a pink stripe and cap to match and pink slippers and red belt. Mahoney, the smallest man in the race at five feet six and 130 pounds wore a green gauze shirt, blue striped calico breeches, blue belt, white stockings, and black slippers.

At the signal to start, a blast from the trumpet, little Pat Mahoney darted into the lead, but nobody regarded him as a serious threat. He had done no training for the race. Working as a porter on Water Street, he pushed and pulled his cart all day long from dawn to dusk and had no time for training. Pat continued to lead throughout the first mile, which he finished in 5 minutes and 36 seconds. The rest of the field remained bunched together some distance behind. At six minute intervals a blast from the trumpet gave the spectators an indication of where the runners stood in their assault upon the time record. Pat was well into the first lap of his second mile when he passed the six minute mark. At the end of the second mile Pat was still leading, having covered it in 5 minutes and 45 seconds. This was creditable time for two miles but nobody believed that he could keep it up. The fast pace soon began to tell on the

The Scots at their annual reunions held a full program of athletic contests, including running events, jumping, and weight throwing.

little Irishman and he fell back to fifth position as Glauer went into the lead.

Glauer with a respectable reputation as a runner had a number of enthusiastic supporters. He had run the distance between New York and Harlem and return, twelve miles, in seventy minutes. It was reported that he had wagered nearly $300 that he would win the prize.

As Glauer moved into the lead, the favorite Downes pulled up into second position close behind. Vermilyea dropped out of the race. Having walked thirty-eight miles earlier in the week to be in time for the race, he had appeared tired and in ill health at the start. Following Downes were Stannard and Wall. Mahoney was now trailing in the rear. Glauer continued to lead throughout the third and fourth miles. After four miles, Mallard, Sutton, and Wall gave up.

Going into the fifth mile, Downes moved into the lead; but Glauer stayed close behind, followed by Stannard, McCargy, and Mahoney. Soon McCargy dropped out, leaving but four contestants. Downes trotted on, apparently in control of the race. In the sixth mile Stannard moved into second, Glauer and Mahoney trailing. Downes continued to lead throughout the fifth, sixth, and seventh miles.

In the eighth mile, Downes faltered, and Stannard moved into first position. Soon Downes dropped out, claiming that he had injured his foot. Stannard had carefully followed a pre-arranged plan. A rider on horseback trotted along by his side, shouting to him to hold back when he was running too fast and to speed up the pace when the schedule required it. At the end of six miles he paused to take a little brandy and water. At this point he was right on schedule in thirty-six minutes. For the last three miles of the race, the three survivors plodded on in the order of the finish, Stannard, Glauer, and Mahoney.

Stannard finished amid wild cheering which became even louder when it was evident that he had succeeded in covering the ten miles in twelve seconds under one hour, for the first American record. The trumpet blast coming twelve seconds after the finish could not be heard above the shouting. Glauer finished in one hour and twenty-seven seconds, trailed by Mahoney in sixty-one minutes and forty-five seconds.

Stannard was called to the stand to receive the award of $1,300, and he was invited to dine with the members of the Jockey Club. The club's president then announced that Glauer and Mahoney would each receive a purse of $200 for their performances.

For the next few years Henry Stannard enjoyed the recognition of champion, and his record would be a topic of conversation in sporting circles for nine years, when it would be surpassed as records usually are. Stannard was much in demand. A year later it was reported that he had collected purses in half of the states of the Union. Shortly after his Long Island victory, he was in Philadelphia for a mile run in three heats. Stannard won $400, top prize for giving a running lesson to the best that the Quaker City could offer. By the end of the year he had amassed a small fortune, enough for him to take a wife in 1836 and to purchase a resort at Killingsworth, Connecticut, which he named the Pedestrian Hotel.

His advertisements in the sporting journals promised visitors "everything that may contribute to their health, comfort, and happiness." In urging patronage for Stannard's hotel, *The Spirit of the Times*, the leading sports journal of the period wrote: "Go and spend a week with him — he's got the homeliest dog, the fastest horse, the prettiest wife, and the surest rifle in all Connecticut, and can run longer, dive

∞∞∞∞∞∞∞∞∞∞∞∞∞∞∞∞∞∞

One Monsieur Bouganville in visiting Detroit in 1757 when that village was a remote outpost of New France, told of the foot races between the French and the Pottawatami Indians which took place each spring. They created as much excitement in Detroit as the horse races generated in England, the visitor recorded. The race was a mile and a half on a course from the village of Detroit to the Pottawatami village and return. Betting was very spirited, the Indians offering furs and the Frenchmen merchandise. One Frenchman named Campau won so easily in previous races that he was no longer permitted to enter the competition.

∞∞∞∞∞∞∞∞∞∞∞∞∞∞∞∞∞∞

deeper, stay under longer and come out drier, than any man this side of where the sun rises." Henry Stannard had become the first athlete of note in the country and he was reaping the benefits of his fame.

Stannard's performance served as a stimulus for the sport. Running races were held at the Union Course, the Beacon Race Course at Hoboken, and at tracks throughout the country. Competition was not limited to distance running, as stars in sprinting and middle distances began to attract notice. Henry Perritt, a speedy Georgian, who beat all comers at fifty yards, was the pride of his state. Opponents came from afar to match their speed against Perritt. His race with John Day of Kentucky attracted national attention.

Professional running continued to be an occupation of the lower classes, although interest in the sport extended into the more affluent classes. One Anson Livingstone, a gentleman, walked fifty-four miles in twelve hours and three minutes. He had bet that he could walk fifty miles in twelve hours and fifty-four miles in fourteen hours, without taking food. Livingstone accomplished his feat on the turnpike in the village of Jamaica on Long Island. Commenting on the long walk, the *American Turf Register* wrote, "We believe it is the first time this or any comparable feat has been performed in this country, especially by a gentleman of leisure, and without any regular training."

Continued the *American Turf Register:* "We have reason to believe that some further matches will arise from this, and we rejoice that so innocent and manly an exercise, and one so conducive to health, should appear likely to gain favor among the youth of our city, with whom athletic and laborious sports have heretofore been rather at a discount."

Livingstone's performance added a measure of respectability to the sport of pedestrianism, much in the same manner that Captain Robert Barclay had done in England. Barclay, a gentleman, had set a number of records for walking great distances. His greatest record was set when he walked 1,000 miles in 1,000 successive hours. For years Captain Barclay was recognized on both sides of the Atlantic as the paramount athlete of the age. The fact that he was a gentleman added greatly to the popularity of pedestrian sports in England.

During the 1830's large numbers of immigrants were arriving at the Eastern seaboard cities, mostly from the British Isles, but with some from the continent as well. The immigrants brought with them a tradition for sports competition which they were not willing to abandon. Some, like the Scottish Highlanders, held annual meetings at which sports competition was the principal attraction.

In September of 1838 the Highland Society of New York held its games which were reported in *The Emigrant* and in *The Spirit of the Times*. The games started with "shinty," which the reporter explained was better known to Southerners as "hockie." The athletic contests described included tossing the caber, putting the stone, standing jump, throwing the hammer, and footraces. The newspaper descriptions of such events demonstrated a complete unfamiliarity with them. In telling of the putting of the stone, the predecessor of today's shot put, or a cousin to it, the reporter wrote, "The stone used for this purpose weighed 18 lbs., and the manner of discharging it, was to poise it on one hand above the shoulder, and push it away as far as possible." The winning distance was 28 feet.

The editor of *The Emmigrant* expressed his pleasure over such exercise. "We cannot conclude without re-iterating our satisfaction on perceiving the spirit with which these national sports were carried on; with similar pleasure we mark the progress of the English game of Cricket, and we shall ever rejoice to perceive Old Countrymen, from whatever section of the British empire they may be derived, cherishing the sports and exercises which are associated with the love of their country and their own people."

For the immigrant, sports meetings provided an opportunity for re-union, for meeting old friends, preserving customs that were a pleasant part of their backgrounds. As sports competition developed and became better organized, the immigrant youngster would find it an avenue to recognition and wealth. It would accelerate social mobility. This would be particularly true of the Irish immigrant, imported for common labor, often the victim of extreme poverty. Most entry lists for professional competition included a number of "Patlanders," as the Irish were called.

The proprietors of the Beacon Race Course at Hoboken announced in June 1838 that they were to hold a meeting that month with a varied list of events. It was announced that Stannard was entered and was in fine condition for the races. Within a few days of the races, it appeared that Stannard would have no challengers. The managers, unwilling to sponsor a meet without such a stellar attraction as Stannard, decided to postpone the meet until September. They announced that the postponement had been granted at the request of many gentlemen who would like to compete against Stannard, but were loath to do so without sufficient training.

In August the proprietors ran advertisements in the sporting journals and newspapers for a program of "Foot Racing and other Athletic Exercises." One thousand dollars in prizes would be offered. The meet would last two days.

The feature of the first day's activities was to be a mile race run in three heats, with a thirty minute rest period between heats, for a purse of $500. Also offered was a purse of $50 for the greatest distance walked in one hour; $25 for "the Highest Leap over a Bar;" and a purse of $25 for a 200-yard race. The attraction of the second day was a 2-mile race for a purse of $250. Other events and purses were $25 for the "farthest three jumps," $40 for a quarter mile race; $25 for the "farthest Pitch of a Bar;" and a $50 purse for a bag or sack race. The variety of events indicates that the influence of the Highland games was being felt.

On the day of the races it was announced that no runners had come forth to challenge Stannard, and since the star himself was ill, the races for the two large purses were cancelled. Peter Van Pelt of New York City won the 200 yard race; William Vermilyea won the walking race; Van Pelt came back to win the quarter mile; a Mr. Brown won the jumps; and Jeremiah Ryan took the purse for "sledge throwing." Samuel Clemens, an Indian from Syracuse, easily won the mile race which was run in three heats of a mile each.

Samuel Clemens was one of the first of a long line of Indian runners who would attract wide attention and fame during the nineteenth century. Tales of unusual feats of endurance and speed performed by Indian runners were published from time to time. In the minds of many the image created by James Fenimore Cooper in his novels prevailed. So great was the impression of the Indian's native ability as a runner, sponsors of races in the towns near Indian reservations set up separate races for Indians, excluding them from competition with white runners. This was particularly true in Canada, where Indian runners dominated the sports scene for many years.

One correspondent from the West wrote to *The Spirit of the Times* in 1835 to tell of an Indian who ran 100 miles in a day. That alone would have been quite an achievement, but this Indian was carrying a sixty pound bar of lead. Another correspondent told of Osage Indians running from sunrise to sunset covering distances of 60 to 75 miles. In relating the pedestrian skills of the Osage Indians to members of the Indian Commission, Mr. Chouteau, the fur-trader, sensing skepticism on their part, proposed a wager. An Indian was to carry a message to Fort Gibson 40 miles away at sunrise and return with the answer before night. Chouteau won the bet.

"Great ambition is felt to be acknowledged the best runner of the town and nation; and no exertion spared to attain the distinction," wrote the correspondent. Races between the best runners of Indian villages were often held. There were races between boys, girls, men, and women. Running to these Indians, the writer pointed out, was of the utmost importance because it was often the key to survival.

Long distance contests designed to test the ultimate limits of human endurance were frequently held in English sporting circles. Accounts of such contests reprinted in the sporting journals in the United States prompted pedestrians to attempt to match the exploits of their cousins across the sea.

Nicholas Low of New York City in February 1841 undertook to walk 200 miles in 200 hours. He would walk 1 mile before the end of the hour and another at the beginning of the next hour. He would thus have a period of an hour and a half for rest or sleep. Low was one of the athletes with "Esq." appended to his name, so he was not competing for money. "We are happy to see manly sports of this kind entered into with such spirit, by gentlemen of fortune, not professed pedestrians," commented *The Spirit of the Times*.

According to accounts, Low was "perfectly fresh" at the finish. His friend had no doubt that

CAPTAIN BARCLAY

he could have gone on for 500 miles. They were so impressed by the demonstration of endurance by Nicholas Low, Esq., that some expressed the belief that he might even equal Captain Robert Barclay's record.

Whenever any athlete excelled at any distance event, he was compared to Captain Barclay; and speculation as to whether he might be able to beat the Captain's record was voiced. Barclay's record of 1,000 miles in 1,000 hours was made in the year 1809; yet for sixty years after, the story of his great triumph was told and retold in the journals. Captain Barclay's system of training was printed in a number of sporting journals throughout the century; and the system was followed by many pedestrians. From time to time there were those who came forth to claim that they had equaled or surpassed Barclay's record, but the claims were generally greeted with skepticism or outright repudiation.

Captain Robert Barclay started his 1,000 mile walk on June 1, 1809, and completed the trial on July 12, forty-two days later. He walked in the rain, the heat, and wind, through day and night. By the time that he had reached the halfway point, walking was becoming painful. In the last week, the pain in Barclay's legs became so intense that he had to be helped to his feet to begin his walk. The first steps required all the strength and concentration that he could muster.

The course for the walk was one half mile out and return. Throughout the contest many people came to watch, and interest mounted each day as the contest progressed. Toward the end the crowd became so great that the half mile route had to be roped off so that Barclay would have room to walk. Every bed in every village and town for miles about was rented. The Dukes of Argyle and St. Albans, the Earls Grosvenor, Besborough, and Jersey; Lords Foley and Somerville; Sir John Lade and Sir Francis Standish were among the excited spectators on the final

Captain Robert Barclay, an English gentleman, enjoyed the reputation of premier athlete of the first half of the nineteenth century. He was best remembered for the astounding feat of having walked 1,000 miles in 1,000 consecutive hours

day. At fifteen minutes after three o'clock in the afternoon of July 12th, Captain Barclay started his one thousandth mile which he finished twenty-two minutes later amid the wild cheering of the immense crowd.

Captain Barclay became a national sports hero that day and his reputation extended abroad to other countries. Although Barclay had been winning races since that day in 1796 when at the age of fifteen he won a six mile walking race against a gentleman from London for 100 guineas, his great trial of strength and endurance made him a legendary figure in athletics. Up until that day on July 12, 1809, his record had been compared to that of Foster Powell, the celebrated pedestrian who had dominated the sports scene in the 1770's and 1780's. Henceforth Powell's record would no longer bear comparison with Barclay's. Engravings of Captain Barclay as a sports hero were sold and biographies of him were published. He had no peer in England or America during the first half of the nineteenth century.

One of the first claimants to the honor of exceeding Captain Barclay's record was a Bostonian named Thomas Elsworth. According to his backer, Elsworth commenced the task of walking 1,000 miles in 1,000 consecutive hours on August 24, 1842, at noon at the Cambridge Trotting Course. He finished on October 5th at sixteen minutes and forty-two seconds after three o'clock in the morning. Not content with having equaled Captain Barclay's record, Elsworth continued walking until five o'clock in the afternoon of that day. Elsworth's backer asserted, "The judges, who were three disinterested men, and had been with him through the whole of the performance, were in full belief that he could have continued walking for ten days longer!"

At one time during the contest the rumor was circulated that Elsworth did not walk every hour of the night. His backer responded by offering $100 to anyone who could prove that Elsworth was not abiding by the rules. He also offered to put up from $1,000 to $5,000 that Elsworth could repeat the performance.

In July 1843, it was announced that Thomas Elsworth was to repeat the trial in company with Simon Fogg at Tafts Gardens at Chelsea,

Massachusetts. If Fogg succeeded in completing the 1,000 miles in as many hours, he would receive $200. Elsworth was to receive $300 plus his expenses. It was claimed that Elsworth successfully completed the contest for the second time.

Elsworth also published a booklet reviewing his life and presenting a summary of his remarkable performances. Whether Elsworth actually equaled or surpassed Captain Barclay's record is uncertain, for sporting journals years later were still referring to Captain Barclay's record as unequaled. Elsworth's name was not referred to in any of the articles, and furthermore, Elsworth's other pedestrian feats scarcely approached mediocrity.

In sprinting, Peter Van Pelt, the young man who had won the purses for the 200-yard race and the quarter-mile at the Beacon Race Course in Hoboken was matched against William Belden, who was regarded as the fastest sprinter in the 1830's. They ran in a 200-yard race at Staten Island before several thousand spectators. The betting was 2 to 1 that Belden would win, and win he did — by 20 feet.

In a few years Belden's reign as the top sprinter would come to an abrupt end. In a 100-yard race on the Centreville Race Course on Long Island, Belden toed the mark against an unknown "Down East Yankee" for $500 a side in December 1841. He was heavily favored to win, but this time the losses were heavy as the Yankee vanquished Belden by a good 6 feet.

The unknown Yankee was George Seward, who should probably be ranked among the all-time greats in the sprinting events. Born in New Haven, Connecticut, on October 16, 1817, Seward displayed his talent for running and jumping at an early age. It was recalled by some of his boyhood companions that he could take a short run and jump over a horse standing erect. One companion related that Seward once jumped over a body of water which when measured was found to be twenty-one feet across.

Thomas Elsworth, or Elworth, walked his way into song with the "Pedestrian Quick Step." He also wrote his autobiography which he sold in pamphlet form.

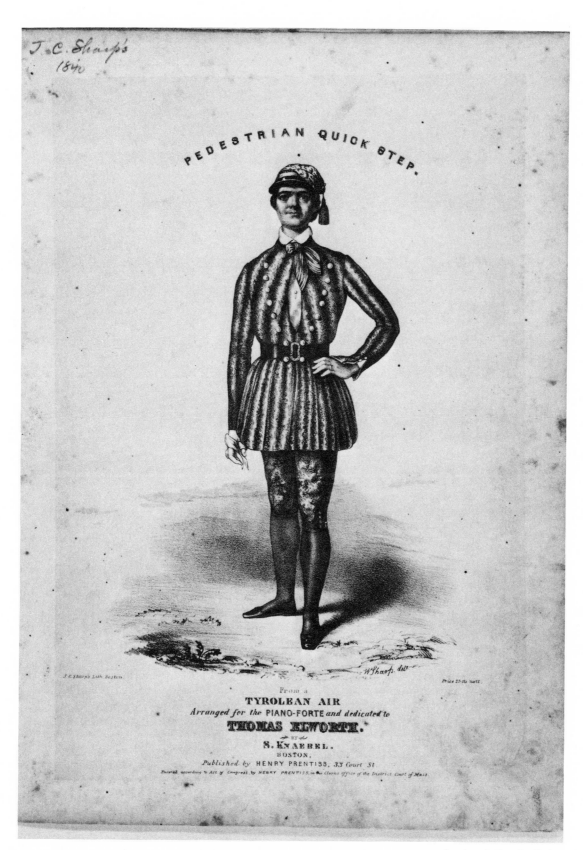

PEDESTRIAN QUICK STEP.

From a
TYROLEAN AIR
Arranged for the PIANO-FORTE and dedicated to
THOMAS ELWORTH.
BY
S. KNAEBEL.
BOSTON,
Published by HENRY PRENTISS, 33 Court St

15

All who saw Seward run in his early races which led to his contest with Belden acknowledged that a truly phenomenal sprinter had appeared.

After his conquest of Belden, Seward found difficulty in arranging races. No runner wanted to compete against him. For a runner to match his talents against Seward, it would be necessary for him to secure a backer to put up the stake. Nobody appeared willing to risk money against such a fleet-footed sprinter. After remaining idle for some time, Seward decided to sail for England, where the opportunities for competition would be greater. Under an assumed name he signed on as a seaman on a sailing vessel bound for Liverpool.

Most athletic matches in England were arranged in the public houses or sporting houses where the "fancy" or fans congregated. Some of these taverns became so closely associated with sporting activities that they constructed running tracks adjacent to the house. In Liverpool George Seward dropped in at a public house run by Jem Ward, the noted pugilist. Here most of the local matches were made. After waiting a proper time, Seward authorized Nick Ward, a brother of Jem, to make a match for him with Jack Fowler, who was recognized as the fastest sprinter outside of London, for a 100-yard race for eight pounds a side, provided Fowler would give him a head start. Fowler's backers jumped at the chance to run their sprinter against this yokel from America. It looked like easy money to them.

Prior to the match when Seward appeared in the rough clothes of a seaman at the tavern, the sporting fans made fun of him. Seward went along with the game and even emphasized his Eastern accent or dialect for the amused bystanders. He managed to keep his identity a secret, not even revealing it to the Ward brothers.

On the day of the race Seward, dressed in his plush cap, worsted overshirt, and cow-hide boots over his pants, walked around before the crowd. The spectators were highly amused at the prospect of this naive person thinking that he could beat so capable a sprinter as Fowler. They shouted derisive calls at the Yankee and laughed at their own taunts.

The betting was ten to one on Fowler with no takers except the Yankee. All that Seward had was a little over £10 in money, which he placed in Jem Ward's hands to be covered. Fowler's backers quickly did that with £100 and sat back to await the outcome with amusement.

⬦⬦⬦⬦⬦⬦⬦⬦⬦⬦⬦⬦⬦⬦⬦⬦⬦⬦

Early in October of 1826, a tall, rather slender, but muscular young man from Ohio appeared in Detroit in Michigan Territory to challenge all comers to a foot race. A young man named Berthelet responded. A space on Jefferson Avenue large enough for a 75-yard race was cordoned off. Excited men paraded about waving banknotes as an invitation for residents to bet on Berthelete against the stranger; but there were few takers. At the signal the Detroiter jumped into the lead and soon had the race won before it was half over.

Three weeks later among the passengers from Buffalo landing from the steamship *Superior* was a celebrated runner from New York City who had come to try his speed against Berthelet. Reports were in circulation that the New Yorker had won several heavy purses on Long Island and in Boston. The fame of the visitor discouraged betting; and again Berthelet had few supporters. The distance was 100 yards, and several hundred spectators had gathered on Jefferson Avenue to witness the race. At 50 yards, Berthelet was about a yard in the lead; but the stranger was gaining gradually. Berthelet struggled to maintain his lead and hit the tape a scant foot ahead of the New Yorker. "It must have been really mortifying for the New Yorker to be distanced by a Michigan lad," gloated the *Gazette*.

⬦⬦⬦⬦⬦⬦⬦⬦⬦⬦⬦⬦⬦⬦⬦⬦⬦⬦

Told that Fowler was waiting for him at the start, Seward sat down on his haunches, threw off his heavy boots, drew his shirt over his head, and appeared before the crowd in a suit of flesh-colored silk tights and shirt and in running shoes. He looked every inch a runner. After Seward practiced a few starts, the charges were voiced that somebody had rung in one of the flyers from the British Isles on them. Still Fowler was confident that he would win. At the shout of the word "Go!" Seward bounded off and in a few seconds had relegated Fowler to a position of second-rater.

Seward after this race could find no other opponents in Liverpool. They all knew him now. He secured the services of a manager named Dan Dinsmore and set out to conquer the British Isles. Running in races from 100-yards to a mile, as well as hurdle races, Seward soon established a record as champion. In his victories he tried to keep his winning margin as close as possible so that the opponents would demand a second match. Since running was his profession, he was more concerned with the purses

than with the honor of a record. Nonetheless, he was credited with several records, most notable of which was set at Hammersmith on September 30, 1844 — the record: 100 yards in 9¼ seconds!

George Seward, according to contemporary accounts, was of a "wonderfully fine physique" and was regarded as quite handsome. He stood five feet seven inches tall and weighed 160 pounds. His running career extended over a period of more than 25 years.

The opening years of the decade of the 1840's saw organized athletics, particularly running

The picnics of immigrant groups such as the Caledonians included in addition to athletic contests such events as sack races, three-legged races, and wheelbarrow races. When collegiate competition started, particularly in the Midwest, these bizarre contests were often included in the program.

and walking, in a much better state than it had been ten years earlier; but the sport still lagged far behind the English. The sporting houses there were prosperous affairs. In America, as in England, much of the sporting interest emerged from the saloons, but in this country these establishments never assumed the highly developed role of their counterparts overseas, nor did they win the respectability of them.

Throughout the nineteenth century there were many who claimed that they had equaled or surpassed Captain Barclay's feat of walking 1,000 miles in 1,000 hours; but each time a claimant came forth, he was greeted with skepticism. There was always some period in the ordeal which had not been viewed by impartial witnesses. In 1879, however, one William Gale, a Welshman, in the presence of many witnesses equaled Captain Barclay's record. Then he went on to walk 4,000 quarter-miles in 4,000 hours; 1,000 miles in 1,000 half-hours; and 500 quarter-miles in 500 quarter-hours.

Sports in America encountered a great deal of resistance. Preachers railed against such activities as sinful. Newspapers, except for a few, ignored such pastimes or opposed them. Horse-racing was the principal spectator sport of the time and prospered because racing was viewed as a means of improving the breed. Horse-racing was represented by two regularly published journals, *The Spirit of the Times* and the *Amer-*

ican Turf Register. These publications gave some attention to other sporting events. In New York City, the newspapers, *The Sun, Evening Post,* and *Mirror,* carried news of sporting activities, particularly those in the area. It would be many years before the newspapers would begin to give notice to sports, first as a sports column and ultimately as a sports page.

Betting was the chief motivation for sports promotion. While speed and endurance were recognized as admirable qualities, they were secondary. The betters could get just as excited over a race between second-raters. Indeed, they might find more excitement in such contests, since the outcome was less predictable. When an athlete acquired a reputation that placed him above all others, it became increasingly difficult for him to find opponents who could acquire backing. This was the case of both Stannard and Seward. The number of good runners in the United States was small, unlike in England, where every province and town would produce its favorites to vie with runners from other areas.

The records of athletic competition which have survived heavily favor the seaboard states, particularly the New York City area. There were running contests elsewhere, however. In the newly settled Midwest, at community gatherings local champions demonstrated their skills. At the county fairs in Western New York State, running races were often one of the attractions but competition was usually local, sometimes featuring Indian runners. Because the beginnings of organized competition took place in the New York City and seaboard area, the historical record which has survived seems to convey the impression that all of the action occurred there.

Visitors from Abroad

Henry Stannard still reigned as the leading distance runner in the United States in the spring of 1844 when the proprietors of the Beacon Race Course announced that they were offering a purse of $500 for the runner who succeeded in covering 10¼ miles within an hour. The race was an auspicious start for a year which would prove to be up until that time the greatest ever in pedestrian sports competition.

If the winner failed to run 10¼ miles within an hour, he would be awarded $300. Second and third place finishers would receive $200 and $100 respectively, provided they ran 10 miles in less than 1 hour. The race was set for Monday, June 3.

As the race time approached, Stannard was still the favorite, but he shared that honor with Anson Livingstone, the socialite who had attracted attention for his distance feats. A third runner who was considered to have a chance to win was David Myers from Poughkeepsie, New York. It was recalled that in 1835 when Stannard set his record, he was only twenty-four years old. There was much speculation as to whether the years had diminished his running ability.

Thirty thousand spectators crowded the stands and grounds at the Beacon Course when the runners lined up for the race. Betting was three to one on time, that is, that no runner would cover the distance within an hour. Missing from the line-up was Anson Livingstone. He had issued a statement informing the public that he had not authorized the use of his name

and that he had never thought of entering the competition for the purse. "An unwarrantable liberty was taken with my name," he declared.

The entries were Henry Stannard, Connecticut; Samuel Clemens, the Indian from Syracuse; George Whitehead, New York; David Myers, Poughkeepsie; John Smith, New York; John Gilder, New York; James Leroy, Brooklyn; James Stewart, New York; and J. C. Oberteuffer, Philadelphia.

A blast from the bugle sent the runners on their way. No riders on horseback paced the runners, although riders did pace back and forth in front of the crowd to keep the spectators off the track. At the start Stewart went into the lead, but at the quarter mile post four runners strode abreast in the lead. Soon after Stannard took the lead and moved ahead of the field. Three runners, Whitehead, Leroy, and Stewart, dropped out in the first mile. The highly-touted Myers stopped in the second mile, the Indian Clemens in the fourth, and Oberteuffer in the fifth. This left only three runners: Stannard, Gilder, and Smith, running in that order.

Stannard continued to lead by a comfortable margin throughout the race, leading Smith by nearly a mile at the start of the tenth mile. In the final mile Stannard, realizing that he had no chance of beating time, slowed to a walk more than once. It was generally agreed that Stannard could have run the ten miles within an hour, if he had chosen. He was within the hour 215 yards from the finish line. Gilder finished twenty rods behind Stannard, collapsing at the finish. Stannard's time for the ten miles was 62 minutes, 10½ seconds.

Following his victory, Stannard leaped upon a horse and galloped around the track. Then he mounted the stand to thank the sponsors in a brief speech. The $300 purse was given to Stannard, a $50 purse was given to Gilder, and the spectators passed the hat for Smith.

Stannard's fame, in spite of his slow time, was by no means diminished. His name began to appear in advertisements endorsing "Brooks Elastic Metallic Shank Boots," a forerunner of a lucrative source of income for professional athletes.

Encouraged by the interest shown in the race, the proprietors of the Beacon Course announced two weeks later that they would offer a purse of $1,000 for the winner of a foot race to take place on the 14th of October. Six hundred dollars would go to the winner who covered the greatest distance within an hour. If the winner failed to cover ten miles within an hour, the prize would be reduced to $300. Second, third, and fourth prizes would also be awarded. Runners from England or any other country outside of the United States would have any winning purses increased by ten per cent to cover travel expenses. An entrance fee of $5 was required "to prevent persons entering their names who do not intend to run." No person would be allowed to run for the purses if they competed for a purse of $50 or more between this time and the day of the race. The advertisement was carried in newspapers as far west as Cincinnati, and notices of the race were sent to the leading sporting journals in England.

The excitement over the race late in September rose to unprecedented heights for any athletic event when it was reported to the press that three noted English runners had arrived in New York City for the race. The prospect of an international foot race for the first time had the sporting fans counting the days until October 14. The English runners, John Barlow, John Greenhalgh, and Ambrose Jackson, had increased the list of entries to thirty-six. Even without the English runners, it would have been a great race, for there were entries from Western New York and seven different states. No other athletic event had ever attracted such a field in this country.

In addition to the American favorites, Henry Stannard and John Gilder, there were two Indians, Samuel Clemens from Syracuse and Steeprock, a Seneca from Buffalo. Three other Americans who enjoyed reputations for speed and endurance in their communities were Thomas McCabe, "an Irishman;" J. P. Taylor, Connecticut; and William Carles, Yorkville, New York.

Gilder, whose full name was Gildersleeve, had distinguished himself in June by finishing behind Stannard in the ten-mile race at Hoboken. A chair-guilder by trade, Gildersleeve was the son of a Suffolk County farmer. He was thirty-two years of age, five feet five inches tall, and weighed 130 pounds.

Greenhalgh, the Englishman, was twenty-four years of age, five feet six inches in height, and weighed 128 pounds. Greenhalgh's successes as a runner in England had been at shorter distance, from a quarter of a mile to four miles. William Barlow was the same age, five feet six and three quarter inches in height, and 140 in weight. He had earned a reputation as a capable distance runner in England.

Unlike the American runners who dressed in colorful "jockey" suits, the English contestants appeared at the starting line clad only in linen drawers from which the legs and waist had been cut off. "Quite naked," remarked one reporter. They also wore "high lows," or "ankle jacks," high pumps laced from a point near the toe to the instep. In contrast, John Gildersleeve was dressed in a blue silk shirt and cap and flesh-colored silk drawers.

A crowd estimated at 30,000 had gathered at the Beacon Course in time for the great race. After the stands were filled, a dense multitude of "tag-rag and bob-tail denizens of New York" got admission to the grounds by breaking

Unprecedented was the excitement among the huge crowd which gathered at the Beacon Race Course in Hoboken, New Jersey, to witness the running race between the visiting English professionals and the American runners on October 14, 1844, in what is recorded as the first inter-national competition in America.

NEW YORK CLIPPER

Vol. VI—No. 10.   NEW YORK, SATURDAY, JUNE 26, 1858.   Four Cents.

GREAT FOOT RACE ON THE BEACON COURSE, HOBOKEN, NEW JERSEY, NOVEMBER 19, 1844.

SPORTING REMINISCENCE.

Great Ten Mile Foot Race,

OVER THE BEACON COURSE, HOBOKEN, NEW JERSEY,
NOVEMBER 19, 1844.

EXTRAORDINARY AND EXCITING CONTEST

BETWEEN

Barlow, Steeprock, Gildersleeve, Greenhalgh, McCabe, etc.

Ten Miles in 54 Minutes 21 Seconds.

As an interesting Sporting Reminiscence, we give the above Engraving, and the following report of one of the most interesting foot races that ever took place anywhere.

THE HORSE TAMER AND THE ZEBRA.

through the fence. The race scheduled for three o'clock was delayed a full hour before the track could be cleared. Finally a dozen men on horseback had to ride before the runners to keep the track clear. As Nathaniel P. Willis described the scene in the *New York Mirror:*

"It was a curious scene. The fence that encloses the mile-ring of the course was guarded by men with sticks and poles to keep out the unpaying rabble, and every minute or two there was a shout by the crowded stands, and the hundreds of pointing fingers showed the knockdown of a fence-keeper, and the pouring in of boxes through a hole in the enclosure, like grain from the nose of a mill-hopper. The rejoicing over every defeat of authority was universal. In half an hour several thousand interlopers had crossed the forbidden field to the Judges' Stand, and stood assembled in the course below, while eight or ten lawless climbers mounted the two-story structure to its roof, and a sailor lay on his stomach upon the back of the gilt spread eagle.

"Ten or fifteen thousand people seemed, by this time, to be on the course. The track itself was black for half a mile. Stannard, the hero of the last race, came into the Club-stand, not yet stripped, looking down with amazement, declared that no force could clear running-room through such a crowd. It began to be doubted whether there would be a race. Some of the discomfitted fence-keepers were now collected to open the track, and they came up in a body, headed by a famous pugilist; an honest, rustic, and powerful-looking fellow in broad-brim and claret coat. The next ten minutes were pretty busy. There were two fights, from each of which a man was carted off by friends, staggering and bloody; a horse ran away in the field with a wagon hopping after him like a tin kettle at a dog's tail; two drunken men in a ludicrous race; the big gate at the distance post was crowded down; one or two carriage loads of rouge and ribbons were bumped about over the grassy knolls within the enclosure; the Indian made his appearance in moccasins and a cloak, and the judges ascended into the stand. The bell was struck, and the course ordered to be cleared. McClusky and three others mounted horses and galloped through the crowd at full speed, knocking people about in all directions, but

leaving, at first, no more track than a ship does in water. Presently long poles were brought and given to the crowd to enable them to keep their own line. By riding upon the toes of the pole-holders they were made to back upon the crowd behind in a retrograding phalanx, every man, of course, keeping tight hold of the pole to preserve his place in front. (A capital idea, by the way, for making a mob 'dress,' and, if American, worth lending to the mob-managers of England.)"

Betting on the race was heavy. Every conceivable form of wager was offered, the Englishmen against the field; Gilder vs. Stannard; for and against Stannard doing ten miles within an hour; the Indian Steeprock vs. Gilder; and the list of wagers went "every which way." The runners also backed their own efforts with wagers, not necessarily to win, but to cover the distance within a specified time. Thousands of dollars were wagered.

A bell would be struck once at three minutes after the start, when the runners should be at the half-mile mark, then the bell would be struck three times at the six minute mark. This pattern of bells would be repeated throughout the race so that the runners would be able to judge their pace. Runners were permitted to have pacesetters to run at their sides. Gilder's trainer, for example, ran a quarter with him in every mile.

Seventeen runners of the original thirty-seven entries responded to the starter's signal. Gildersleeve bounded into the lead but was soon passed by Barlow, Greenhalgh, and Jackson. Steeprock then spurted into the lead which he held until the end of the first mile which he covered in 5:16. At this point his trainer ordered him to fall back as his pace was too fast. Barlow and Greenhalgh then moved into the lead, running smoothly, within a yard of each other. The style of running of the Englishmen was different. They ran with their hands clenched and held elevated, and with their elbows close to their sides.

Around and around Barlow and Greenhalgh ran, lap after lap, with scarcely a yard separating them. Two runners dropped out in the second mile; and another dropped out in the fifth mile. Barlow and Greenhalgh were still leading at this point, which they passed in 27:38, well under the expected pace. They were fifty yards ahead of Steeprock, Gildersleeve, and McCabe; and Stannard and Fowle followed twenty yards back. Those who had bet on the Englishmen were beginning to wonder if they could keep up this fast pace.

At the end of the seventh mile they were still leading with Gildersleeve 150 yards behind in third place. Still farther back by about 75 yards was Steeprock, who had now become a favorite of the crowd. He ran leaning forward, every two or three rods "bounding like a buck," much to the amusement of the crowd. Whenever he came into the quarter stretch there were shouts of "Go it, my wild Ingine!" Behind him but all within time were McCabe, Fowle, Stannard, Taylor, and Jackson. One dropped out in this mile; but three others, although behind in time, still held on.

Going into the tenth mile, Greenhalgh moved into the lead, with Barlow close behind. Gildersleeve had moved up to within forty yards of the leaders. Steeprock came next, followed by McCabe, Stannard, and Taylor. Seven runners were still in the race. Greenhalgh passed the ten mile mark in 57:01½, with Barlow no more than a second behind him.

By this time the men on horseback had all they could do to keep open a lane for the runners. Many of the spectators, thinking that the race was over, crowded onto the track. But the runners still had three minutes to run for the purses. Gildersleeve picked up his pace and passed Barlow on the backstretch. Showing the effects of his fast pace, Barlow slowed to a dog trot as Gildersleeve took off after Greenhalgh. As Gildersleeve drew abreast of Greenhalgh, the Englishman held him off with a spurt of speed; but cheered by the thousands, Gilder hung on and went past Greenhalgh by ten or fifteen feet. Greenhalgh, all done, slowed to a walk. Gildersleeve kept on beyond the half mile until stopped by one of the officials on horseback when the hour was up. Gildersleeve had run ten miles and a half, plus seventy-five yards.

Greenhalgh, Barlow, Gildersleeve, Steeprock, McCabe, and Stannard were all within one hour at the ten mile mark. Only Taylor failed, and by only one second, at that. The first four con-

tinued on, but the others having covered their bets stopped at that point.

One reporter who covered the race, in describing the immense crowd, wrote, "Extra boats had been provided for the occasion, but it was long after dark before we could leave the Hoboken side of the Hudson; even the boats for Canal and Christopher streets, let alone Barclay, were crammed like cigar boxes."

Prior to the race at Hoboken, the proprietors of the Eagle Course at Trenton, New Jersey, had announced a program of seven races, from 100 yards to ten miles, for the 12th of November. They further announced that the English runners had expressed their intentions of competing for the prizes. The great success of the race over the Beacon Course made the prospects of a re-run appear very favorable. This was not overlooked by the proprietors of the Beacon Course. Soon after the big race they announced that a purse of $1,200 would be offered for a ten-mile race at Hoboken on or about November 14. The larger purse and the commitment of the leading runners to the Beacon Course left the Trenton promoters no alternative than to cancel their proposed meet.

C. S. Browning, the proprietor of the Beacon Course, announced that $700 would go to the winner of the race, $250 to the second-place finisher, $150 to the third, $75 to the fourth, and $25 to the fifth man. Gildersleeve, Barlow, and Greenhalgh had already entered, and it was expected that Steeprock would also be among the starters. Each runner would be permitted to have two or three of his friends to guide him or assist him during the race. This was deemed of especial importance to those runners who lacked experience, explained Mr. Browning. Their handlers could restrain them from running too fast in response to the cheering of the crowd.

The date of the race was advanced to November 18th because of the elections which were taking place. Added to the program was a three mile race with $200 in prizes.

As the day of the race approached, Gildersleeve was a slight favorite to win over the English runners; but the closer to the race time, the closer the odds became, until the betting was just about even. Steeprock, the Indian, was given a chance, as were McCabe, Carles, and Taylor, participants in the last race. Only a few harbored any doubts that the race would be run under one hour. The doubters based their judgment on the condition of the track which was quite spongy because of the two days of rain which had caused a postponement of the race. The odds were ten to three on time. Predictions were that this would be the best race ever run in America. "All the world and his wife will be in attendance," wrote one reporter.

In reporting the race, *The Spirit of the Times*, in describing the crowd, wrote: "We doubt if so many spectators have ever been assembled on an American race course as was present on this occasion. A single steam-boat from Albany brought down four hundred; New Jersey, Long Island, and the river towns along the Hudson, furnished immense crowds, while this city sent over materials for an army three times larger than that with which Napoleon made his Italian campaign. From the head of the quarter-stretch quite around to the drawgate, the enclosed space was so densely crammed as to render it nearly impossible to clear a space wide enough for the pedestrians to run through, though they were preceded by two dozen men on horseback. Thousands filled the stands, but it would have required the Amphitheatre of Titus to have accommodated all."

It was a clear, cold day. The course was sodden and damp. Each step of the horses "cupped up" a shoe full of earth, rendering the track rough.

Gildersleeve, suffering from a cold, appeared "as pale as the ghost of his majesty of Denmark," but full of confidence. Steeprock looked impressive. It was reported that he had been training hard since the last race. If Steeprock had the advantage of a first rate English trainer, it was doubtful if any man in the world could beat him, speculated one sports writer. McCabe had slipped in the betting. When it was learned that he had married a few days after the last race, his trainer ordered a separation; but one night he stole away to spend the night with his wife. The news got around as *The Spirit of the Times* reported: "Indeed, not a prominent man in the race has made a trial without being secretly watched by a host of touters; as nothing escaped their vigilance, the backsliding of McCabe was as well known all over town the next day, as if advertised in the newspapers." The Englishmen Barlow and Greenhalgh appeared to be in superb condition. They were "nearly as naked as Correigo's 'St. John in the Wilderness,' having their 'loins girded' with a simple strap of linen, and a blue and yellow fogle about their heads."

A few false starts as Barlow bounded forth before the signal, then the starter shouted, "Go!" Barlow and Greenhalgh darted into the lead together, followed closely by the seven other runners. They soon disappeared from sight, hidden by the dense throng which lined the railing on both sides of the course. Even at the start the men had to run the gauntlet through the crowd. As the runners sped down the opposite side of the track, the judges could only determine their position by the horses which trotted on before the leaders.

Through the first mile, which Barlow covered in 5:10, the four leaders remained bunched together. Going into the second mile, Barlow opened up a slight lead over Steeprock, while Gildersleeve and Greenhalgh followed some distance behind. The rest of the field was strung out far behind. Barlow lopped off the second mile in 5:15.

By the end of the third mile, Barlow had opened up a lead of fifty yards, while Greenhalgh and Gildersleeve ran stride for stride behind. Spectators conjectured that Greenhalgh was sticking close to Gildersleeve while Barlow ran Steeprock into the ground. If Barlow should falter in doing this, Greenhalgh would be able to contend with Gildersleeve for the purse. Barlow passed the three mile mark in 15:47. In a preliminary race of three miles on the same program, the winning time had been 16:16. Barlow was moving along at a pace that few believed he could sustain.

At the five mile mark the order remained the same; but the gap between Barlow and Steeprock had widened, and Barlow showed no sign of weakening. Gildersleeve and Greenhalgh still ran together. McCabe and Taylor, though far behind, were still running at a pace which would bring them into the ten miles under one hour.

After eight miles Barlow was leading Steeprock by 200 yards; Gildersleeve and Greenhalgh were a minute behind the leader; and McCabe and Taylor, the other survivors of the field, were far behind. Barlow increased his lead to 250 yards in the next mile. Steeprock had made a rush to overtake Barlow but he had expended so much energy in this endeavor that he was now struggling to keep going. Barlow going into the tenth mile was the apparent winner; the fast pace that he had set had had no effect upon him. "An incredible piece of machinery," wrote one sports writer, "instinct with life, is the only thing to which the rapidity and regularity of his style of going can be compared."

Suddenly there was the cry of "There goes Gilder!" All the spectators strained for a glimpse at Gilder making his dash for the leader. When they finally gained a glimpse of the runners above the crowd, it was the yellow fogle of Greenhalgh which they espied fifteen or twenty yards ahead of Gildersleeve's blue and white striped cap. Greenhalgh, who had been running one stride behind Gildersleeve throughout the race, suddenly, as they moved into the tenth mile, passed Gilder, turning to him and exclaiming, "Good-bye, Gilder!" The next three quarters were run by Greenhalgh faster than the distance had ever been run in this country. He had run his last mile in 4:48, an amazing feat for that time.

However, Greenhalgh's amazing finish was not enough to enable him to overtake Steeprock, who trailed Barlow across the line by 173 yards for the second place purse. If Greenhalgh had started his drive for the finish earlier, it was quite likely that he would have overtaken and passed Steeprock. Gildersleeve kept on at his pace, apparently with plenty of reserve energy but unable to increase his speed. McCabe followed a long way behind, but under one hour, for the distance. Taylor, with Stannard running along with him, shouting cries of encouragement and clearing a passage through the crowd, managed to run the ten miles within an hour, "by the skin of his teeth," only having two seconds to spare.

Thus ended the "most extraordinary" race in the sports history of the United States. It would be a subject for reminiscising for years to come. "They won't believe this in England, even if you *do* print it, Mr. P.," remarked Barlow to William Porter of *The Spirit of the Times*. He had run the ten miles in 54 minutes 21 seconds, faster than any recorded time for the distance hitherto. The six runners who finished all ran the distance in less than an hour, five of them beating Stannard's best time. The crowd went wild with excitement.

"Yankee Sullivan caught Barlow up in his arms on his coming in, and rushed with him into the Judge's stand, where he was immediately dressed and cared for. A closed carriage was drawn up into the rear of the crowd, into which, in a few moments, he was placed, having left the stand upon Sullivan's shoulders, waving his blue bird's-eye fogle in the air, amidst the most tremendous cheers," wrote William Porter.

In the days following the great race, challenges were hurled about; and efforts were made to promote another race. However, the lateness of the season discouraged prospects of another race. Barlow and Greenhalgh made arrangements to sail for home the following Tuesday on board the packet ship *Roscius*. During the short stay in America they had won $1235 in purses alone. What they won in bets of their own was not disclosed.

They stopped at the office of *The Spirit of the Times* to express their gratitude for the treatment they had received in this country. "They desire us to express their grateful acknowledgments for the uniform courtesy and kindness they have received here from the press, the sporting world, and the public generally," wrote *The Spirit of the Times*, "And we here take great pleasure in assuring their friends at home, that during their visit to this country, they have borne themselves with such a degree of propriety as to have won the good wishes of all, and acquired a host of friends who will extend to them a cordial welcome should they determine hereafter to repeat their visit."

When the packet ship *Roscius* sailed for Liverpool, Barlow was on board, but Greenhalgh had yielded to persuasion to stay on for yet another race. A twelve mile race with Steeprock had been arranged, to be run on the Beacon Course on December 15. Five hundred dollars would go to the winner, and $300 to the second place. A week before the match Steeprock's Buffalo friends induced him to withdraw from the race and wait until spring for further competition. Greenhalgh was not to be permitted to take the purse by walking over the course without contest, for Gildersleeve agreed to run.

The day of the race was intensely cold. A piercing wind blew across the course, and the track was frozen as hard as flint. Sports fans en route to the track saw crowds of boys skating on the Hoboken meadows. "Every gentleman wore the collar of his overcoat turned up about his ears, and the stamping and dancing to keep warm was most amusing," wrote one observer.

Gildersleeve had been training indoors at the rope walk near the Union Course on Long Island; Greenhalgh had been training at Hoboken.

As the starting time approached, Gildersleeve appeared from a room in the club stand, accompanied by his trainer. He was dressed in a striped silk night cap, a blue silk shirt and flesh-colored drawers. Greenhalgh, who had been waiting in a closed cab in the rear of the club stand, emerged, peeled to his nearly nude state as before; and wearing a yellow bird's-eye fogle entered the judges' stand with Gildersleeve. Three other contestants who had entered decided at the last minute to withdraw, so the contest was to be between the two stars only. Again the crowd broke through the palings onto the course, although this time there was little excuse, for the stands were not at all crowded. In the stands were "a great number of gentlemen of the highest respectability."

Betting was vigorous. "One could not ask 'What's o'clock,' without being answered '10 to 6!' and if you only looked a man hard in the face he roared out 'Done, Sir!' Such difference of opinion, such interest and betting, such shouting and stamping, made up a scene that will not soon be forgotten. Half the people's hearts were in their mouths, and the pitiless cold was forgotten in the anxiety to see," wrote one reporter.

At the word "Go," Gildersleeve jumped into the lead, followed by Greenhalgh a yard behind. The Englishman trailed Gildersleeve throughout the first mile by that single yard, stepping exactly in Gilder's tracks. Time for the first mile was 5:53. It started snowing in the second mile, which was finished in 5:57. The snow increased in the third mile, slowing the runners to 6:02 for that mile; but the order remained the same, Gildersleeve followed closely by Greenhalgh. In the fifth mile the sun broke through the clouds, but it was snowing again before the mile ended. Times for the first five miles varied little, ranging from 5:50 to 6:02. In the sixth mile Gildersleeve picked up the pace in an effort to open up a space between him and his opponent; but Greenhalgh stayed with him as they ran the mile in 5:33. The seventh, eighth, and ninth miles were run at a fast but even pace, each being covered in 5:40. There was no change in position, and it appeared to be anyone's race yet. While the crowd shivered, the runners perspired freely. The color from Gildersleeve's blue striped shirt extended down to his flesh colored drawers. The tenth mile was run in 5:38 for a total of 57:52, with neither runner showing any distress or sign of weakening. The eleventh mile was also run in 5:38. Now the odds turned in favor of Greenhalgh, who still followed Gildersleeve a pace behind. The spectators remembered the amazingly fast finish in the last race and looked for a repetition of it here.

Going into the twelfth and final mile, both men looked as fresh as though they had not run a yard. The crowd shouted encouragement to both of them. They shouted to Gildersleeve, "Shake yourself, miboy!" "Cut loose Greenhalgh!" "Give him fits!" Gildersleeve exerted himself but could not shake off Greenhalgh. Down the backstretch they raced stride for stride. "At the half mile post, you could just see a glimpse of daylight between the two. Around the last turn it was still Gildersleeve running strong; but Greenhalgh was still on his heels."

Let the reporter from *The Spirit of the Times* take it from here:

"They swung into the head of the quarter stretch. We could occasionally catch a glimpse of Gildersleeve's blue shirt, as we thought, in advance, but as the men were coming directly towards us, it was impossible to say which had the advantage. A mighty shout of 'Gilder's got him!' was the cry. 'No Greenhalgh!' 'Three to one on the Englishman!' 'Greenhalgh's got him for a thousand!' 'No, Gilder!' 'Greenhalgh!' 'Greenhalgh!' 'Gilder!' '*I told you so!*' 'Gilder hasn't got him!' 'Greenhalgh wins it like a d—n!' 'Hurrah for Greenhalgh!' 'Didn't I tell ye?'

"After getting into the quarter stretch Gildersleeve's trainer shouted to him, 'Spread yourself, old fellow!' 'Think of the *people at home*, Tommy,' was the response of Harrison, Greenhalgh's faithful trainer. Every muscle was exerted, the last link was let out, and the most desperate struggle ensued on both sides. At first Gildersleeve seemed to have the best of it, but the unconquerable Englishman had yet a run left; he 'bottled himself up,' as it were, for a final rush, and this being the critical moment, he collected all his energies, and at the instant thousands were felicitating themselves that the favorite was beaten, lo, here he came with the force, the certainty, and the precision of a locomotive! The contest was not for a moment doubtful. Gildersleeve, if he had not over-marked himself, had 'done all that might become a man.' Without 'hanging fire' an instant, Greenhalgh, with a last tremendous effort, rushed past him, and *the thing was out!* Gildersleeve, as game a man as ever breathed, did not make another effort; nobly had he acquitted himself, and 'justified his training,' if he could not 'command success' he had 'done more — he had deserved it;' but limbs of steel and sinews of catgut, animated by the dogged courage and sullen obstinacy of the heroes of the Peninsular, only, could have achieved the victory on this occasion. Long before Greenhalgh reached the drawgates (some 200 yards from the Stand) he was alone, with the crowd of spectators so closely packed behind him that the Judges, for some moments, could not distinguish Gildersleeve in the dense mass. Mr. Browning rode by his side and advised him to 'run it out,' which he did, but by the time he reached the drawgates, Yankee Sullivan had brought Greenhalgh in his arms up into the judges' stand, the twelfth mile having been run in 5:18!"

Greenhalgh appeared exhausted. He could not have run 100 rods farther to save his life.

Connecticut-born George Seward may have been the greatest sprinter of all time. For twenty-five years he competed in England as a professional, vanquishing all challengers with ease.

Gildersleeve, however, was not nearly so distressed. He looked as though he could have run another mile without difficulty, but to run any faster was beyond his capability. As soon as he was able, Greenhalgh came forward and waved his yellow fogle to the crowd, which responded with mighty cheering. "Come back and give us another turn next spring," shouted a voice from the crowd. Yankee Sullivan then hoisted him to his shoulders and carried the English runner to a waiting carriage.

The running season of 1844 was over. It had been the greatest season in the history of sports in the United States. For years to come the sporting journals and fans would look back upon these international contests with undiminished excitement. It would be more than a quarter of a century before a spectacle of equal importance would capture the public's attention.

Greenhalgh sailed for England on the packet ship *Siddons* in the following week, carrying with him a greater fortune than he had ever owned before. His winnings had been substantially increased by a public subscription which had been raised in his honor by appreciative followers. They also raised a fund for Greenhalgh's trainer Harrison.

With such an exciting year behind them, the sporting fans were looking forward to the next year's competition. Already they had received notice that the celebrated American sprinter George Seward was coming home. He had notified *The Spirit of the Times* that he was planning to sail for America in the following April or May. In England he had won seventeen races and had taken the silver cup in recognition of the championship of the British Isles.

The reports of the great races at Hoboken in 1844 stimulated interest in foot racing throughout the country. Gildersleeve, now a famous figure in sporting circles, went on tour. In April he was reported training at the Metairie Course in New Orleans for a ten-mile race. On the day of the race, although nine runners had signified their intentions of competing for the purse, only three runners actually responded to the starter's signal. Before the largest crowd ever assembled on the Metairie Course, Gildersleeve lined up with one Archer and Thomas Elsworth, the Bostonian who had earlier claimed that he had surpassed Captain Barclay's record.

At the start Gildersleeve jumped into the lead, and at the end of the first mile, which he ran in 5:30, he was far ahead of Archer, while Elsworth trailed far back in third place. At the end of two miles in eleven minutes, Gildersleeve was a half mile ahead of Elsworth. The latter ran awkwardly and laboriously and his pre-race favorite status was no longer recognized. Now the betting was on when Gildersleeve would pass the Bostonian on the mile track. This he accomplished at the start of his fifth mile as Elsworth finished his fourth mile, collapsed and was carried from the track. Archer was on the stretch toward the end of his sixth mile when Gildersleeve was about to overtake him. He slowed to a walk and left the track. Gilder-

sleeve continued on to finish the ten miles in 59:50.

In the meantime, C. S. Browning was making plans for another stellar season at the Beacon Course. He had placed notices in the English sporting journals and expected that contestants were now on their way across the Atlantic. In May, Browning announced that $1,500 to $2,000 were to be offered for a program of races which would include a ten mile race, a three mile race, a one mile race, and a sprint. There would also be a purse offered to the person who walked the greatest distance within one hour.

Soon it was announced that George Seward, accompanied by William Jackson, who billed himself as "the American Deer," had arrived in Philadelphia on board the *Champion*, after a very rough passage of forty-two days. Jackson, although he ran under the title "the American Deer," was an Englishman making his first trip to this country. (It was the practice of many professionals to adopt a title or name.) Upon arrival, Seward and Jackson departed for Providence, Rhode Island, where they would go into training. On another ship, Harrison, the trainer of Greenhalgh, arrived to serve in that capacity on behalf of Gildersleeve.

The first competition took place June 17th at the Cambridge Course near Boston rather than at Hoboken. The English star Jackson was not among the starters, however. Ambrose Jackson, the English runner who had won at the shorter distances in 1844, was among the entries. This Jackson had remained in the United States and had become an immigrant. In addition to Ambrose Jackson, the only other runner of note was John Gildersleeve. Thirteen runners from Boston, New York, and Maine answered the starter's signal.

Gildersleeve, after leading the whole distance, ran the ten miles in 57:19 to win the first prize purse of $350. Cavanagh of New York and Desmond of Boston took the second and third place purses.

The big racing program at Hoboken was scheduled for June 30th, July 3rd, and July 5th. On the program for the first day was the one mile race and the one hour walking contest. In the mile race, Ambrose Jackson was the favorite, although Major Henry Stannard still had a loyal following. An Iroquois Indian from Canada named Ignace Katanachiate was also expected to be a contender. William Barlow, a nineteen-year-old youth from nearby Williamsburgh, had considerable backing because of his local reputation as a speedster. Barlow was no relative of the English runner of 1844. His real name was William Freestone; Billy Barlow, his professional name, had been adapted from a popular song of the day. Although born in London, he had come to America with his parents when he was but nine years old.

At the word "Go!" the Indian shot into the lead which he held through the half-mile which he covered in the fast time of two minutes and eleven seconds. After the three-quarter mark Barlow overtook the Indian and passed him. The Indian came back, drew abreast of Barlow, and pushed him, knocking him off his stride, nearly into the railing. Barlow recovered quickly and pulled ahead of Ignace, winning in 4:36, fast time for the mile in that day. Ignace followed in 4:42, trailed by Ambrose Jackson in 5:06 and Stannard in 5:09.

In the walking race an athlete who billed himself as "North Star of Canada" won the purse, doing seven miles within an hour. These races introduced two professional pedestrians as winners who would remain a part of the sports scene for more than a decade.

In the five mile race William Jackson, "the American Deer," was the favorite in the betting by two to one. At the start Barlow took the lead but was soon headed by Jackson, who continued to hold the lead to the finish in 27:39. He was clearly the class of the field with no close rivals.

On the third day Seward won the quarter-mile race over 15 hurdles in two heats of 1:11 and 1:09. North Star took the two mile walk, beating a single competitor. The ten mile run proved to be a big disappointment. Only two entries appeared to contest William Jackson for the purse; these were John Gildersleeve and Robert Williams, "the Welsh Bantam." Williams stopped in the third mile; and Gildersleeve gave up in the ninth mile, as Jackson went on to win easily in 56:29.

In spite of the appearance of stars of the caliber of William Jackson and George Seward, the racing program of 1845 at Hoboken failed to generate the level of excitement of the races of the year before. It may have been the hot weather, but more likely it was the recognition of the apparent supremacy of Jackson and Seward. With wagering as the principal stimulus of interest in the races, it helped if the outcome of a contest was uncertain. Contributing also to the lack of attendance was the fact that those who could afford to leave the city during the summer months did so. The memories of the dreaded cholera epidemics of the 1830's made city life in the summer months unattractive.

Steeprock, the Seneca Indian, yet remained to try his running skill and speed against Jackson. Soon after Jackson's victories at Hoboken, Steeprock's backers started to promote such a contest but they were not able to come to terms until fall.

Early in September Jackson issued through the newspapers and sporting journals a challenge to any man in America to run against him at any distance from two miles to fifteen. The challenge, Jackson states, would remain open until September 25, after which date he would sail for England. Steward was also experiencing difficulty finding suitable opponents over the shorter distances. Finally both runners were able to schedule races at the Beacon Course late in September. Jackson's departure date would be deferred.

Billy Barlow, the young runner from Williamsburgh, Long Island, found the necessary backers to put up the $500 needed to accept Jackson's challenge. The race would be over the two mile distance. Barlow had proved his competency at the mile run, but it was not known how well he could do over the longer distance. Thus Jackson enjoyed the advantage in the odds. Barlow's backers were so confident in their man that they ignored the odds and readily took dollar for dollar in their bets.

The race was a spirited one in which the lead alternated between the two contestants. It appeared to the spectators that Jackson was making a waiting game of it, hoping to outdistance Barlow at the finish. Some thought this an error in judgment on his part. Since endurance was his forte, they thought that it would have been wiser for him to have run Barlow into the ground from the start. As the two runners entered the quarter stretch, it still looked as though it was anybody's race, but Barlow easily outdistanced his rival in the final dash for the finish line, which he crossed in 9:44½. It was announced that this was the fastest two miles on record, better than the best time of 9:45 which had been recorded in England.

After the race Jackson called at the office of *The Spirit of the Times* to offer to run Barlow at five miles for $1,000.

When suspicion was expressed over Jackson's defeat by this youngster from Long Island, it was pointed out that this was the fastest time on record. Barlow's backers offered to put up the money for a two mile race with Jackson or any other man in the United States. Their man had won the race honestly, and they would go to any limits to prove it.

Unable to promote any further contests in the New York City area, Jackson and Seward took to the road. They appeared in Montreal on October 22, where Jackson easily won a three mile race, but Seward had the misfortune of falling in the 250-yard hurdle race and finished third. A large crowd of spectators appeared at the race course, some even coming from as far away as New York City and other cities across the border.

In a ten mile race at Toronto, seven entries signified their intentions of competing for the purse, but only two appeared at the starting line, Jackson and Gildersleeve. The American led throughout most of the distance. Midway through the race Jackson appeared to be in distress; Gildersleeve widened his lead. At the end of 9 miles Gildersleeve was running smoothly 200 yards in front of his opponent. It seemed inevitable that he would win. Suddenly, Jackson came to life and picked up his pace. With three quarters to go, he was still 150 yards behind, but he was closing the gap with each stride. Coming into the quarter stretch, Jackson was only a stride behind; then he drew abreast of Gildersleeve amid the wild cheering of the crowd, and in a lunge for the tape he won by a scant foot in 59 minutes and 55 seconds.

A week later at Toronto Jackson again defeated Gildersleeve in a ten mile race in 56:52 but Seward had to be content with running over the hurdles without opposition. Before the touring athletes had left Toronto, Seward made a match with one Leakdigger to run a 150-yard race on College Avenue. Seward gave his opponent a five-yard start and failed to overtake him. There were cries of "hoax" and expressions of doubt over the outcome of the race. Some thought that the defeat might have been engineered to encourage opponents to try their speed against Seward. Even when it was revealed that Mr. Leakdigger was actually an army officer with quite a local reputation as a sprinter, doubts persisted over the outcome of the race.

They went on to Albany, where Jackson and Gildersleeve again took turns in leading over the ten mile course, with the Englishman winning in 55:30. It was reported that Steeprock, the Seneca Indian, was present but chose not to run.

Again Jackson issued a public challenge to race any runner in the United States, specifically naming Steeprock and Barlow. He offered to race at any distance from two miles to twenty and would give head starts at any distance from three miles upward. He stated that he would like to race Barlow at two miles again "to satisfy the public and myself which is the better man of the two." Any takers would have to respond within three weeks, he wrote, for he planned to sail for England "if all remain silent."

On November 24, at Baltimore, he ran against the clock, successfully running 10½ miles within an hour. In January 1846, he still had not sailed for England. He was now in New Orleans issuing challenges to the "Cherokee Indian" and anybody else who would face him. He had to be content with running against the clock in an effort to run 11 miles within an hour. He failed to accomplish this goal by ten seconds.

In February, Jackson and Seward had succeeded in generating sufficient interest in their

William Howitt, alias Jackson, "The American Deer," was the English professional runner who made two triumphant tours of the United States and Canada in the 1840's and 1850's.

PAINTED & ENGRAVED BY W. BROMLEY, N° 9, NEW CHURCH STREET, EDGWARE ROAD.

William Howitt

running prowess to induce Colonel Oliver of the Metairie Course in New Orleans to offer purses totaling $1,000 for a pedestrian program. Jackson would give a 600-yard start to his opponents in a 15-mile race. An added purse was offered if the distance was covered in less than an hour and a half. Gildersleeve and two other New York City professionals had come down for the race. Seward, too, had found an opponent in Cornelius Fitzgerald, an Irish immigrant, for a 300-yard race over hurdles.

A writer for the *Daily Delta* expressed his fears that Jackson had undertaken a feat in which he could not possibly succeed. "Of those whose feats have placed them in the exalted positions as the first pedestrians of the world, it is unnecessary to say a word except to express our fears that in the arduous task to be performed, Jackson, 'the American Deer,' is about to attempt a feat in which his highest hopes will be frustrated;" he wrote, "it really seems to us impossible that a man of Gildersleeve's power and compactness of form, added to his peculiar facility of 'go along,' can be beaten by 600 yards in the given distance of 15 miles."

Jackson without difficulty soon passed all of his competitors save Gildersleeve, whom he overtook in the sixth mile but did not pass. Throughout the rest of the race Jackson ran close behind Gildersleeve, who without much contest won the race by a yard. The time was two and a half minutes above the goal set for the race; but Colonel Oliver, considering that the heavy rain which fell during the latter half of the race impeded the runners, divided the purse as if they had met the goal.

There were serious questions raised about the outcome of the race. The *Picayune* wrote: "We are sorry to say that a very general impression prevails that *Jackson threw off the race;* his running was surely most unaccountable upon any other hypothesis." The *Daily Delta* commented: "It was strongly hinted that Jackson's rider held him in, and pulled him to one and the other side of the course, without any apparent necessity. Whether those hints were well founded we will not pretend to say, but we did make up our mind to follow the example of a tall, weatherbeaten Kentuckian on the course, who, when bantered to bet, replied, 'Look here,

I've made an amazin' heap of money bettin' on races, but I got damnably chiseled once, an I can't afford to bet a red cent on anything that talks.' "

Because betting was the chief incentive for the runners, doubts about the honesty of professional runners persisted throughout the century. Sometimes they could make more money losing than by winning by placing the right kind of bets. Running against the clock was thought to be one way of keeping the runners honest; but still even in such races the amount that could be won in wagers easily exceeded the size of the purse. Then, too, as had been observed in Seward's experiences, it did not pay for a pro to win consistently. If he did, he was not good wagering material, so he had trouble finding anybody to race him. The Kentuckian's observation caught on; and many a sportsman resolved not "to bet a red cent on anything that talks."

Jackson and Seward continued their tour, making appearances in South Carolina, Kentucky, and racing towns in other states. Gildersleeve usually made his appearance, too, so that Jackson could at least make some semblance of a race.

Jackson and Seward's tour marked a change in the American sporting scene. The improvement in travel had broken down the local isolation of sports competition. *The Spirit of the Times* marveled at the speed and mode of modern travel: "This may be emphatically characterized as the age of improved travel. Of late years it has advanced in a geometrical ratio. Compare it with the traveling of the last century, or of thirty years ago: and what a change! Only seventy years since it took a fortnight to convey the news of the battle of Bunker Hill to Philadelphia! Not many years since, one who thought in advance of the times, was considered insane for believing the time would come when one might travel in two days between Philadelphia and Boston. In 1776, when the British army under Sir William Howe came from England, the voyage was so long that Baron Knyphausen, commander of the Hessians, had serious apprehensions of having passed America! In less than forty years since, the packets were something more than a fortnight between Albany and New York. Now a traveller goes in less time from Albany to London! Your correspondent, not an old man, remembers having been four days on the route, in 'the accommodation stage,' between New York and Philadelphia. Will not four hours soon be the average time? He crossed the river at the ferry from Paulus Hook, now Jersey City, in a rickety sail boat. He once crossed in a similar way, from Elizabeth Town Point. . . . About the year 1816, on the Hudson River, the magnificent and incomparably fast steamer, "The Chancellor Livingstone,' was advertised to perform the trip between New York and Albany, in the astonishing short time of eighteen hours, for only $7 a passenger! The more splendid 'Niagara' and other fast boats of the last season, have performed the same route in less than half the time, for $1 a passenger!"

At the end of February Billy Barlow in the columns of *The Spirit of the Times* offered to accept Jackson's challenge for a two mile race. However, Barlow wished to limit the wager to $200 a side, rather than the $500 asked by Jackson in his challenge. The $200 was the highest amount that he could raise, stated Barlow, who added that he was requesting no backers.

Jackson's response was less than enthusiastic. He acknowledged having seen Barlow's proposal but regarded $200 "a trifling sum." He wrote: "As I have better fish to fry in England, it will not suit me to stop for so small a sum; but if Barlow will make the amount $400, I am at his service for a two mile race, to take place at Baltimore or Philadelphia the latter end of April or the first day of May."

Apparently Barlow and Jackson were unable to come to terms, for on April 11, Jackson was once again announcing his departure for England, this time on May 1. He expressed "his grateful acknowledgments for the uniform courtesy and kindness extended to him in the twenty-three States of the Union he has visited as well as the Canadas." The simple reason that he was leaving, he stated, was that he could find no competitor, in spite of generous odds offered. However, if anybody should wish to meet him for any amount above $500 a side before sailing time, he would be available. He offered to delay his departure if any gentleman wished to bet $1,000 to $700 against his running 11 miles within one hour.

Jackson's departure was to be postponed, for his offer was accepted by a gentleman from Philadelphia; the attempt to run 11 miles in an hour was set for June 15 at the Hunting Park Trotting Course near Philadelphia.

Jackson trained carefully for this race and weighed 105 pounds when he started. Before the contest, he inspected the track carefully, even having it measured by a surveyor. It was found by the surveyor that the track exceeded one mile by five feet three and a quarter inches. For this reason the starting line was moved forward. Jackson failed by twenty-eight seconds to do the eleven miles in the hour and lost the wager.

The crowd at the track was immense and little preparation had been made for managing it. In the final stages of the contest they crowded onto the track in such numbers that Jackson had to push spectators from his path. "It is the general opinion of every one that witnessed the Jackson race on Monday week, that he would have won it with ease had he but had fair play and a clear course, and not to have been obstructed by men who ran before him, that he had to push down before he could pass, and the immense crowd of people that obstructed him on every part of the race course, which gave him no chance to win," wrote the Philadelphia *Daily Chronicle*. The *Chronicle* writer maintained that in all fairness Jackson should not be the loser of $700 under these circumstances. He and a friend were contributing $50 toward a fund for Jackson and he hoped that other gentlemen would follow suit.

The Spirit of the Times expressed its amazement at the speed with which they had received the results of this race. At the conclusion of the contest an express rider had sped from the track to the office of the Magnetic Telegraph in Philadelphia and had sent the message: "Jackson has lost by 20 seconds! More presently!" *The Spirit of the Times* received the message from the Jersey City terminus in ten minutes. They exclaimed, "The distance between our office and the course is over One Hundred Miles! In less than half an hour we had the particulars of the race!" That they knew the results of the contest as soon as their Philadelphia contemporaries was almost too much to believe.

Jackson, although he lamented the lack of competitors, had had more success in finding rivals than his companion George Seward. Finally, from Washington, Seward received an acceptance of his open challenge. A sprinter named G. W. Morgan, who had made quite an impression among the sports followers, agreed to run Seward in a 100-yard race for $500 a side. Morgan, about 32 years old, six feet two in height, with long slim legs, slightly bowed, broad shoulders and large chest, had won several races in the Washington area. It was reported that he was from the West; other sources said that he was a Cherokee Indian. His running style was somewhat awkward as he turned his body alternately right and left with each stride. He was credited with prodigious strength and speed, however.

Although the challenge was accepted in May, the race did not take place until August 8. It was a torrid day but this did not discourage the spectators who turned out in large numbers, some coming down from Philadelphia to bet on Seward. The odds for the week before the race were two to one that Morgan would win, but on the day of the race the odds were even. Morgan was to receive a three-yard start from Seward. Seward had been in Washington with Jackson for six weeks in training for the race and appeared to be in top shape. Just before starting Seward offered Morgan $10 to $50 that he would beat him by six feet, but Morgan declined.

Both runners got off to a good start. Morgan led by from two to three feet for 75 yards when Seward sped by him to win by a yard. The time was announced as eleven seconds.

The correspondent of *The Spirit of the Times* described Seward's running as smooth and fast, but he speculated that if Morgan had the benefit of competent training he could beat Seward. If he could be taught to run in a smooth, direct manner without lurching alternately from right to left, he would be unbeatable, thought the writer.

Jackson and Seward soon after sailed for England. Whether they returned any wealthier than they arrived is not known. Jackson would within a few years return for another visit, but Seward would spend the rest of his years in England. He continued to race professionally until 1866, running in races from fifty yards to two miles.

Seward, at his best in the sprints, was credited with the best times on record in the 100 yards, 9¼ seconds; 120 yards, 11⅛ seconds; and 200 yards, 19½ seconds. If one can attach any credence to these times, Seward was an extraordinary sprinter. These times would have been made from a standing start, in unspiked shoes, and over a surface far removed from the smooth, resilient surfaces of today's tracks. The fact that he dominated the professional running scene for more than twenty-five years indicates that he must have possessed outstanding talent as a sprinter. He was in the winner's circle until the end of his long career. Following his retirement from professional running, he resided in Liverpool, where he worked at his trade as a silversmith.

Seward's 9¼ seconds for the 100-yard dash remained on the books until 1890, when the *New York Clipper* expunged it from its records. The fact that the fleetest runners of modern times with better tracks, improved equipment, and superior training had failed to approach Seward's mark made it appear unlikely to the *Clipper* that Seward had ever run that fast. Furthermore, forty-five years after the event "an eye-witness" had come forth to testify that the record had been made from a running start and that the section of the turnpike on which the race had been run was downhill. None of this testimony coincided with the published reports in 1844 when the record was established. Oddly enough, the *New York Clipper* was content to allow Seward's other records to remain on the books, and they were just as spectacular as the 9¼ second mark.

Vol. IV.—No. 11.   NEW YORK, SATURDAY, JULY 5, 1856.   Four Cents.

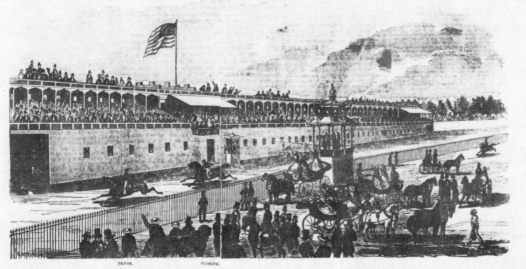

FASHION COURSE, L. I.—FOUR MILE DAY, JUNE 19, SPRING MEETING, 1856.

The Fashion Race Course on Long Island was not only the scene of great horse races; many of the famous professional foot races were also held there.

THE NEW YORK CLIPPER

1880
ALMANAC

Published annually, the Clipper Almanac presented a summary of the year's activities in theatre and sport. It became the recognized repository of athletic records.

Father of American Sports

If it seems that New York City was the center of sporting activity in the first half of the nineteenth century, it is no illusion. The City was well on the way to becoming a metropolis. Farms were being transformed into city blocks, commercial enterprises were flourishing, and ships disgorged immigrants and cargoes in unprecedented quantities as the 1840's progressed. The other population centers along the coast were experiencing remarkable changes but New York City had clearly commandeered the lead.

In the Midwest, Ohio, Indiana, and Illinois, had become broad expanses of farms; Michigan, Wisconsin, and Iowa were still vying for settlers. Chicago was rapidly becoming a giant real estate office where land speculators were laying the foundations of great fortunes. In the South agrarian interests ruled, and New Orleans was emerging as a large city, the trade center for the Mississippi Valley. Settlement extended beyond the Mississippi into Arkansas, Missouri, and Iowa, but beyond these boundaries were immense tracts of largely unexplored lands, known only to the traders and trappers. Much of the land at the beginning of the decade lay beyond the boundaries of the United States, yet within ten years Texas, the Southwest, and California would be added to the nation.

Railroad tracks were stretching across the settled parts of the country, bringing communities closer together. The telegraph was further shortening the distances. The Clipper ships and steamboats were even bringing Europe closer to America, attracting distinguished visitors, artists, and critics from overseas.

It was a decade which witnessed many mechanical and industrial advances. It was a time for movements, religious, social, and political. It was a decade of war and conquest. Destiny reigned. The people knew that they were making history and even paused occasionally to marvel at the changes they had witnessed.

New York City, now beyond 300,000 inhabitants, was the largest city in the nation. Its luxurious homes, amusement centers, and business establishments attracted the attention of foreign visitors — but so did the poverty, the hovels of the poor, the pigs roaming through the streets.

It was by no means an egalitarian society. There were people of great wealth who shunned those in the lower economic strata. And those in the lower levels, if they were native born, looked down upon the immigrants. One was an immigrant throughout one's life, and this attitude continued on even through the life span of one's children.

The class distinction in the East and in the South exerted an influence upon the sports scene. For the affluent, horse-racing, field sports, yachting, and cricket were the favorites. The lower economic groups found amusement in rat-catching contests, dog fights, and an assortment of tests of endurance, speed, and physical dexterity among humans.

The members of the polite society looked to England for example. The sporting journals often carried as much news of activities abroad as at home. Running and walking contests in England were reported at great length in the American sporting journals, while similar contests in this country passed unnoticed. In England pedestrians sports were witnessed by princes and members of the nobility who offered the professionals encouragement and sometimes financial support. In the United States, after the great races of 1844 and 1845, the interest in pedestrian sports among the upper classes waned. They were relegated to the lower classes, or at the highest level to the middle classes. The rich could match their horses and wager large sums of money; the poor could find comparable amusement in wagering upon the outcome of a race between professionals from their own class.

On the frontier and in the small towns and villages of the Midwest, these class distinctions were not visible. Sports there were still of a spontaneous nature. At a holiday gathering, a race, wrestling match, or some other contest might be staged to determine who was the better man. A horse race might also be staged from a starting point to a post and back, but it was not a race between blooded stock and for hefty wagers. The class distinctions would have to await the emergence of an urban society.

William T. Porter's *Spirit of the Times* reflected the interests of the upper classes. Much space was devoted to horse-racing and to hunt- and fishing, and little attention was directed toward the activities of the less prosperous. Porter frankly asserted, "We are addressing ourselves to gentlemen of standing, wealth and intelligence — the very corinthian columns of the community."

Athletic competition was for money. No gentleman would consider it proper activity. For the poor man, or the recently arrived immigrant, however, the prospect of winning a purse of $50 or $100 was an attractive inducement. In a day when wages for labor amounted to something between fifty cents and a dollar a day, $100 represented a handsome sum of money — as much as a man might earn in a year, if he were fortunate enough to be employed throughout the year.

The 1840's witnessed a remarkable increase in the volume of immigrants from the British Isles and Germany, particularly toward the end of the decade when famine in Ireland and a political upheaval in Germany sent thousands of refugees to the United States. This influx of immigrants had a definite influence upon sports. As early as 1826 German political exiles had organized gymnasiums and had stimulated interest in gymnastic exercises. Annual gathering of the Scottish Caledonians and the Hibernians promoted running races and weight-throwing contests, all of which contributed toward the growing interest in athletics.

All across the settled part of the nation, cities and towns were springing up and growing. Some of these cities achieved notice and were recognized for their future prospects, but many of them never grew much beyond that initial burst of prosperity and promise. They rested at the eminence reached then. This growth of cities exerted much influence upon sports as rivalries developed between adjoining communities.

The cities required fire protection which was provided by volunteer fire companies. Depending upon the size of a city, a community might have a number of different companies among whom rivalry developed and contests ensued. Since the fire-fighting equipment of that time was hand-operated and drawn to the scene of the fire by men on foot, the life of a fireman was athletic. Companies engaged in contests against others in the same city and even traveled to distant points for the grand competition.

The American scene was changing.

The great races in the first half of the decade of the 1840's belonged to the visiting Englishmen. The second half of the decade would belong to the Indians, with the close being highlighted by a return visit from William Jackson, "the American Deer."

A group of excursionists in visiting the Indian village near Batavia, New York, in July, 1847, made a point of seeking out the famous Seneca runner John Steeprock. Desiring to see the Indian run, the party offered Steeprock a purse to race the wagon to the council house, a distance of slightly over a mile. Steeprock readily assented.

Divesting himself of his boots and hat,

Steeprock signaled that he was ready. The wagon, drawn by a four-horse team, carried four passengers. At the word "Go," they were off. Steeprock, running in a smooth, easy style, had little difficulty outdistancing the carriage which had to negotiate a rough, winding road through the forest. The Indian arrived at the council house six rods in advance of the carriage.

Walking the plank during the 1850's became a popular athletic endeavor in the saloons. The objective was to keep moving back and forth on a plank which might be anywhere from 15 to 40 feet in length for a specified number of hours. Here the versatile Mickey Free nears the end of 100 consecutive hours in a Flushing, Long Island, saloon.

Following this impromptu contest, Steeprock offered to come to the village of Batavia to run five miles against time for a purse. In preparation for the contest, a surveyor measured a half mile east on Genesee Street from the corner of Summit Street. This would be the track.

Steeprock loafed through the first three miles in slightly over six minutes per mile. His companion, Ely Parker, urged him to pick up the pace, lest he fail to run the five miles in under thirty minutes, and thus lose the purse. At this admonition, Steeprock increased his speed, finishing the fourth mile in five minutes and four seconds. Still fearing that Steeprock might not yet make the goal, Parker urged him to run faster yet. On the last mile Steeprock sprinted up and back over the course in 4 minutes 35 seconds.

Steeprock's performance evoked memories of the great races at Hoboken and raised a clamor for a match between the Seneca and Gildersleeve, who was still around and running. The match was not long in being arranged. A ten-mile foot race was scheduled to be run by Gildersleeve, Steeprock, and some other Indians at Buffalo in October.

On October 23, the day of the race, the streets of Buffalo were crowded with carriages, horses, and pedestrians wending their way to the race course. The race had been the chief topic of conversation during the week. The Indian runners were paraded through the streets in carriages preceded by a band. Much to the dismay of sports fans, the celebrated Steeprock was not among the starters. The betting which favored Gildersleeve at long odds before Steeprock's withdrawal became totally in his favor. It was almost impossible to make a wager. However, there were some few who favored the Indian John Canada. He was better than Steeprock, they claimed.

A blast from the bugle called the runners to the starting line. Alongside Gildersleeve were the Indians Canada, Armstrong, Smoke, Sprague, and Simon. At the word "Go!" Gildersleeve took the lead, followed closely by Armstrong and Canada. The rest of the field trailed behind. The order remained unchanged for six miles when from the pack there emerged a tall Indian youngster, George Smoke. He took off after the leaders, passed them on the backstretch of the seventh mile and held this lead for the rest of the race, finishing ten yards in front of Canada. Armstrong finished in third place, and Gildersleeve fourth, just seconds within the hour. The winning time was 58.17.

Smoke, a member of the Cattaraugus tribe, was only eighteen years old. "This George Smoke is the prettiest and smoothest runner I ever saw," commented a reporter from Buffalo.

At the end of the race Gildersleeve and Armstrong left for Chicago, where they were scheduled to compete. For the next few years the Seneca Indian runners would travel throughout the country in search of competition. They would be a major attraction in sporting circles.

In Albany, a month after the Buffalo race, Steeprock, Smoke, Sprague, and Cooper ran in a ten-mile race on a rain-soaked track. The race became a contest between Steeprock and Smoke, with the latter winning by a narrow margin in one hour, twelve seconds. In January 1848, Gildersleeve and Steeprock met in a ten-mile run at Montgomery, Alabama. Gilder was the winner.

Later in the year Coffee, a new Indian runner made his debut at Buffalo by vanquishing Steeprock, Canada, Armstrong, and Smoke in an eleven mile race. This year the Indians performed at Cambridge, Massachusetts, Providence, Rhode Island, and in a number of other Eastern cities. Wherever they went they attracted large crowds.

Somehow, Jackson, the "American Deer," learned of the interest in running which was being generated by the remarkable Seneca Indians. In 1849 he sailed for America. In August he easily won a ten-mile race against an unidentified Indian at Saratoga. In October, however, he was vanquished by the Seneca Canada at Buffalo in 55:49½.

Immediately Jackson began to hurl challenges at Canada and Coffee for a race to be run at New York City. His challenges apparently went unheeded; for Jackson closed the year by competing against a New Yorker, an English immigrant named Robert Poole, in an unusual type of race which enjoyed popularity at the time.

One hundred stones were laid out one yard apart for each competitor. At the signal to start, each runner brought the stones one at a time back to the starting line. If the contest seems like a harmless picnic contest, it was far from being so. It was a series of dashes run in consecutive order, a very strenuous exercise.

Jackson's race with Poole took place in the street at the Red House on Third Avenue on December 3. The betting was that the winner would fail to finish the task within forty minutes. Jackson and Poole had each put up $200 for the purse, with Jackson giving the last stone to his opponent. It proved to be a close race, with Jackson winning by 5 yards in 38 minutes 20 seconds.

Poole's friends, claiming that he lost the race

when he misplaced a stone, demanded a re-match and offered to put up $100 for a second race. Jackson agreed, offering to give Poole the fifth and last stones. Again Jackson won, this time in 37 minutes 28½ seconds.

Jackson then went south to race against horses when he could not find human opponents. In April 1850 Jackson raced William Barlow at New Orleans in a race of five one-mile heats. The runner who took three of the mile heats would be the winner. After the third heat Barlow was unable to continue. Jackson's next race at New Orleans was a five-mile hurdle race in which he gave his seven rivals a 200-yard start. After the second mile Jackson had passed his rivals and went on to win with ease. This race introduced a young Irish immigrant who would be performing as a professional pedestrian for some years to come. He was Mickey Free, who took the third place purse.

By May, Jackson was working his way north. In Cincinnati he was joined by the Seneca Indians. Here he ran the ten miles in 56 minutes 10 seconds to beat Coffee and three other Indians, Armstrong, Jones, and Canada. A week later in the same city Jackson ran Coffee in a five mile race. Jackson led from the start and was 300 yards in the lead at one point, yet Coffee overtook him and went on to win. Loud were the accusations of a sell-out, and there were even threats of a lynching.

Jackson returned to New York City, where he again issued in *The Spirit of the Times* another challenge, offering to race any man in the United States, any Indian, or any horse. A few weeks later he was in Rochester running against Steeprock and other Indians in a ten mile race which he won.

In October Jackson was in Buffalo but this time as a spectator at a one-mile race between two Indians, an eighteen-year-old Tonawanda Seneca named Hill and an unidentified Canadian Indian from Montreal. The latter won the mile race in the unprecedented time of 4 minutes 33 seconds.

On October 29, 1850, Jackson was in Nashville, Tennessee, where he was to race against the clock in an effort to run 10½ miles within an hour for a $300 purse. He won the purse, having covered the distance with ten seconds to spare. In November the "American Deer" was in St. Louis running against horses. The horse was to trot ten miles to Jackson's five and a half miles. In this race Jackson trailed the horse by three yards at the finish.

In May of 1851 Jackson was back in St. Louis for a ten-mile race with Coffee. For the first seven miles of the race the lead alternated between the two contestants until in the eighth mile when Jackson opened a gap of thirty yards and was never headed after that point. He won in 58:34. Jackson again beat Coffee at ten miles at Nashville in June.

On Jackson's second tour of the United States, his earlier opponent, Gildersleeve, was conspicuous by his absence. This was not because of any reluctance on Gildersleeve's part to face his English rival. Gilder had responded to the lure of California. In 1851 he won a 20 mile race at San Francisco against one William Peck. In the land of gold the stakes were high; the backers of the two runners raised a purse of $4,000 for the race.

Jackson returned to England in 1851 and a year later astounded the sporting world by running the ten miles in 51 minutes 34 seconds. He beat the champion of England by a third of a mile.

Jackson's tour of the United States demonstrated the difference in ability between the English and the American runners. While the Seneca Indians appeared invincible to many, they were easily outdistanced by the English professional. Running and walking in England rested upon two centuries of tradition. Time had permitted the development of techniques and training methods. In the United States the sport was in its infancy, any techniques or methods having been borrowed from the British.

The interest in running and walking in the United States was growing, however. Much of it was in the form of match races in which one runner would issue a challenge to another, stakes would be posted, and the race would be held in the streets, at a track, or on a cricket field. There were no recognized champions in the country, although there were claimants to titles. In the western New York area the Indians held title, while in the New York City

Patrick Buckley, "The Lynn Buck," was a successful pro, who boasted victories over Boston Buck, Shooting Star, and Young Sport at the five mile distance.

clamoring for more sport then took up a collection to raise a purse for a half-mile race between William Barlow and North Star. Barlow won with ease. North Star, whose specialty was walking, then stood on the judge's stand to challenge any man to walk a mile for a small stake. He offered a 30-yard start to anyone who would compete against him. One Thomas Regier accepted and won in 8 minutes and 49 seconds.

There was little organization in the program. It was sport and entertainment for the working class. Few from the upper class would have patronized the Red House and few would have had an interest in the sport of the laboring

area William Barlow was regarded as the best, especially at distances under five miles.

A typical meet of the time would be one like that held at the Red House, a tavern or public house in Harlem. A purse of $25 was raised for a five-mile race. A crowd of 1,500 people assembled for the race which had three contestants, Amos Saunders, who called himself "the Brooklyn Pet," Robert Poole, an English immigrant and one who simply billed himself as "Yankee Bob" of New York. Poole won the race in 29 minutes 28 seconds. The crowd

Athletic competition among the Irish immigrants in the Boston area became intense during the 1850's. Large crowds, which were not always peaceful, attended the races and sometimes assaulted the athletes if the outcome of the race did not please them. George Brown was a prominent ten-miler in the Boston area.

William Hughes did a lot of wandering in his time. Born in Liverpool, England, he emigrated to Boston as a child, competed in walking races there during the 1840's, then went to California during the gold rush period. In the 1850's he returned to the East as a Californian and introduced the plank-walking feat.

class. While a race between a well-known English star and an American at a regular track might have some appeal which would cut across class lines, the average sports event would be for the lower classes and would often pass unnoticed by the press.

The appearance in 1853 of a new sporting publication, *The New York Clipper*, changed this picture. Edited by a Philadelphian named Frank Queen, the *Clipper* carried articles on all sporting events, pedestrianism, horse-racing, dog fighting, cock fighting, rat catching, pugilism, cricket, baseball, rowing, and a host of

other sports activities, as well as news of the theatre and the circus. It became the clearing house for most sports. Challenges were issued through its columns; stakes were held by the editor; and abuses were exposed by the paper which had become something of a watchdog of the sporting world.

Issued weekly, the *Clipper* enlisted the aid of correspondents from coast to coast to record the results of sporting events in towns and villages throughout the nation and abroad. Suddenly the winner of a contest in Iowa or Wisconsin became news. No other publication contributed to the popularity of sports more than the *Clipper*. The acceptance of baseball as a national sport owed much to Frank Queen.

James Smith upset William Sheehan, "Boston Buck," in a one-mile race in the National Theatre at Boston, winning in 4 minutes 57 seconds.

Pedestrianism and athletic sports received much attention from the *Clipper* and the interest in the sport increased as the results of the contests were reported. Each year for two decades Frank Queen also published *The New York Clipper Almanac*, an annual summary of sports and theatrical events, which became a repository of records of all kinds. If anyone merits the title "Father of American Sports," the honor belongs to Frank Queen, for he has no rivals. He exposed fraud whenever he detected it; he called for the adoption of standards, and he stimulated organization in a chaotic era of competition. Most important, he provided recognition to athletes at a time when their achievements were generally ignored by the press.

With the advent of the *Clipper*, the names of pedestrian stars became known, and the recognition of certain figures as American champions gradually evolved. In the 1850's William Barlow was still the outstanding runner at distances from a half mile to five miles. Gildersleeve was last heard from in California, but his day as a distance star was all but over. The Seneca Indians continued their dominance in the western New York area and occasionally made trips to the East for races. New names began to appear, and from among these names emerged figures who would be labeled champions.

Mickey Free, a young Irish immigrant, who was born Robert Harriott in Castle Blarney, Ireland, in 1819, started his professional running career at the age of fifteen. From 1834 until 1850, Mickey competed in races throughout the British Isles for small stakes. None of the big names of the time appeared among his opponents. He came to America in 1850, making his debut in a five-mile hurdle race at New Orleans, where he finished third behind William Jackson. Running the hurdles, particularly over the long distances, was the specialty in which Mickey Free laid claim to the title of champion. The hurdles, three feet three inches high, were placed 100 to a mile. Mickey claimed the record for leaping 1,000 and 1,200 hurdles.

Although Mickey by today's standards would hardly have a claim to championship laurels, he was regarded as a capable performer in the 1850's. Much of his fame rested upon his ex-

hibitions and contests against time. From time to time he had opponents in his long distance hurdle races; but just as often he ran by himself, betting that he would accomplish his task in a specified time. When the novelty of the hurdle races began to wane, he performed "Nine Athletic Feats," a series of contests against time. Mickey was a busy traveller who took his show to New England, western New York, and into the Midwest. His personality probably contributed as much to his success as a gate attraction as his legs. The *Clipper* often referred to his smiling countenance, "his good-natured mug," and his "blarney."

Mickey received frequent notice in the columns of the *Clipper,* which attempted to follow his career as he traveled about. "It is hard to keep the run of this jolly pedestrian and hurdle leaper. He is here, there and everywhere," wrote the editor. Mickey at this time was in Rochester and Buffalo. A week later he was performing in Hamilton, Ontario, en route to London, Ontario.

William Barlow still competed when the opportunity offered itself. Employed as a pilot on a ferryboat, Barlow now confined himself to races in the New York City area. His career was coming to a close just as pedestrianism was becoming popular. In March 1854, he was matched to run a mile race against one Hiram Horton, who had won a number of matches at shorter distances, principally as a sprinter.

The match, which had been arranged in a saloon in February, had become the source of much excitement in sporting circles. Betting on the race was heavy, much of it in favor of Horton, a factor which puzzled many, since Barlow was regarded as the best mile runner in the country. On the day of the race more than 2,000 spectators crowded the stands and the rail to witness the race.

Horton went out into an early lead, but was soon passed by Barlow. They remained close together until the half-mile point when there appeared to be some jostling. Horton then left the track and walked to the judge's stand to claim that he had been fouled and should be declared the winner. Barlow kept on running and finished the mile in 5:02½. After consultation the judges announced that there was no evidence of a foul and that Barlow was the winner. There was a great deal of rumbling about the outcome of the race which prompted accusations of a "fix." Actually, the race turned out to be a double cross. Barlow in a letter to the *Clipper* revealed that he had been offered $100 in cash and a note for $250 to let Horton win. He had taken the cash but had ignored the agreement to let Horton win.

At the same meeting a purse of twenty dollars was raised and a match was made between the veteran Mickey Free to run two miles against a young unknown named John Grindall. Since Mickey Free was well known to all present, the odds were heavy in his favor with few takers. Grindall, a young butcher, had a few years earlier won a five dollar purse in a mile race at the Red House in Harlem. In a lot adjoining the saloon, impromptu races of this sort were often held.

At the signal Mickey Free darted into the lead, but young Grindall stayed close to him. On nearing the half mile, Grindall drew abreast of Mickey. Soon both runners were on the ground. Grindall scrambled to his feet in an instant and was running again. Mickey chose to walk across to the judge's stand to claim a foul which the judges quickly denied. Grindall was awarded the purse.

The young butcher had now officially entered the professional ranks. Through the columns of the *Clipper* he issued challenges to Horton for a mile race and to Mickey Free for a two-mile race. Grindall's challenges passed unheeded. It was not until July that he was able to find a chance to compete. This was at a race held at the Hippodrome on a small track around the interior of the building. The race was twelve times around the track for a prize of fifty dollars in gold. Attracted by the purse, nineteen runners started, including Barlow and the leading short distance runners, Jack Williams and James Dorcy, both of Brooklyn. In an upset Grindall won by two yards over Barlow.

This upset by such a close margin raised a clamor for a rematch. Barlow, to retain his dominance as a professional runner, had to win

over Grindall. The proprietors of the Hippodrome lost little time in offering a purse of sixty dollars for the winner of a two-mile race on August 9, 1854. In this race Barlow retrieved his reputation by overtaking Grindall on the last lap to win by three yards.

Two weeks later a five mile race was scheduled on the same track with a purse of fifty dollars being offered. Six competitors started on the 44 laps around the Hippodrome, but by the 21st lap only Barlow and Grindall remained in the race. At the halfway mark Barlow gave up, and Grindall went on to cover the five miles in 28:40⅖. Not content with having been vanquished twice by a novice, Barlow promptly issued a challenge for a rematch which Grindall accepted. In this race on the 30th lap Grindall, far in the lead, passed Barlow to lead him by a full lap. Soon Barlow gave up and Grindall went on to finish the five miles in 28:39. Grindall was now hailed as "Champion Pedestrian." "The mere fact of his thrice defeating Barlow, who has heretofore stood at the head of the list in this country, is sufficient to place him as A No. 1 runner, especially at long distances. In a distance race of five or ten miles, we do not believe there is an individual in New York, at present, who can beat him," wrote the *Clipper*.

Now the clamor was for a ten-mile race between Barlow and Grindall; but at this distance Barlow had no desire to contend. Grindall had to content himself with issuing challenges and racing against the clock. For a purse he ran a race against time on the Newark plank road. The time allowed for the three miles was 18 minutes, but all that Grindall required was 16 minutes 30 seconds.

In search of competition Grindall traveled to Rochester to race against the fleet Senecas. In a one-mile race there, he beat the Indian Sundown in a 4:42 mile. Matched against the Indian Albert Smith for a ten mile race, Grindall trailed his Seneca rival to the tape by ten yards. Upon his return to New York City, Grindall issued a challenge to Smith for a return match to be run in the City. William Baker of Buffalo, Smith's manager, responded with an offer to race in Buffalo. Later he offered a compromise — to race halfway between Buffalo and New York City at Syracuse. Grindall did not appear too anxious to run against Indian Smith at any place but New York City.

In 1855 Grindall competed in a number of races, vanquishing opponents at five and ten miles throughout the East. The most notable race of this year was a victory over John Stetson, the New England champion, in a ten mile race at Cambridge.

The year 1856 saw him repeat the victories at five and ten miles. His only losses were in a two-mile race indoors when he became ill and a quarter mile race at Lynn, Massachusetts. He lacked the speed for so short a distance. In September of this year he had undertaken a wager to run twenty miles in under two hours at the Lynn Trotting Course. Just before the race, when a hoodlum attacked Frank Queen, editor of the *New York Clipper,* for statements published in the newspaper, Grindall in attempting to defend Queen was soundly kicked in the knee. In spite of this injury he started on his twenty mile run and ran within the time for thirteen miles. However, after the sixth mile, he began to complain about the pain in his knee where he had been kicked. The pain increased as he ran, finally compelling him to give up the attempt in the fourteenth mile.

Published challenges for races from other runners began to exclude Grindall. The runners wanted races with anyone except him. When he appeared for a five mile open race in Boston, he was told by the sponsors that he could not compete. In spite of the reluctance of runners to accept a race with Grindall, some questioned his right to call himself "champion." He responded with a challenge to any man in the United States and Canada to race him at any distance from five to twenty miles at the Union Race Course. There were no takers.

In 1857 he went on tour in search of competition but had to settle on races against horses in St. Louis.

When a Mr. Travis made the offer to race the Indians Albert Smith and Louis Bennett against any other two men in the United States, Grindall offered to run either of them; but no match resulted. The *Clipper* remarked: "It is a little strange that no ten mile runner has had the nerve to accept the double match

William Sheehan, who competed under the name "Boston Buck," stands proudly by some of his running and firemen's trophies.

with Mr. Grindall, considering the many pedestrians there are in this section of the country."

The 1850's had witnessed a veritable explosion of interest in sports. Toward the end of 1856 the editor of the *Clipper* looked back over the past few years and marveled at the increased interest in sports. It would make a difference in the general health of the nation, the editor asserted, pointing out that immigrants arriving from the old country always appeared "hale and hearty," a factor which could be traced to the exercise which they derived from participation in sports. In the past few years cricket and baseball clubs had been organized, competition in rowing and pedestrianism had spread throughout the country, boxing had become a popular activity, and just about every competitive activity had experienced a growth in its following. For this remarkable increase in the popularity of sports the editor of the *Clipper* claimed a portion of the credit. As the pioneer in general sports publication, the *Clipper* made it possible for its readers to learn of the performances of others. It opened a window on sports activities in Boston, Philadelphia, Buffalo, Cleveland, Chicago, Milwaukee, St. Louis, and California. No town was too small and no athlete too much of a novice to win the attention of the *New York Clipper*. Gradually, newspapers which for the most part had totally ignored sports began to run items on local and national sports feats. Before long there would be sports columns in the newspapers, and before the end of the century the sports page and the sports sections would be an integral part of most newspapers.

The sports mania spread throughout the country. Boston developed a number of runners and walkers whose names and exploits appeared frequently in the sports news in the 1850's. In addition to John Stetson, who claimed the New England championship, there were such figures as the Boston Buck, the Lynn Buck, the Boston Greyhound, Shooting Star, Bunker Hill Boy, the Cambridge Deer, and the Worcester Pet. The adoption of professional names had long been a custom in England. Competition among

Kennovan, the champion of California, born in Boston in 1814, won fame for his walking exploits in San Francisco and in the gold mining camps.

the Boston area runners who were largely Irish was intense. Large crowds attended the races, and they were not always peaceful crowds. At one contest a group of hoodlums assaulted John Stetson. The assault upon Frank Queen was in retaliation for his exposé of hoodlums who had tried to win control over the races for the mob.

Chicago and Milwaukee were enjoying sports activities. Local champions had a chance to match their talents against the traveling Senecas. At the distances the Senecas were invincible, but when Indian Smith accepted a match with a Milwaukee runner at 100 yards, he was easily outclassed. Runners were on the move. The St. Louis Pet ran against the Illinois Footpad, and Philadelphia George stopped in Detroit long enough to try his speed against the locals. Even in such an out-of-the-way place as Saginaw, Michigan, which was a lumbering community in 1859, a visiting pedestrian was sufficient cause to raise a purse, rope off a street, and test the speed of the local favorites against the outsider.

In California, miners on their Sundays enjoyed sports events which often included running races. One diarist recorded the interest and excitement generated by a match between a man and an Indian squaw for a mile race. Spectators came from miles around to the mining camp to watch and wager. The Squaw won.

From California came William Hughes, who had astounded the sports followers there with his feats of endurance by walking 100 hours without rest. Born in Liverpool, England, in 1819, he had started his walking career in the Boston area as early as 1843, but in 1853 he went to California where his long distance feats attracted so much attention that he felt that it might be profitable to return to the East. Hughes performed his endurance trials in saloons or small halls before an audience by walking back and forth on a three-feet wide plank which might be anywhere from fifteen to forty feet long. The objective was to continue walking without rest for 100 consecutive hours. The performance provided many possibilities for wagers. The spectators could bet that he would or would not finish, they could bet on the hour he would give up, and they could bet on the times or miles covered.

Soon this activity became popular throughout the country. The long, narrow platform was erected in the saloon where the patrons of the sport came to imbibe and lay their wagers on the outcome of the performance. Before long Mickey Free was in on the act along with a host of other performers. Even the respectable John Grindall, who found himself in need of money one winter, traveled to Boston to walk the plank in a saloon for 100 hours.

Walking the plank became a popular "sport" for women, too. There was the Highland Maid, Flora Temple, Mrs. Bentley, Mrs. Dallison, Mrs. Jackson, the Lynn Prioress, and Mrs. Mickey Free. Kate Irvine had early in the decade attracted large crowds to watch her walk 500 miles in 500 hours. Mrs. Mickey Free had also performed as a hurdler in company with her husband. The plank walking feat by women in saloons was hardly regarded as a respectable activity, but it was enjoyed by the men. "The prettiest walker I have ever seen," commented a Milwaukee male follower of the sport in evaluating Mrs. Bentley's performance.

Mrs. Bentley, reportedly from Ohio, performed in the Midwest before coming to New York City to walk the plank for thirty hours at

Thomas Woods, born in England in 1837, won his first race at the age of 12 in Lowell, Massachusetts, where he dominated the pro runners.

the Broadway Tabernacle on April 27, 1857. This was the twentieth time that Mrs. Bentley had performed this feat, having accomplished it seventeen times in the past year. Much sympathy was expressed in her behalf when it was discovered that she was in the advanced stages of consumption and had resorted to this activity to support her three children.

Napoleon Campana, alias "Young Sport," born in Petersburg, Virginia in 1836, first won fame as a runner when he beat Billy Lee in a race around Tompkins Square in New York City. He remained one of the professional stalwarts for 25 years.

"Mrs. Bentley was originally a vocalist, well known on the Western 'boards,'" wrote the *Clipper;* "but in consequence of a serious throat infection was compelled to resign that profession, and, for the maintenance of herself and three children, adopted that of the pedestrian. While we regret her sanguine feelings have prompted her to undertake so severe a task in her present prostrate condition, yet the promptings of a mother's heart are above censure and we wish her success for the nonce..."

By the end of the decade there was some falling off in the general interest in running and walking. Perhaps the theatrical aspects of some of the performers did much to diminish interest; but it is more likely that professionalism with the elements of inherent dishonesty attached to it was a more effective deterrent to acceptance. There were indications that amateurism would eventually displace the professional. In Philadelphia a Pedestrian Association was formed. "The main objective of the association," it was reported, "is the improvement of its members in pedestrian and athletic exercises, which are so well calculated to promote the bodily health and vigor of all who indulge in such sports." Elsewhere contests were being sponsored for amateurs, with medals and trophies for prizes.

When the manager of the Hippodrome offered cash prizes for the winner of a one mile footrace for firemen, the participants were soundly condemned for competing for money and thus disgracing the uniform of "such a noble institution." The seeds of amateurism were sprouting.

For runners and walkers the 1850's were a memorable decade. It had produced the champion John Grindall; it had introduced organized competition to communities throughout the nation; and it had brought together large numbers of people in a bond of common interest. The records made by the athletes are not very impressive by today's standards. Professional runners won mile races in five minutes or more, times that today would embarrass a competent junior high school runner. Although Barlow was credited with having run the mile in 4:36, this time was in a class by itself, never equaled in his time, or even approached. At the beginnings of the 1850's, the English record for the mile was 4:28; and by the end of the decade an English runner had lowered the mark to 4:22¼. A long, steady trial of competition would be required before the American runners could claim any records, especially in the longer distances, to match those of the English. Nevertheless, the decade of the 1850's marked a beginning toward that goal.

The 1860's had barely started when the dissension which had been mounting between the North and the South broke into war. The *New York Clipper* editor wrote in May 1861: "The season just opened for outdoor sports does not promise to be very successful. Before the attack on Fort Sumter, prospects were excellent for a brisk campaign, but now the chances are the other way. Many of the young men belonging to Cricket, Baseball, and Boat Club organizations have joined their fortunes to some military company, and now are serving their country where duty calls them. Those who are left behind, will not enter into the spirit of their respective games with the same feelings as heretofore. Everything must give way to the all-absorbing business of the day, the defence of our government against rebellion; and outdoor sports and pastimes for the year 1861 will meet with little attention."

Two weeks later a Mr. Evans called at the office of the *Clipper* to post a challenge for a 10 or 12 mile race with John Grindall for $500 or $1,000 a side. Just after the challenge was received Grindall walked into the *Clipper* office to announce that he had enlisted in Colonel Kerrigan's 25th Regiment, New York Volunteers. He thought it strange that after waiting for three or four years for a competitor that someone should come forward with a challenge accompanied by the right amount of money just as he was no longer available for competition. He promised that if he should return from service "sound in wind and limb," he would be willing to accept the challenge.

The Noble Savage:
The Story of Deerfoot

At mid-century at the county fairs in western New York in the 1800's one of the featured spectacles was often an Indian running race in which the native runners tested their skills against each other for cash prizes. It was at such a fair at Fredonia, New York, in 1856 that Lewis Bennett, who was later to win fame under the name of "Deerfoot," first came into public notice as he won the purse of fifty dollars in the five-mile race in twenty-five minutes, a time so fast that few believed it to be accurate.

Two large Indian reservations, one at Tonawanda and the other at Cattaraugus, contributed the Seneca runners who won widespread fame for their athletic feats. Extraordinary performances of endurance and speed were attributed to these native runners who dominated the athletic scene to such an extent that some scheduled races excluded Indians, or the sponsors included a race for Indians only.

Deerfoot was born on the Cattaraugus Reservation in Erie County, New York, around 1830. Some sources give 1828 as the year of his birth, while others attribute dates as late as 1837 for his birth. At his death in 1895 Deerfoot's son insisted that his father was sixty-five years old, which would support the 1830 date.

When Deerfoot's name first began to appear in the reports of results of running races, a Seneca named Albert Smith was the leading runner among the Indians; and Steeprock, the dominant Indian runner of the 1840's, was still competing.

In 1854 John Grindall with Mickey Free, who was as much a performer as an athlete, journeyed to Buffalo to try their skills against the Indian runners. Mickey Free in a quarter-mile race beat his opponent, the Indian Armstrong, in 56 seconds. He was then matched to race the Indians Burton, Armstrong, Bennett, and Steeprock, in a five-mile race over hurdles, twenty-five hurdles in each quarter mile. In this contest Burton emerged the winner. A seven-mile race over 700 hurdles a few weeks later was won by the Indian Sundown, although Albert Smith finished first but was disqualified because he had knocked over a hurdle and had refused to replace it. The rules required that the hurdles which were three-feet high had to be returned to upright position if knocked over.

In other races Grindall defeated Sundown in a 4:42 mile but ran second to Albert Smith at ten miles. In all of these contests Bennett failed to find a place among the winners.

It was not until October 30, 1857, that Bennett was able to threaten Albert Smith. In a ten-mile contest at the fair in Buffalo, Bennett out-lasted a field of seven Indians and one John Stetson, who was billed as the Massachusetts champion. In this race Bennett posted the respectable time of 56 minutes 19 seconds for ten miles.

A year later the sporting journals reported that Albert Smith at a fair in Rome, New York, had beaten Lewis Bennett at five miles in the time of 25 minutes 18 seconds. The *New York*

Clipper expressed doubts about the time, saying, "... either the distance has not been correctly measured, or the time has not been accurately noted."

In the same issue of the *New York Clipper* appeared a challenge from two Indians stopping at the Merrimac House in Boston offering to race any comers at the distances of 5, 10, or 15 miles for $200 to $500 a side. The Indians were Albert Smith, who was billed as the champion of the Tonawandas, and Lewis Bennett, who was the champion of the Cattaraugus. Their challenge fell on deaf ears for the most part. John Grindall responded with an offer to meet them in a series of races at 5, 10, and 15 miles in the following May with each side to put up $500. Subsequent comments by others indicated that the impression prevailed in some circles that Grindall was not very anxious to face the Indians.

Two weeks later the promoters succeeded in arranging a race over the fifteen mile distance to be held at the Franklin Trotting Park in North Chelsea. Smith and Bennett were scheduled to meet a field of five local runners, but only two appeared at the starting line, James Griffin of Boston and one who was simply listed as the "Reading Champion." Prizes would be awarded the runners who were leading at 5 miles, 10 miles, and at the finish. The grand prize would be awarded only if the winner covered the distance in less than 1½ hours.

Bennett covered the first five miles in 26 minutes even and passed the ten mile mark in 55 minutes, 54 seconds. The "Reading Champion" dropped out after a mile; Griffin left the track after five miles; and Smith gave up at fourteen miles.

Bennett's announced time for the distance was 1 hour, 29 minutes, and 50 seconds, narrowly within the time goal. A long letter from a "Sportsman" published in the *New York Clipper* disagreed with the announced time and questioned the honesty of the event. Since betting was an important aspect of pedestrian contests, often the principal reason for racing, the time goal was a very important consideration. The "Sportsman" said that he had timed the race from the stands with different results, as

had others. The corrected time, he insisted, was 1 hour, 30 minutes, and 36 seconds.

The Indians a week later engaged in one more contest, a five mile race, at North Bridgewater. John Stetson was scheduled to run but withdrew because of unfavorable track conditions. Lewis Bennett won over his competition and one non-Indian competitor in 27 minutes.

Bennett and Smith continued their running but failed to attract any notable opposition. On

∽∽∽∽∽∽∽∽∽∽∽∽∽∽∽∽∽∽

The famous New York diarist, Philip Hone, recorded that the race had developed as the result of a large wager between two wealthy sportsmen, John C. Stevens and Samuel L. Gouverneur. Stevens had bet that he would produce by a given time a man who could run ten miles within one hour. To accomplish this feat he offered the prize of $1,000.

On the morning of the race, diarist Hone found himself on the road to the race course, "jostled by every description of vehicle conveying every description of people." The crowd at the track, Hone recorded was as large as that which gathered to watch the horse race won by the famous Eclipse. Hone wrote, "... immense sums were betted by men who find it difficult to pay their honest debts." Henry Stannard, the winner, at 24, tall and thin, weighing 165 pounds, was just the right build for running, Hone concluded.

∽∽∽∽∽∽∽∽∽∽∽∽∽∽∽∽∽∽

July 13, 1859, they were reported as having attempted to run 100 miles with 13 hours at the Empire Trotting Course at Albany, New York. Running in a ninety degree temperature on a sultry day, Bennett gave out on the 28th mile, and Smith stopped at 61 miles. He had passed the 50 mile mark in 7 hours and 28 seconds.

In June of 1861 an English promoter named George Martin arrived quietly in New York City with three runners, Nevin, Mower, and White. They were what we would today call "ringers," but at that time the term was "planters." Nevin and White were runners of unusual ability in England, but to the large mass of Americans they would be relatively unknown. The prospects of their challenges being met by runners of less ability were promising; the lure of easily won purses, to say nothing of wagering, was attractive. However, they had not reckoned with the vigilance of the *New York Clipper,* which soon exposed them as "planters."

A series of races did take place at the Fashion Pleasure racing course on Long Island, the first of which saw White and Mower matched against Lewis Bennett and Albert Smith in a ten mile contest. Mower and Smith dropped out before the halfway point; and for a while the race was between Bennett and White, until the latter spurted into the lead at the seven mile mark, at which point Bennett retired from the race. White went on to finish the distance in a few seconds under one hour.

In a racing program on July 1 at the Fashion course Nevin easily won the quarter mile in 52¼ seconds. A half hour later he toed the mark with White, Bennett, and three other runners in a mile contest. This race soon settled down to three runners, Nevin, White, and Bennett. The Indian stayed close to his English rivals until the home stretch when they easily pulled ahead to win in a dead heat in 4:39¼. The runners were allowed thirty minutes to rest before running the second heat of a mile. Nevin scratched, and only White and Bennett answered the starter. This race appeared to be a close contest with the lead changing from time to time until the last quarter when White dashed ahead to win by seventy yards in 4:55¼.

As the fans were about to leave the stands, it was announced that a purse of fifty dollars had been raised for a ten mile race and that White, Bennett, and Grindall would be the contestants. Grindall, now a volunteer in the Union Army, had been there to watch the races. The race provided ample elements of uncertainty for wagering. Grindall was admittedly out of condition, and Bennett and White had exhausted themselves in two grueling mile races. At the start of the race Grindall led, followed closely by Bennett, while White trailed along some distance in the rear. After a few miles White came to life and took over the lead, toying with his

opponents over most of the distance. Bennett, nearly in a state of collapse after eight miles, was led from the track by his friends. White finished the ten miles 100 yards in front of Grindall in 58 minutes 40 seconds.

It may be perceived from this review of Deerfoot's career and his encounters with Jack White, the English champion, that the Seneca Indian had not achieved a record as a runner that would cause him to be remembered beyond his time. The encounters with White, however, introduced Bennett to the promoter George Martin, who arranged to transport Bennett to England for a series of races. They saw the possibilities of the grand promotion, for in England there was a mysterious, romantic concept of the American Indian. The handsome young Deerfoot, tall at 5 feet, 10½ inches and husky at 162 pounds, would serve as a good gate attraction. In August a notice appeared in the English sports journal, *Bell's Life:*

An Indian of Catterangus, North America, known by the names of Deerfoot and Red Jacket, has visited England for the purposes of testing the fleet powers of our pedestrians and aims at nothing lower than the 10 miles Champion's Cup and 6 miles Champion's Belt. Ready to make a match at each distance, he has left £10 with us, and the acceptor has only to cover this sum, and meet the Indian (or his representative) at Mr. Wilson's 'Spotted Dog', on Friday next, and the match will go on.

Few athletes who visited England provoked such curiosity or aroused so much interest as did Lewis Bennett, and his promoters missed no opportunity to enhance the romantic image of their protege. The London *Sporting News* went into ecstacy over Deerfoot.

. . . Although meetings between representatives of different countries have not been uncommon in England, yet hitherto, we question whether a genuine child of the prairie, like Deerfoot, of the tribe of the Senecas, has ever tried his skill, stamina, and speed, against an Englishman in England. There have been instances in which men represented to be aboriginal inhabitants of the tropics have contended, but they have been detected deceptions. It was evident, however, from their first moment, that Deerfoot was no imposter. Any one who read the elaborate narrative of Catlin's experiences among the wild tribes of America, or the equally faithful delineations of Fenimore Cooper, could not doubt for one moment that the aspirant who had been induced to cross the 'big sea water,' to contest with English pedestrians was a pure bred son of that interesting and intelligent race of people. The authors to whom we have referred have made us thoroughly familiar with the dexterity and muscular skill of the tribes and the names which they have appropriated to themselves, of 'Deerfoot,' 'Arrow,' &c., &c., would show that, for generations, they have especially prided themselves on being fleet of foot. Longfellow, the American poet, who, too, has devoted great time to the study of the American aboriginal character, in his charming poem, 'The Song of Hiawatha,' represents the hero of the song, who is an ideal creation of the national character endowed with superhuman speed.

'Out of childhood into manhood,
Now had grown my Hiawatha,
Skilled in all the craft of hunters,
Learned in all the lore of old men.
In all youthful sports and pastimes,
In all manly arts and labors,
Swift of foot was Hiawatha.
He could shoot an arrow from him.
And run forward with such fleetness,
That the arrow fell behind him.'

The *Sporting News* went on to explain that Deerfoot had never been in a match race in his life. His running had been done in the hunting field where he demonstrated that he was the swiftest runner of his tribe. The article disclosed that Deerfoot's managers were enhancing the image with all of their imagination. The Indian appeared in public wrapped in a wolfskin blanket and wore a headband and an eagle feather. "In personal appearance, Deerfoot is majestic, with remarkably handsome features, and is mild and unobtrusive in his demeanor," wrote the London *Sporting News*. He could speak no English, the reporter explained, relating that his trainer Jack MacDon-

old had to communicate with him through signs and gestures. When he appeared for his first race against a young English runner named Edward Mills, the excitement built up by the promotion was intense.

The race was scheduled for September 9th at the Metropolitan Grounds at Hackney Wick, just outside London. Six o'clock was set for the time so that spectators could come from work to witness the great contest. All the trains from London were jammed with men of all stations in society — no ladies though, for race tracks were regarded as pretty rough places. By six o'clock 4,000 spectators lined the 260-yard track in anxious anticipation of the great race. The reporter for the *Sporting News* wrote, "The Indian, on his arrival was walked round the ground by Jack MacDonald, and his appearance caused a great rush to obtain a peek at him, as he stalked in stately manner, with his wolf skin around him, looking the very model of one of Fenimore Cooper's Mohicans or Pawnees."

When Deerfoot and Mills stood at the starting line and when Deerfoot had dropped his wolf skin from his shoulders, the Indian's size was accented by the contrast with his opponent who was only 5 feet, four inches tall, and 112 pounds in weight. "A loud buzz of admiration" rose from the crowd as Deerfoot stripped to the buff. "He wore a slight red apron around his waist, and a band around his head, with one eagle feather, and altogether presented a very picturesque appearance."

At the pistol shot Deerfoot dashed into the lead making Mills appear like a pygmy as he trailed behind. Mills soon overtook him and went into the lead. From time to time Deerfoot in a burst of speed would pass Mills, only to relinquish the lead to his little opponent. In this manner the lead changed over the six miles, creating much excitement among the spectators. On the last lap Mills pulled ahead, winning by twenty yards in 32 minutes, 31½ seconds.

Although he had lost his first race on English soil, Deerfoot was still a favorite of the crowd. The spectators stood around and cheered and called for Deerfoot and would not go away until he came to the window in acknowledgment of their cheers.

This enthusiasm was not shared by the *New*

DEERFOOT,
THE SENECA INDIAN RUNNER.
IN ONE OF HIS CELEBRATED MATCHES.

York Clipper which looked upon the whole promotion as a swindle. After the race with Mills, the *Clipper* expressed its skepticism, saying that the Indian had played "his points" well. "The contest seems to have been quite interesting, and, whether the race was square or not, the spectators were well pleased," the *Clipper* concluded.

In the next race when Deerfoot defeated Jack White in four miles, the *Clipper* in an item headed "SHREWD PERHAPS, BUT IS IT HONEST?" thought Deerfoot's English tour was pure humbug.

First the Indian loses a race, now he is permitted to win one, and we suppose, for the sake of keeping up the excitement, he will be allowed to 'turn about and wheel about and do just so,' winning and losing alternately, although perhaps not in regular order, until the tour of England has been made, and the 'flats' there have been duped out of their spare cash, as well as the cash they cannot spare. It appears, too, that they are making quite a fool of the poor Indian, dressing him up in all manner of queer costumes, putting 'rings on his fingers and bells on his toes,' and all that sort of thing, besides issuing all sorts of lies in reference to his sleeping and eating, etc., for no other purpose than to make him a laughing stock by parading him before a gaping multitude. What a sad thing it is that men will resort to such low, petty measures, to raise the wind. When shall we see the end of it? This is being done we understand under the auspices of Jack Mc-Donald. How the mighty have fallen!

Pedestrian contests in England originated for the most part in public houses, which in some cases owned tracks adjacent to their places of business. This was the case at Hackney Wick, where Deerfoot made his English debut, which was owned by the White Lion. It was a small track, 260 yards in circumference, part of it lined with trees on both sides of the track. The grading and laying out of the curves on such tracks left much to be desired for running.

So completely had Deerfoot captured the public imagination that he faced a deluge of challenges. For the next two months he would be facing the best runners England had to offer in races every Monday evening. Following his initial race with Mills, Deerfoot, with the aid of a fifty-yard start, defeated White in a four-mile race at Manchester. A week later he was back at Hackney Wick to race Mills, White, and John Brighton at ten miles, all four of the runners starting from scratch. This time they were vying for the ten-mile Championship Cup.

Mills went into the lead at a fast pace, being relieved by White, with Deerfoot spurting occasionally to take his turn in front. White lasted but three miles, then the race became a contest between Mills and Deerfoot. The Indian's style of running in irregular bursts of speed was upsetting to the professionals who were trained to run at an even pace. Mills would take over the lead for a time, only to be headed by Deerfoot in a sudden explosive sprint which would require Mills to apply pressure to overtake him. Mills would then settle down to an even pace, only to face a repetition of Deerfoot's sudden spurt. Finally after eight and a half miles, Mills yielded and left the track. Deerfoot chose to continue on to the end of the distance which he covered in 54 minutes, 21 seconds.

On the following Monday Deerfoot was in Dublin to race the Irish champion, John Levett. The Indian's reception here was as enthusiastic as it had been in England. When he emerged from the inn to walk to the nearby track, he was greeted by a cheering throng which filled the street trying to get a glimpse of the colorfully attired Indian. In the ten-mile race Deerfoot gave his opponent a one minute start which he won back shortly after the five mile mark. Levett retired from the race utterly exhausted at this point, and Deerfoot went on to win in a record 53 minutes, 35 seconds.

A week later on the same track in Dublin Deerfoot engaged in a twelve-mile race with Mills and Levett, finishing alone in fast time, having covered some 200 yards over 11 miles within the hour, a feat rarely accomplished up until that time. After this race Deerfoot with his manager George Martin returned to England for weekly races at Hackney Wick.

The Indian made good newspaper copy, a challenge to writers to describe his bizarre costume, his war whoops which he yelled as he sped on to victory, his eating and sleeping habits, and anything else that they recognized as unusual. Artists drew sketches of him which were sold as colored lithographs. The Prince of Wales attended the races and presented a purse containing 10 pounds to be added to the prize money. He was also introduced to Deerfoot. The Indian's popularity extended beyond the racing crowd. Ladies began to appear at the tracks to see the runner, a factor which compelled Deerfoot to cover his naked chest and loins for the sake of propriety.

As the year came to an end Deerfoot must have been in a state of exhaustion, having raced nearly every week since September. His immense popularity in England and his running successes did not impress the *New York Clipper*, which wrote:

"Elsewhere will be found a report of another race won by the American Indian, Deerfoot, and witnessed by the Prince of Wales. The Prince gave the Indian a purse of money, and had a 'talk' with his Indian nibs. Deerfoot is playing his points nicely, in England, and has already eased the Britishers of a clever little pile. He dresses up in Indian gear for the benefit of our transatlantic 'neighbors,' and gives the war whoop to the great delight of the crowds that follow him. In this country, as Bennett, he appeared dressed up in good store clothes, without paint or polish. He is 'doing' all England with a vengeance."

The schedule of races undertaken by Deerfoot and his promoter during the first few months of his visit—a race every week and sometimes more than one a week—was more than could be expected of any athlete. By December he was showing signs of fatigue. In an eight-mile contest with Teddy Mills on December 16 before a crowd of 6,000 at Hackney Wick, Deerfoot ran his last race of 1861. The race was a close contest throughout, so close that the excited crowd rushed to the finish line leaving little space for the runners. Deerfoot, running beside Mills, collided with a spectator and jostled Mills, nearly upsetting both runners, with Mills losing one of his shoes. The runners recovered and sped on to the finish, ending in a dead heat in 42 minutes, 55 seconds. Immediately after the race Mills declared that he could have won by twenty yards if the ac-

cident had not occurred and stated that he would win in a rematch. Deerfoot's manager in a meeting the next day declared that his runner was tired and wanted to rest.

In reviewing Deerfoot's arduous schedule over the autumn months of 1861, it is not unreasonable to recognize that the Indian must have been utterly fatigued. However, the London newspapers began to point the finger of suspicion at Deerfoot and his manager George Martin. The *New York Clipper* in its January 18, 1862, issue commented:

"Some of the London papers are pretty severe upon the Indian, Deerfoot, who has been defeating the most celebrated pedestrians of Great Britain. They charge that he has not won his races fairly, but that his opponents have been bribed to lose. We knew the bubble would burst some time. The whole affair is a speculation, or home and home series of races . . ."

In another item in the same issue of the *Clipper* the supicions were enlarged upon:

"Elsewhere we have referred to the speculative doings of the Indian, Deerfoot, in England. Since that article was written, we have stronger evidence that the bubble has burst, and that the frauds being practiced upon the credulity of the Britishers were coming to a finale. Several matches between the Indian and others had been declared off, for obvious reasons. His match with Pudney is off, the latter 'having business to look after.' Deerfoot's ten mile affair with Brighton is also knocked in the head, and numerous other matches have been squelched very quietly, and no explanation offered. There were murmurs of 'seeking satisfaction' among the 'gulled peoples,' and the Indian, through his manager, Martin, considers it better to subside while he has a whole skin. If Deerfoot is molested, we trust that White, of Gateshead, may come in for a share of the punishment."

Deerfoot enjoyed a much needed rest at the home of George Martin before returning to competition. He returned to the track in February, winning an impressive victory at six miles over Job Smith. He followed this win with triumphs over Brighton at ten miles and Lang at six miles. The London *Sporting Life* commented after the race with Lang: "The Deerfoot mania is evidently on the wane in the metropolitan district. As proof, although the day was beautifully fine, not more than 2,000 persons assembled on Monday, March 3, at Hackney Wick. . ."

Perhaps concluding that they had done as well as they could in the London area, Deerfoot's promoter and manager decided to take the show on the road in order that the people in the provinces might see Deerfoot in action. For this purpose he constructed a portable track which consisted mainly of a wood and canvas screen which would prevent non-paying spectators from seeing the runners in action. Early in May the Deerfoot show left Martin's home on the grand tour. Included in the troupe, in addition to Deerfoot, were four professional runners who were to perform at four pounds per week.

The runners were to perform every evening of the week, Sundays excepted, in a four-mile running race. In each of the contests Deerfoot was consistently the winner. In spite of all of the publicity Deerfoot had received, the attendance at the shows was disappointing and receipts were low. After one evening's performance before a meager crowd, it was necessary for the troupe to walk through the night over the thirty-five miles to the next town because of a lack of funds. Finally Martin was forced to conclude the tour for a period.

Martin reorganized the tour on July 12 and continued through the northern counties and into Scotland, concluding the tour with a visit to Ireland. When the tour ended on September 10, Deerfoot had run in competition over 400 miles and had performed before about 150,000 people.

In the fall William Jackson, one of the hired competitors, sued Manager Martin for breach of contract, testifying in court that all of the races had been pre-arranged to allow Deerfoot to win. John Brighton, another of the hired runners, supported Jackson's testimony. The judge ruled in favor of Jackson.

In October Deerfoot returned to legitimate competition, running a disappointing twelve miles in 1 hour, 7 minutes, and two weeks later he failed to finish in a ten mile match with John Brighton. It seemed that Deerfoot was exhausted from his strenuous tour of nightly races, and rumors were in circulation that he was drinking heavily.

Just when it seemed that Deerfoot's career was over, he faced John Brighton, Jack White, and three runners Andrews, Newman and Knowles, in a one hour contest. At first the race was between Deerfoot, Brighton, and White, with the other contestants running a second race far in the rear. White dropped out at seven miles and the race settled down to a contest between Deerfoot and Brighton. Deerfoot soon began to pull ahead of Brighton, leading him by nearly a lap. When eleven miles were covered by Deerfoot, a gun was fired; 2 minutes and 44 seconds remained yet in the hour. At the end of the allotted hour Deerfoot had traveled 11 miles and 720 yards, a new record.

Four thousand spectators had watched Deerfoot set this record. Many of them, according to the London *Sporting News,* had come to see him run against the clock, and "following so closely as the event did upon the explosion of what has been termed the 'Deerfoot bubble,' public excitement ran unusually high . . ."

The remaining months of Deerfoot's stay in England were marked by a series of erratic performances which were difficult for the running enthusiasts to comprehend. Early in January he lost a six-mile race to Mills, but on the 12th of the month at Hackney Wick on a track made soft and spongy by a heavy rain, he beat Mills in a one hour race, increasing his record to 11 miles, 790 yards. Two weeks later he failed to finish a five-mile race.

Running with the aid of pacemakers, Deerfoot was able to increase his one hour record to eleven and a half miles. This he did with 16 seconds to spare, pulling off the track before the hour's end. His last great race in England was before 5,000 spectators at West Brompton on Good Friday, a twelve-mile handicap race in which Deerfoot started from scratch, offering head starts to the best runners of England. William Lang with a 100-yard start was leading in the last lap of the race when Deerfoot brought the crowd to their feet by passing him. Lang responded and drew abreast of the Indian and they ran toward the finish line abreast of each other. In a lunge for the tape Lang won by a yard over Deerfoot. In this race Deerfoot succeeded in setting a new record for ten miles, 51 minutes, 26 seconds, and for the twelve mile distance, 1 hour, 2 minutes and 2½ seconds. He had passed the one 'hour mark with 11 miles, 970 yards.

This was Deerfoot's last stellar performance in England. Throughout April he ran in races, finishing far behind or dropping out before the finish. On May 11th in his last race on the track at Hackney Wick, where he had become the darling of the crowd some twenty months earlier, Deerfoot faced Lang and White in a contest for the ten mile belt. The race started out at a blistering pace with the lead alternating between Lang and White, Deerfoot trailing far behind, being lapped on the twenty-second and retiring from the race in two more laps. He left the track "amid the derisive cheers and hisses of the assembled thousands." A few days after this race Deerfoot embarked on the *Great Eastern* for home.

In twenty months he had electrified the English sporting scene, setting records and attracting larger crowds than had ever appeared at running races hitherto. He had captured the imagination of the people and enjoyed the role of hero for a time, only to suffer the scorn of the fickle crowd when he failed to perform as a champion.

The court suit in which Jackson and Brighton testified that they had been paid to allow Deerfoot to win cast a cloud of suspicion over the Indian's performances. Even before the grand tour newspapers had been suggesting that Deerfoot's races were fixed, that his opponents had been bribed to lose. There were brief periods of renewed enthusiasm for the Indian when he performed his record-breaking feats; but when he failed to perform as a champion, he won only abuse and accusations of fraud for his efforts. Throughout most of Deerfoot's English tour the *New York Clipper* regarded the whole thing as a fraud. When Deerfoot outlasted Lang in a fast six mile race on March 3, 1862, the *Clipper* commented:

"The Indian Deerfoot. This now celebrated pedestrian seems to be taking all the British

peds down, one after another, as easy as 'breaking sticks,' but whether with or without their connivance remains a question. We give place elsewhere to a report of his last victory over Lang in a six miles race, which was run after a dashing struggle, apparently, in 31 min. 15 secs. Deerfoot also threatens to run 11¼ miles within the hour for any part of 1,000 pounds or $5,000. Bravo Deerfoot."

This was as close as the *Clipper* had during the whole tour come to praising Deerfoot until the Indian ran his remarkable twelve-mile race in which Deerfoot set a new ten-mile record and ran the greatest distance within one hour. At this astounding performance the *Clipper* for once had only praise for Deerfoot:

"In a pedestrian handicap, run at one of the public arenas in England, on April 10th, in which the American Indian—Deerfoot—was the only one that started from the scratch, he made the unequalled time of 51 min. 26 secs. for ten miles, and 62 min. 2¼ secs. for twelve miles, and all but defeated Lang, who had 100 yards' start. Deerfoot, by his extraordinary effort, came well nigh fulfilling the prediction of the *Clipper,* that he would one day do twelve miles in an hour. Bully for Deerfoot, to whom all praise is due for giving us this opportunity to record this truly native American triumph, and the fastest time on record."

In spite of the *Clipper's* concession to Deerfoot's triumph, no hero's welcome greeted Deerfoot upon his return to the United States. He returned home during the Civil War when sports contests were not of primary news interest. In a series of local races at Rochester, New York, on the 4th, 5th, and 6th of July, 1864, Deerfoot appeared in the five mile race, running against other Indians and winning in less than 27 minutes.

It was not until March 4, 1865, that Deerfoot made what was considered a head-liner appearance. On this occasion he was matched in a five mile contest against Jimmy Griffin, the leading Boston area professional at the time, and Patrick Cokely. The race was held indoors in the National Theatre building on a track which required forty-two laps to the mile, two hundred and ten laps for five miles. From the early stages in the race, Griffin dominated the contest and had lapped Deerfoot four times by the ninety-ninth lap. At this point Deerfoot withdrew from the race.

Deerfoot's name seldom appeared in the sporting journals for the next two years, and most of his competition seems to have been limited to local appearances in the western New York area. In November of 1867, he and his friend Steeprock appeared at the Riverside Park in Boston in a race against horses. The Indians were to run 3⅛ miles to six for the horses. A large crowd gathered to see this performance which the Indians won. In the same month Deerfoot and his Indian companions raced against horses in Cleveland, Ohio, indicating that they were probably doing the circuit with this routine.

Five days later Deerfoot was matched over five miles with Jimmy Griffin. A large crowd expecting a good race gathered at the park. At the start Deerfoot took the lead which he increased with little effort as the race progressed. From time to time Deerfoot paused and looked around to see how far Griffin was behind, sometimes stopping completely until his rival caught up. At the finish Deerfoot jogged along easily while Griffin went on to win. To the judges this was obviously not an honest race, they termed it a "sell-out" and declared all bets off.

At the Cold Spring racing course near Buffalo, New York, in August 1868, Deerfoot was matched in a five-mile race against two Indians, one of whom was to receive a quarter-mile start, and the other, a half mile. Deerfoot appeared in rare form this day, passing his opponents before the third mile was reached. He was timed in 24 minutes and 15 seconds, a faster time than had ever been posted for the distance. The *Clipper* suspected that the course was short or the clock was stopped too soon.

Deerfoot's name appeared from time to time in the sporting journals over the next few years, sometimes for races won against men and at other times against horses. By 1870 other notable Indian runners were achieving notice. In Canada the Indian Keraronwe and the two Daillebouts, father and son, were winning races and attracting widespread attention. It was inevitable that the aging champion of the Tona-

Deerfoot was depicted in this English lithograph clad in native garb, standing by a table upon which rests the wolfskin cloak which he often wore in public in England.

wanda Senecas would be matched against the champion of the Iroquois. The race between Deerfoot and Keraronwe took place in Montreal on August 27, 1870, with the younger Indian emerging the victor in a close race of three miles. Pleading that three miles was not a long enough race for him to demonstrate his skills, Deerfoot challenged Keraronwe to a six-mile race which the latter declined. They did meet at four miles a week later, but in this race Daillebout was the winner.

In vain Deerfoot challenged the Iroquois runners to a race over longer distances. Now in his forties Deerfoot continued to perform at fairs and went as far west as Chicago to participate in a race against horses. His last public appearance, but not as an athlete, was at the Chicago World's Fair in 1893. Deerfoot died on the Cattaragus Reservation in Erie County, N.Y., on January 18, 1897. He was buried on the reservation, but three years later his remains were removed to be placed next to the grave of the celebrated Seneca orator Red Jacket in a cemetery in Buffalo. In the passing of years Deerfoot has assumed a position among the legendary greats of the past, frequently alluded to by feature writers, but in all a shadowy figure about whom little is really known, except that he was a great runner.

As has been pointed out, Deerfoot's running career before leaving for England was confined to races in the Buffalo area, with the exception of a few forays into Boston and New York City. None of his performances indicated that he was a runner of the stature that his English performances would later establish him, but times and distances in races in the United States could not be relied upon for accuracy. Tracks were often laid out for the event and were merely ungraded, unimproved areas which were simply roped off for the occasion.

In England the tracks were much better. In most cases tracks there were owned in conjunction with public houses. At Hackney Wick, where Deerfoot ran many of his notable races, the track was under the management of the "White Lion," an adjacent pub. It was 260 yards in circumference with trees lining both sides of the track. Spectators who paid an extra fee were permitted to witness the races from the inside of the track. The track was graded and was in fairly good condition.

Timing, although not as sophisticated as today, was reasonably accurate. Watches could measure to within a quarter of a second. Since large sums of money were wagered on the races, spectators who had large amounts riding on the outcome of races against the clock could be expected to do their own timing. Thus it is not unreasonable to assume that Deerfoot's sensational times made in England were accurate.

That he failed to provide any performances in the United States before going to England that would justify a prediction of his ability

～～～～～～～～～～～～～～～～～～～～

A Kansas correspondent to the *Clipper* wrote in the 1870's that one of the popular sports spectacles was Indian racing. When the Pottawatomies came to town, the offer of a coin as small as a dime would be sufficient inducement to promote a running race. The Indians, the writer explained, took off their trousers before the race. This caused a scurrying of the ladies to their houses; but a rustle of the curtains indicated that they were not missing anything.

～～～～～～～～～～～～～～～～～～～～

to set records may be explained by the competition which he enjoyed there for the first time in his career. Facing runners of the caliber of Mills, Brighton, and Lang probably enabled Deerfoot to achieve times beyond what his earlier performances indicated he might reach. It is quite possible that Deerfoot reached the peak of his ability as a runner under the impetus of competition.

That some of his races were fixed is not denied. However, the races against time were generally acknowledged as records, even by such a hostile critic as the *New York Clipper*. His time for the greatest distance run within one hour remained on the record books unimproved until 1953, when an amateur named Jim Peters exceeded it by a narrow sixteen yards.

The inconsistency of Deerfoot's performances, though they excited suspicion at the time, may have been explained by the arduous schedule of competition which he faced on his English tour. That he failed to perform at the record-setting level upon his return to the United States may have been the result of inadequate competition and the fact that he was aging.

Lewis Bennett's reputation as a great runner rests upon that brief period when he conquered the best athletes of England and ran to records beyond what man had achieved before. That the aura of the "noble savage" and the promotional gimmicks of his manager had much to do with the establishment of his fame is undeniable. It is equally undeniable that his records establish him as a great runner. Had he lived in another era when training conditions, tracks, competition, and social mobility were more favorable, his career might have been more sensational; but that is merely subject for speculation. Had he failed to make the English tour, he might have been just another Indian runner relegated to oblivion, for the competitive edge provided by the English athletes stimulated Deerfoot to run at the peak of his ability.

The Civil War and After

Frank Queen's *New York Clipper* in the 1850's stimulated interest in sports activities throughout the United States. The Civil War in the 1860's completed the task.

Young men from all over the country were brought together in large groups. Although they were summoned to training camps for preparation for battle, they had ample time for activities other than drilling. Even beyond the training period, it was not all marching and fighting; there were frequently extended periods in camp. Sports filled the void. Wrestling matches, running races, sparring bouts, and baseball games helped to occupy the idle hours. The fact that most soldiers volunteered or were enlisted from their own home towns and were kept in the same units throughout their enlistment helped to create inter-sectional rivalries, thus sharpening the competitive edge.

On New Year's Day in 1862 in General Kearney's Brigade, which was in camp at Alexandria, Virginia, a marksmanship contest was held. The best shots from each company were vying for the prize which consisted of three barrels of ale for the company and a fine rifle for the winning marksman. Private John Mowers of Company F had little trouble in carrying off the honors. As soon as the competition was over, a tall slim fellow, R. D. Crandol rose and shouted a challenge, saying that he would beat any man on the field in a 100-yard race. A little fellow, called "Yankee Notions," jumped up with the response, "I'm your boy!" Stakes of five dollars a side were raised, the ground was measured off, bets were made, and the race was run. "Yankee Notions" won the match by half a yard.

In another camp at another time two privates, Swing and Royal, made a one dollar bet for a 100-yard race with knapsacks and full equipment. Swing won by five yards. In camp at Columbus, Ohio, Dan Bushnell, who had raced professionally, was challenged to a 100-yard race. He agreed to run for $100 a side. The pro won the race by a margin of 20 feet.

An item in the *New York Clipper* in May of 1862 reported that Mickey Free, the celebrated Irish pedestrian, the "humorous and good-natured individual," was in the hospital at Newport News recovering from wounds. He had suffered the loss of three fingers and had sustained other injuries in battle. He assured his friends that his "under-pinning" was still sound and that he would soon be home in search of competition.

Grindall, home on a brief furlough from his regiment in November 1863, issued a challenge from Michael Boyle's saloon to race any man in America at five miles for $200 a side. There were no takers, but a year later he was able to arrange a race with Young Sport, which he won easily.

One soldier wrote home from camp in Maryland to relate how Christmas day was spent. The officers had a baseball game which lasted but three innings, with Captain Mitchell's side winning, 32-12. A wheel barrow race and a contest to catch two greased pigs filled out the day's entertainment.

James C. Smith, of Troy, New York, stationed on the U.S.S. Portsmouth, on the Mississippi River, 120 miles from New Orleans, made a bet that he could pull a 65-pound sulky around the track on shore for six miles within an hour. Much to the delight of his shipmates he finished the distance in 59 minutes 35 seconds. Men from Company B, First Indiana Cavalry, boasted that they had a fleet-footed man whom they would match against any man in the Army of the Potomac in a 200-yard race for $50 or $100 a side. The challenge was accepted by the boys from the 75th Pennsylvania, but the

~~~~~~~~~~~~~~~~~~~~~~~~~~~

Some of the feats performed were even more bizarre than walking the plank. The challenge issued by Professor H. G. Varner, Boston, is an example: "I will match any man in the United States, for $50 or $100, to pick up 50 eggs, placed one yard apart, with my mouth, and deposit them in a bucket of water; making a separate trip for each egg, having my hands tied behind, and not touching my knees to the ground;; and pick up 50 stones placed in the same manner with my hands, run 1 mile, walk 1 mile, walk 1 mile backward, all at one start, or will match against time, doing all in one hour. Match to be made within six weeks."

~~~~~~~~~~~~~~~~~~~~~~~~~~~

distance was 150 yards and the stakes but $10 a side. The Hoosier Benjamin Conners easily won the prize from Gottlieb Hosmer, the Pennsylvanian.

On the home front there were still some foot races, but they were usually for small stakes and were run by relatively unknown athletes. From time to time there were races at the Red House in Harlem. In California, far from the battle scenes, Parson Rix beat Mr. Dyer in a 100-yard spin for $300. Seth Cain, of Grass Valley, California, bet that he could run from that city to Nevada City and back a distance of 14 miles, within an hour and a half. He missed by 23 minutes.

The big news in pedestrian sporting circles came from England, where Deerfoot, the American Indian, was showing up the English professionals and setting records. Week after week the *New York Clipper* filled columns with reprints of sporting articles from the English sporting journals.

With the cessation of hostilities in March of 1865, the sponsors lost little time in resuming competition in running and walking. Boston led off with a full program of foot races. The *New York Clipper* acknowledged the resumption of competition with enthusiasm but also uttered a warning: "Our pedestrian friends in Boston are beginning to bestir themselves in resuscitating the health-imparting, invigorating, and exciting sport of foot-racing, which for the past four years, or since the breaking out of the rebellion, has been lying dormant, and with such a promising commencement as the races referred to below, we have reason to hope that the coming spring and summer will witness a series of good, honest, straight-forward contests in the pedestrian arena. It lies with the peds, themselves alone, to see that no double-dealing is allowed, and when it is once known that everything is regular and on the square, the sport will not die out for lack of patronage."

Soon notices were appearing in columns of the *New York Clipper* of races and challenges from cities and towns across the nation. Although the interest in distance running continued to maintain a high level, competition in sprinting, jumping, and other events began to attract contestants and followers. Names of frequent winners began to appear in the press, and athletes came forth from all directions to claim the title of champion. Newspapers in general began to give attention to sports events. Those which had noticed sports before the Civil War were the exception; now the reverse was true. At first items on sports events were mixed in with the general news; but by the close of the decade of the seventies, a column was set apart to report exclusively on sports events.

The common events of a typical athletic meeting as described in a little book on sports published in 1866 were walking, running, leaping, standing leap over a height, standing leap over a width, a running leap over a height, run-

John Dane, who came from the remote logging village of Alpena, Michigan, became one of the leading jumpers in the country, but met his match when he encountered George Hamilton.

ning leap over a width, the hop-step-and-jump, and the leaping pole.

Norman Bortle, of Monroe County, New York, in 1866, claimed the title "Champion Jumper of America." The friends of Bob Way, Orlean, New York, equally proud of the jumping feats of their fellow townsman, arranged for Bortle to come to Orlean for a contest which would determine who was really champion. It was reported that each side put up $500 for the purse. The contestants were to be permitted an hour to perform as many jumps as they wished or could. The longest distance jumped in the attempts would be the winning effort. After a half dozen tries on the part of each jumper, the hour was over. Norman Bortle had jumped 12 feet 5 inches, leading his rival by a mere three inches. Since nearly $10,000 was wagered on the jumping match, there were many disappointed betters who leveled accusations of a sell-out at Way. They were somewhat mollified when it was pointed out that the distance jumped was the best ever recorded in the United States.

In New Paris, Ohio, a young man claimed that he had jumped 43 feet in three standing jumps. Efforts to match him with Way or Bortle failed. Soon Ed Searles of Utica leaped 13 feet, 5¾ inches to lay claim to the title of champion.

The jumping was done from a standing position with the aid of weights. The jumper held in each hand a weight which might be as heavy as 17 pounds. He swung his arms back and forth until ready to take off, the weights helping to propel him farther than would have been possible without such aid.

Sprinting became popular. Races were not restricted to the 100-yard dash and the 220. Such odd distances as 70 yards, 125, 150, and 170 yards were contested. Sprinting introduced the traveling runner or "ringer" who would upon arrival in a town visit a sporting saloon. After a few drinks he would make a few boastful remarks about his running speed. Dressed shabbily and unkempt, the "ringer" gave no impression of speed or athletic talent. Soon his boasts were challenged, and the local sprinter would be brought forth to race the stranger. Sometimes the contest would be arranged for the local race track, but just as often a street in town would be roped off and the race would be held there. The visiting pro usually won the bet but he had to be careful to win by a close margin lest he disclose his identity. If that were to happen, he would need all of the speed at his command to escape the wrath of those he had deceived.

Henry Crandell, of Niles, Michigan, was one of these wandering professional sprinters. Although he competed in matches against the best sprinters in the country, winning and losing big races, he spent most of his time traveling. In California, running under the name of Grainger, Crandell became a sensation and was eventually regarded as good enough to face the Pacific coast champion. In a 75-yard dash he won by 20 feet.

One account of Henry Crandell's mode of operating is thus described: "Hen Crandell has for some time past been engaged in duping the sports of the far West, and so successful has he been that his store of 'dust' has considerably accumulated. His plan is the old, and by no means honorable one of assuming an alias and effecting a match with the crack runner of some town, whom he knows he can easily beat; and as the latter has generally troops of friends only too glad of the chance to back him against so slovenly a customer as Crandell can make himself appear when in ordinary clothes, they put out their money freely, and of course never see the color of it again. After easily defeating Millard Stone of Colorado Springs, Colorado, and thereby scooping up much lucre, Hen recently turned up in Pueblo, same state, and from there wrote to the backers of Stone, telling them that he had a very soft thing on hand, and advising them to put their loose change on him, and thereby win back their previous losses. The unsophisticated Spring sports swallowed the tempting bait, planked their cash and other articles of value on Crandell, who on this occasion was second in reaching the tape. *The Mountaineer* says that, had he shown half the speed in the race that he did in reaching the out-going train, he would have sent home happy the deluded Colorado Springers, who had to be fed and housed for the night, and sent home at the expense of Pueblo the next day."

Two months later Crandell was in Minne-

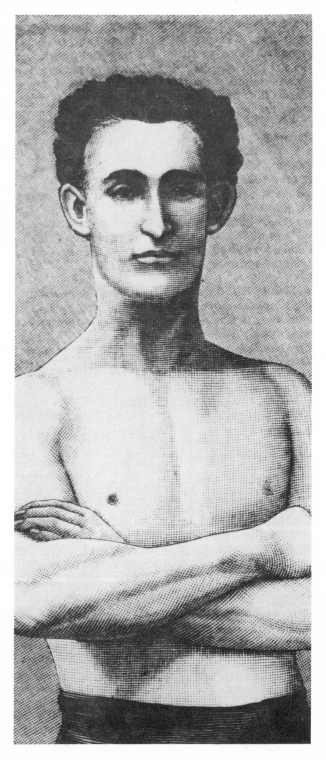

George W. Hamilton, of Fredonia, New York, who enjoyed the reputation as the best jumper in the United States, down-played his achievements in order to lure contestants and stimulate interest in betting.

apolis for a 100-yard race against Ed Moulton, a leading sprinter who had been turning up conveniently at towns throughout the West at the same time as Crandell. Two thousand spectators paid fifty cents admission to see the race which was won by Crandell. Three watches caught him in three different times, 9½ seconds, 9¾, and 10 seconds. Shortly before the race a Minneapolis newspaper published the story of Crandell's Colorado exploits, thus making the betters wary of wagering on the affair.

"Professional jumpers are, as a class, the scurviest of all tribes known to modern sport, and their life seems to be spent in trying to avoid the possession of money honestly earned or won," commented *The Spirit of the Times* in an article which told of the devious ways of a pair of professional jumpers.

George W. Hamilton, of Fredonia, N.Y., *The Spirit of the Times* acknowledged, was probably the best jumper of the time, but no accurate record of his performances existed "because the pecuniary interest of these fellows demand that they should falsify the reports, and thus conceal their real ability." It seems that Hamilton had had a falling out with one of his old friends and associates. In retaliation for supposed wrongs, the former friend published a pamphlet which contained a full description of Hamilton and a list of his records, as well as some of his less than honorable performances.

A series of contests between Hamilton and Jack Dane of Alpena, Michigan, was described. Fred Emerick of Ypsilanti, Michigan, had written to Hamilton to propose a jumping match with his man, Jack Dane. Hamilton persuaded them to come to Buffalo, New York, for a jumping matching at $200 a side. Hamilton won the toss and decided that Dane should jump first. The young Michigan jumper swung his weights and leaped 13 feet 10¼ inches. "How do you like that?" he queried. Without responding, Hamilton swung his weights just once and jumped a quarter of an inch farther than Dane's effort. Dane then took his turn and made 13 feet 10¾ inches. Hamilton came back with a leap of 14 feet ¾ inches. In five more leaps Dane failed to better that mark.

When *The Spirit of the Times* wrote to Hamilton to ask him to confirm that mark of 14 feet

¾ inches, he down-played his achievement, saying that it had been done on a slight downhill ground and with spring shoes. The angry pamphleteer denied that this was so.

Dane, who had suffered his first defeat as a jumper, returned to Michigan, where he took employment as a porter in the Howard Hotel. Emerick told the manager and some of the guests about Dane's great jumping talent. Conveniently, Hamilton appeared on the scene under an assumed name. The manager and guests backed Dane against him and lost.

Soon after, Hamilton appeared in Oil City, Pennsylvania, where he impressed the local sportsmen with a jump of 13 feet 10 inches. He convinced the natives that he could jump over 14 feet. Dane and Emerick now appeared in Oil City, and a match was made, with the local sports backing Hamilton heavily. Dane jumped 13 feet 7 inches; and Hamilton jumped 14 feet 5 inches on his last effort, but fell back. Emerick and Dane collected the winnings and were supposed to meet Hamilton at the hotel to divide the loot. Instead, they took the first train out of town.

Hamilton sent wires to the police in every direction. Dane and Emerick were apprehended in Cleveland just as they had checked into their cabin on the steamer bound for Detroit. They were held by the police until Hamilton arrived to collect his money.

A number of outstanding professional sprinters emerged during the decade following the Civil War, but the one who was generally acknowledged as the champion was John Wesley Cozad of Iowa, who ran under the title "Plow Boy of California." Relatively unknown in 1868 when he accepted the standing challenge of Edward Depew Davis, the reigning sprinter, for a race of 125 yards on the Fashion Race Course on Long Island, Cozad was given little chance of winning. The date set for the race was November 23, 1868.

"Pew" Davis, Kingston, New York, had defeated all rivals in races throughout the East and as far west as Chicago and Rock Island, Illinois. Cozad had won several races against big-name sprinters, including the wandering Henry Crandell, but most of his running had been done in the West.

The stakes for the race were high. Davis was to put up $2,000 and Cozad $1,500. The winner would also collect all the gate receipts above expenses. The betting before the race was quite spirited with the odds much in favor of the more experienced and better known "Pew" Davis. At the shot of the starter's pistol Cozad took a slight lead which he managed to hold to the tape, winning by 8 feet in a record 12¼ seconds. Two weeks later on the same track he beat Poke Perry at 70 yards in 7¼ seconds for another record.

As a result of this race Cozad won the title of champion sprinter and issued a public challenge to all comers. However, as with others who had risen to the rank of undisputed champion, Cozad found few takers. The lower echelon of sprinters preferred to race each other. Their challenges published in the sporting journals would be directed at all runners "bar Cozad." He had to content himself with exhibitions and handicap races in which he would offer a head start to his rivals. That John Wesley Cozad was an outstanding sprinter was supported by the fact that his record times remained unexcelled for more than twenty years.

On Wednesday, November 14, 1866, two runners met on a track on Long Island to race

In the post-Civil War years, John Wesley Cozad, an Iowa native, who billed himself as the "Plow Boy of California," came East to become the reigning professional sprinter of the era.

two miles, one mile in each heat with a half hour rest in between. They were accompanied by a few friends and supporters. The runners were Ike Rooney of Long Island and William E. Harding, who was identified as a Canadian. Rooney was tall and slim, looking every inch the runner. Harding was short and stocky and did not look the part of a runner. Rooney's friends offered odds of four to one on their man, but Harding's friends had little money so they had to let their runner do his own betting.

In the first mile Ike Rooney started off at a fast pace and had built up a comfortable lead by the half mile point. On the third lap Harding moved up and passed Rooney to go on to win the first heat. In the second heat Rooney led for the first quarter but yielded to Harding who went on to win by 300 yards. This was the introduction of William E. Harding to the pedestrian arena.

Harding had been born in Toronto but had long been a resident of New York City. In 1866 he was employed as a reporter for a city newspaper. His victory over Ike Rooney soon brought a challenge from John Rowan of Albany, who possessed a champion's belt and so regarded himself.

On a frozen track in Albany on January 27, 1867, William Harding toed the mark with Rowan in a five mile race for the belt and a purse of $1,000. Harding won the race in the astounding time of 23 minutes 11½ seconds. The time was faster than any previous effort for the distance and appeared incredible, but the official timer insisted that it was correct. It is highly improbable that Harding's time was accurate; however, the victory was enough to win recognition for Harding as an American champion.

In the following summer after having defended his title in a number of other races, Harding was matched against DeKelso, the Canadian champion, at Aurelia in Canada. DeKelso, an Indian, appeared on the track with the Union Jack around his loins; Harding wore star-spangled blue trunks and a red belt with the word champion on it. It was truly an international match. The appearance of Harding in the Yankee colors elicited from the crowd loud groans and hisses. Again phenomenal times

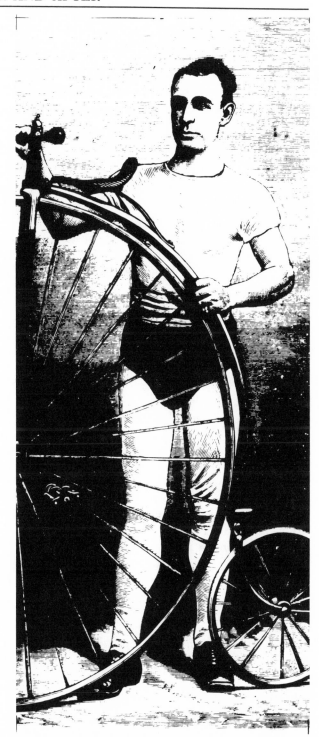

William Harding, a New York City newspaper reporter, after having defeated the leading runners of the United States in the years immediately following the Civil War, claimed the title of "Champion of America." Harding later became sports editor of the National Police Gazette.

were reported, 4:14½ for the first mile, which was far better than the existing world mark for a single mile. The official time for the three miles was reported as 13 minutes flat, far better than anyone else had ever run the distance. Times were often unreliable; tracks improperly measured were frequently short of the announced distance. Gradually to offer some credulity to performances the sponsors of races engaged a surveyor to measure the track and published an affidavit from the surveyor. At any rate, in winning the race, Harding collected a purse of $2,000. Before leaving Canada, Harding agreed to give DeKelso a return match. At Aurelia, Canada, on December 9, 1867, he repeated his conquest of DeKelso in fast time.

Harding, upon claiming the title of champion of America, issued a challenge to the English champions, Teddy Mills and Andrew Lang, for a three mile race for a purse of $5,000. The prospects of such a match created a great deal of excitement in sporting circles. Although most people questioned the accuracy of the fast times attributed to Harding, his conquest of a runner of the caliber of DeKelso was enough to recommend him as a star runner. In October 1868, Lang arrived in Philadelphia, where he issued an offer to race Harding at any distance from a half-mile upwards. Efforts to bring the two parties together to arrange for a race failed. Harding stated that he had not raced in nearly a year and had as a matter of fact retired from running to concentrate his energies on his newspaper job. However, to accommodate Lang, Harding stated that he would race him in the spring. When the time came for the principals to meet to sign the articles of agreement and put up the money, Harding failed to appear. Soon after, Bill Lang sailed for England. In later years Harding briefly tried the longer distances but never lived up to the promise of his early triumphs.

The interest in endurance contests, stimulated to a large extent by the publicity given to Edward Payson Weston's walk from Portland, Maine, to Chicago, spread into every village and town. Theatres, drill halls, and any building which would answer the purpose were con-verted to tracks where spectators watched contestants vie for honors at 50 and 100 miles. They talked of the "walking mania," as every village and town brought forth a local champion. No longer was New York City the only center of competition. Paterson, New Jersey, Pittsburgh, Cleveland, Chicago, Milwaukee, Council Bluffs, and San Francisco were scenes of major contests. "Everybody seems to have contracted the foot fever," commented the *Clipper*.

Walking was distinguished from running by careful definition. The official rule described it as "progression by steps in such a manner that unbroken contact with the ground is maintained throughout." Judges stood around the track to make sure that one foot was on the ground at all times during the contest.

Professionalism in the post-war years still reigned. The *New York Clipper* and the daily press decried the abuses of professionalism. "Despicable frauds" and "swindling dodges" would have to be eliminated if professionalism was to survive, noted the *Clipper*. Time after time a race was designated a "sell-out;" as often, riots and fights over the outcome were reported. A lack of organization to establish a code of conduct or to regulate was the chief weakness of the professional movement. Also undermining it was the gambling. Book-makers moved freely about in the crowds at meets or races, and the event became more an object of speculation than sport.

The great expansion of participation in athletic contests created a demand for some sort of organization which would establish standards and bring some order out of the chaos which existed. For a person to become a champion he simply declared himself one. If his declaration was supported by the *New York Clipper* or one of the other sporting journals, his claim was that much stronger; yet there was no process of elimination or effort to ascertain that the athlete was truly supreme. In the matter of records, the situation was much the same. If the time or distance claimed was reasonable, it might gain recognition by the *New York Clipper*, be published in the *Clipper Almanac*, and become generally accepted as a record; but there was no effort to determine whether the distance was accurately measured, whether the

FORTY-EIGHT HOURS WALKING CONTEST!

—AT—

SEELY'S HALL,

Coldwater, Commencing

THURSDAY, APRIL 3,

At 10 o'clock P. M, and Ending Saturday, April 5th, at 10 o'clock P. M.

8 CONTESTANTS!

Open Day & Night.

The Management will spare no expense to make this the FINEST WALKING TOURNAMENT ever held in the State. The Track has been built strictly with the Astley plan.

SEATS WILL be RESERVED ON THE STAGE FOR LADIES, DAY AND EVENING.

THIRTY DOLLARS

—AND AN—

Elegant Champion Belt

Will be given to the person walking the greatest number of miles in FORTY-EIGHT HOURS.
FIFTEEN DOLLARS TO THE SECOND, AND TEN DOLLARS TO THE THIRD.

Admission during the day,	-	10 Cts.
Evenings,	- - - -	25 "
Season Tickets,	- - -	$1 00.

☞ Ten Cent Tickets not good after 6 P. M. ☜

C. L. HUNTER, Manager.

REPUBLICAN PRINT, COLDWATER.

ground was level, or whether the timing devices used were calibrated for accuracy. Some efforts were made to hold meets which would determine the bona fide champions in certain events. One meet sponsored by a group of Philadelphia sportsmen at Newark for that purpose in July 1869 failed to attract the leading athletes and proved a great disappointment to both the sponsors and the spectators. Other efforts to hold similar open championship events suffered the same fate, as did a movement to organize the professional pedestrians in an association.

For many years there had been sports organizations among the Scots immigrants, who held annual meets in the metropolitan areas. There were Caledonian Clubs in the Boston area, New York City, Detroit, and elsewhere. Competing for modest prizes, often cash, the Caledonians held a full program of events; putting the stone, weight throwing, tossing the caber, jumping, running, and vaulting. However, with few exceptions the Caledonians paid little attention to records from year to year. Other immigrant groups, the Germans in the Turnvereins, the English in the Society of St. George, and the Irish in Hibernians also had athletic competition at their annual gatherings. In the post-war period such organizations as the printers, masons, and other tradesmen, as well as veterans and militia units, held annual athletic meetings. All these were gradual steps toward organization.

In 1868 a group of young men organized the New York Athletic Club. This was not the first athletic club in the United States. The Atlantic Club of Philadelphia and the Olympic Club of San Francisco were organized earlier, and there had been a number of rowing clubs and baseball clubs which had become quite prominent; but the New York Athletic Club was to exert such an influence upon the whole athletic movement, the amateur aspect of it particularly, that it has earned a unique position in the history

The interest in long distance contests spread throughout the country into cities, towns, and villages. Here a poster advertises a 48-hour race in the town of Coldwater, Michigan.

of American sports. The objectives of the New York Athletic Club were different from those of their predecessors. These young men, modeling their organization on the London Athletic Club, intended to promote competition in amateur sports and provide acceptable standards and rules for the various athletic events. They were in sports for the love of sports. In recording the history of sports it has become a common assumption that the amateur movement and the organization of such clubs as the New York A.C. was an effort on the part of the upper classes to exclude those from the lower strata of society. While this may have been true in some instances, the principal motivation behind the organization initially was to provide an opportunity for participation in sports for enjoyment and healthful reasons. They did not expect to do as well as the professionals who spent all of their time in training and preparation for competition. The amateurs had other occupations and could engage in sports activities only in the evenings and on weekends.

That there was some class distinction cannot be denied, but there is a danger of placing too much emphasis upon that aspect. Up until the outbreak of the Civil War, almost all of the competitors in pedestrian contests were professionals who came from the lower economic levels, often recent arrivals from overseas. The professional lists were dominated by Irish names and continued to be throughout the nineteenth century. This was true also in prize-fighting. As the Irish moved up from the bottom rung of the social scale, they were replaced by other groups. Professional contests often originated in the saloons and many times rather rough places. It would have been beneath the dignity of young men from the upper levels of society to enter into competition with the professionals. Thus the amateur club offered to them the only avenue for sports competition. In the end it would have a salutary effect upon all classes, bringing an understanding of the lower levels of society to the more affluent and providing social and economic mobility for those at the bottom of the heap.

When all of the classes were thrown together during the Civil War, the interest in athletic sports spread across class lines. From the Mid-

west where class lines were not so clearly drawn, young men acquired a desire to compete in running and walking races. Thus after the war the list of participants in professional contests included men who did not fit the general pattern set before the war. There were stars who came from Rock Island, Illinois; Niles, Michigan; Ames, Iowa; and many other towns as foreign to the Easterners as if they were overseas. Sports activities were bringing all classes of people together.

The desire to compete in athletics invaded the college campuses. As early as 1826, Yale University had a gymnasium and encouraged exercise, but not competition. Harvard in the 1840's had its rowing clubs, and in the 1850's these clubs started the rivalry with Yale University in a rowing race which soon became one of the chief sporting attractions in the nation. This competition was not between the universities, however. The oarsmen came from the clubs, and the early races were held without university sponsorship. Indeed, the young men from the Harvard clubs sometimes competed against the professional oarsmen. Initially track competition was developed in such clubs on the campus. Gradually athletic associations met in the colleges, and an annual athletic meeting was held for the athletes on campus. At this stage the competition was intra-mural, although some college meets added a race for "strangers." In the 1870's inter-collegiate competition in track and field was started. Before the end of the century inter-collegiate competition would be well on the way toward being the major arena of track and field athletics.

The New York Athletic Club in its first year numbered about thirty men. On November 11, 1868, this new amateur club held its first meet in a partially completed skating rink with the Caledonians as opponents in a program of six running events and eight field contests. The large number of field events favored the Scots who succeeded in winning nine first place medals.

In the third annual New York Athletic Club games held for members at their newly leased grounds at Mott Haven at One Hundred and Thirty-first Street between Third and Fourth Avenues, on October 21, 1871, the program was limited to six events. Henry Buermeyer, one of the club's founders, won the 16-pound shot put with a toss of 36 feet 5 inches. The time for the half-mile was 2 minutes 27 seconds; the quarter mile was 1 minute 2 seconds. The running broad jump was 15 feet 3 inches, and the high jump was 4 feet 7½ inches. No contestants appeared for the one mile walk.

With a few years after the organization of the New York Athletic Club, other groups organized with similar objectives. Soon the New Jersey Athletic Club, the Harlem A.C., the Yonkers Lyceum, Staten Island A.C., and a number of other amateur clubs would be sending their athletes to compete against the young

When W. H. McMillan, first president of the Amateur Athletic Union, toured the country in 1888, he reported "large stone clubs" in Chicago, Milwaukee, St. Louis, Atchinson, and Topeka. Here is the California Athletic Club in San Francisco.

men of the New York Athletic Club. The growth of the amateur movement was evident in the games held by the New Jersey Athletic Club on October 3, 1874. Although most of the events were won by boys from the New York A.C., there were contestants representing the Montreal Club, the Lotos Place Club of Chicago, and the Columbia Club of New York. Before the end of the seventies the list would grow beyond all expectations and would include such outstanding clubs as the Short Hills A.C., Williamsburgh A.C., Manhattan A.C., and Boston A.C.

In the spring of 1875, the New Jersey A.C. announced that it would offer gold medals for the amateur championship of America in two events, the 100-yard dash and the one-mile walk. Both of the events, held at Ridgewood, New Jersey, on July 5, 1875, were won by New York A.C. athletes, Daniel Stern taking the walking race crown and William Curtis winning the 100-yard dash. Thus Stern and Curtis became the first amateur champions of the United States.

The fall games of the New York Athletic Club had become an established affair in athletic circles by 1876. In this year the members of a number of clubs petitioned the New York A.C. to offer its games as the first official national amateur championships. In this meet the mile was won in 4:51.5 by H. Lambe of the Toronto Argonauts, and the high jump title was taken with a leap of 5 feet 5 inches by one H. E. Ficken. The New York A.C. in winning six of the twelve events became the first national amateur champions.

It was during the seventies that some pattern of organization began to develop in inter-collegiate circles. Representatives of Amherst, Cornell, Columbia, Harvard, Trinity Union, Wesleyan, Williams, Princeton, Yale, Brown, and Dartmouth met to form the College Athletic Association. This group held the first college championships at Glen Mitchell near Saratoga, New York, on July 20, 1874, before a large and fashionable crowd. The athletes competed for handsomely engraved silver cups and gold medals. E. Copeland of Cornell won the mile run in 4:58¼; A. B. Neven, Yale, won the 100-yard dash in 10½ seconds; and William H. Downs, Wesleyan, won the three mile race in 18:17½. A hurdle race was won by C. Maxwell of Yale, and the seven-mile walk was taken by J. F. Eustic, Wesleyan.

By 1876, the collegians had added the 440, 880, baseball throwing, running high and long jumps, the shot put, 200-yard race, and the three-legged race. As an inducement to keep the meet at Saratoga, the Citizens' Committee at that place promised to build a quarter mile track within a short distance from the hotels and "in other ways to do all in their power to insure the success of the meeting."

At the meeting of the representatives of the association, now operating under the name Intercollegiate Athletic Association, on April 4, 1877, Mr. Webb of the out-going executive committee denounced "in severe terms" the failure of the Saratoga Citizens' Committee to live up to its promises to prepare a suitable track. It was decided by the delegates that they should look elsewhere for a site for its annual meeting. There was no debate when the New York A.C. track at Mott Haven was proposed, and all agreed that this should be the place for the annual meeting.

The leadership of the New York A.C. provided standards which other amateur clubs and colleges quickly adopted. Standards were set for judging, timing, and measuring. This made a record set in one year or in one place eligible for comparison with other records set under the same circumstances. An announcement for a meet in May 1877 illustrates the care taken to insure that all competitors were truly amateur: "A declaration of colors must be made with each entry, colors to be described in this order: first, color of handkerchief or cap; second, color of trunks or drawers. It is particularly requested that blue and white (together) be not chosen. Dress to consist of shirt and trunks or drawers to the knee. No person will be allowed to compete unless properly attired. Members of athletic or rowing associations, unless known to the club, will be required to furnish a certificate of membership, and any person not a member of a recognized club must be properly introduced by some well-known person who can vouch for his being an amateur. No competitor will be allowed to enter under a false name, and the right to refuse or strike out any entry is reserved."

The New York A.C. was not anti-professional; in the tradition of true amateurism it wished to keep the two groups separate when it came to competition, but from time to time the New York A.C. sponsored meets especially for professional athletes. The club also employed Jack Goulding, a professional walker and runner, as its trainer and coach.

When the third annual national championships were held by the New York A.C. on October 12, 1878, it was apparent that amateurism was meeting with success. The list of entries was much larger and included a number of college stars, and the records made by the contestants were generally much improved. Although the New York A.C. won six of the fifteen events, the laurels for outstanding performances went to other club contestants. William C. Wilmer, Short Hills A.C., won the 100-yard dash in 10 seconds and the 220-yard dash in 22⅞ seconds, times which were recognized as "the best on record." Two of the New York A.C. contestants won national titles for the third year in a row. Fickens won the high jump again at the same height as his previous performances, 5 feet 5 inches, and Henry Buermeyer threw the 16-pound shot 37 feet 4 inches. A recently graduated Yale University runner, Frank W. Brown, running under the colors of the Glenwood A.C., won the quarter mile. Thomas Smith, Manhattan A.C., won the mile in 4 minutes 51¼ seconds.

Professionalism in running and walking still reigned, but amateurism had come to stay. The progress made by the amateurs in the decade of the seventies was indeed impressive. On the other hand, the professionals were continually facing charges of fixed races and general dishonesty. Dr. Dudley Sargent, director of the Harvard College gymnasium, in a speech denounced professionalism as the "evil of modern athletics." "The national tendency of all sports is towards professionalism, and we must regard it as the evil of all evils. Fair play and no favor, or let the best man win, is no longer recognized in sports. The contestants are in the hands of the trimmers, who in turn are controlled by the gamblers. A contestant loses to win from a pecuniary standpoint. Betting is ruinous to athletics. It biases the judges, it injures the contestants and excites the people. Men bet to win."

By the end of the seventies meets were being sponsored by the Manhattan A.C., Yonkers Lyceum, Harlem A.C., Staten Island A.C., Short Hills A.C., Plainfield A.C., and the Knickerbocker A.C., as well as the Scots-American Clubs, Sons of St. George, and other immigrant groups, Rowing Clubs also sponsored track and field meets for amateurs. There was now no shortage of opportunties for the amateur to compete for medals and trophies.

On the college scene, in spite of the fact that an inter-collegiate association had been formed and a championship meet was being held annually, teams as such did not exist. Annually most of the colleges held an intramural meet in which the students competed as individuals or as members of a class. Programs included such events as sack races, three-legged races, potato races, and a tug-of-war, in addition to the regular track and field events. Representative times for winners of college one-mile races in 1878 were G. L. Thayer, University of Pennsylvania, 5:43; Nelson, Trinity College, 5:27¼; White, Amherst, 5:28; J. C. Wetmore, Columbia, 5:40; and T. D. Cuyler, Yale, 5:38.

In 1878 several of the amateur clubs met to organize the American Association of Amateur Athletes. The growth in the number of clubs made some form of general over-all organization imperative. Represented at the meeting were the following clubs: American, Fanwood, Greenpoint, Harlem, Knickerbocker, Plainfield, Scottish-American, and Yonkers Lyceum. The absence of the New York A.C. indicates that all was not harmonious in the movement; some expressed the belief that the New York A.C. was dominating the movement. The delegates adopted by-laws and made plans for holding a championship meet. The members of the association also considered charges of professionalism against two athletes from the Knickerbocker A.C. A year later the clubs were able to come to terms with the New York A.C., and they reorganized as the National Association of Amateur Athletes of America.

With the widespread growth of amateurism, difficulty with the definition of the term amateur began to develop. Each club had its own definition which in general barred competition to any athlete who had competed for money. In March 1879, Columbia College B.C. in announcing a program of athletic contests open only to amateurs, presented its definition: "An amateur athlete is one who practices athletics for his own physical improvement or pleasure, and not as a business or for gain." Further rules prohibited an amateur athlete to compete for a stake or a wager; it banned competing in a meet with a professional, even if money were not involved. The amateur could not teach or engage in any athletic endeavor for gain, could not compete in any meets unless they were conducted by recognized amateur clubs, and could not compete in public games unless the gate receipts were used for charitable purposes or for the promotion of amateur athletics. No amateur athlete could accept prizes of merchandise, nor could he sell or trade any prizes won in competition. The amateurs were working toward a uniform definition, but it would still be some years before an effective organization would be formed which would be acceptable to all clubs.

The results of the fall games of the New York A.C. in 1879 showed that in the decade there had been a remarkable improvement in the performances of the amateur athletes. In the meet held on September 20, 1879, Lawrence E. Myers set a record of 49½ seconds in the quarter mile, far better than the winning times in excess of a minute made by the earlier runners. Myers also won the 220 in 22¼ seconds. The mile was won in 4:37 by W. J. Duffy of the Harlem A.C. A week later in the amateur championship meet held by the New York A.C., Myers won the 220 in 22⅗ seconds, the 440 in 52⅖ seconds, and set a new record in the 880 at 2 minutes 1⅖ seconds. The appearance of the phenomenal L. E. Myers at the close of the decade signaled a new era in amateur athletics in America.

In summing up the sports scene at the end of the decade of the seventies the *New York Clipper* stated: "But the greatest advancement noticeable in any branch of sport is observable in amateur athletics, which includes a series of games such as walking, running, hammer-throwing, weight-lifting, jumping, etc., the list being in the main modeled after the annual field-gatherings of the brawny and exercise-loving Scots, known as the Caledonia games. Ten years ago the New York Athletic Club, the first organization of the kind in the States, was but a bantling, not yet having been incorporated, and, although energetic and enthusiastic athletes were among the organizers and those subsequently admitted to membership, the roll did not for years present a very imposing appearance, and the public did not pay very much attention to the devoted band of brothers who had their headquarters and took their indoor exercise in Maitre's Gymnasium, St. Mark's place. Gradually, however, the public began to manifest greater interest, and to patronize the infrequent competitive games then given more liberally, which stimulated and gave encouragement to the members of the Pioneer Club, and a few years later they obtained possession of a plot of land in Mott Haven, on the banks of the Harlem River, which they transformed into the model athletic ground to which metropolitan lovers of athletics now point with pride. The athletic boom, however, commenced in earnest less than five years ago, and since then there has been no abatement, but rather an augmentation of the interest manifested by the youths of America in these health-giving and manly sports, which do much to remove the young from temptation and assist nature in building up strong, vigorous, courageous and self-reliant men, who, as a result of the lessons in patience and perseverance here learned, and the strengthening exercise taken, will be better able to make their way through the world, whatever may be their lot in life. A large number of clubs have been formed in this city and vicinity, as well as in other prominent cities of the East, West, and South, the majority of which are in a highly prosperous condition; a number of them are possessed of well-appointed grounds and gymnasiums, and some high class 'talent' has been developed. The past year was remarkable for record-breaking, and it will not surprise us if the season of 1880 should prove equally fruitful of noteworthy events, not only in athletics, but in the rowing and other departments."

Edward Payson Weston: The Man Who Invented Walking

Edward Payson Weston, born in Providence, Rhode Island, on March 15, 1839, first won notice as an athlete in 1861, when he undertook to walk from Boston to Washington within ten days. From this time for nearly three-quarters of a century he continued to win attention in the sports headlines, and upon his death in 1929 at the age of ninety, he was saluted by newspapers throughout the country and abroad.

From the start of his career as an athlete Weston combined his ability as a walker with a special talent for winning attention and gaining publicity. His initial effort was linked to President Lincoln's inauguration, ostensibly as payment for an election wager.

Dressed in tight-fitting blue woolen knit drawers and a blue coat with brass buttons, Weston departed from Boston before a crowd which had assembled in front of the State House at noon on Washington's Birthday. Heading west toward Worcester, he arrived at that town at midnight, having covered forty-four miles. After having a lunch there, he continued his trek, covering an additional fifty-five miles before retiring at 8:00 p.m. at Longmeadow, Massachusetts.

Next morning he continued on to Hartford, Connecticut, where he attended church in the afternoon, it being Sunday. That evening he retired for the night at 10:00 p.m. at Wallingford. Heavy snows had delayed him and had cut into the goal of miles that he had set for himself.

Weston finally arrived in Washington at 4:00 p.m. on Monday, March 4, a full day behind his schedule, and too late to witness President Lincoln's inaugural ceremony. Although he had failed to accomplish what he had set out to do within ten days, Weston's feat was recognized as an outstanding pedestrian performance. He had averaged fifty-one miles per day in covering the distance between Boston and Washington.

After service in the Union army as a dispatch carrier, Weston was employed briefly as a reporter for the New York *Herald* but soon returned to the sports headlines with the announcement that he was going to attempt to walk from Portland, Maine, to Chicago within twenty-six walking days.

George K. Goodwin of New York City was Weston's backer in this endeavor, putting up the sum of $10,000 in a wager with T. F. Wilcox, who bet a like sum that Weston could not walk the distance within thirty days. The articles of agreement which were drawn up on August 7, 1867, specified that Weston would cover the ground within thirty days, exclusive of four Sundays, leaving twenty-six walking days. During the course of the walk, Weston, it was agreed, would cover 100 miles within a twenty-four hour period. He was to be allowed five attempts at this record; if he failed, he and his backer would forfeit six-tenths of the wager. If he failed to reach Chicago within the specified limits, he and his backer would lose the entire $10,000.

Each backer was to be represented by two witnesses who would accompany Weston in a conveyance, and they would make all of their statements and reports on the walk under oath.

"If at any time, or under any circumstances, the said Weston enters any vehicle or mounts any animal, or conveyance, for the purpose of riding, or does ride one foot of the distance to be walked, then this wager is forfeited against the said Weston and his backer," the agreement stated.

Weston's walk was preceded by a grand promotion which helped to create much excitement and interest in the event. Newspaper stories were widely distributed; and the New York News Company prepared a paper containing the time schedule of Weston's itinerary, the articles of agreement, instructions to the witnesses, a journal of Weston's walk to Washington, and a number of other articles about Weston. These papers, selling at ten cents a copy, were offered for sale at newsstands, and agents traveled on ahead to sell them in the towns through which Weston would wak.

By the time that Weston started his journey, the excitement was intense. Attired in dark coat, red leggings extending to the knees, high laced walking shoes with substantial soles, and a light colored hat, Weston started from the Preble House in Portland, Maine, at noon, on Tuesday, October 29. Walking with Weston was the celebrated ten mile running champion, John Grindall, who would serve as both witness and trainer. Grindall's presence enhanced the integrity of the event, since he was one of the few professional athletes of the time who enjoyed a reputation for honesty.

From the start Weston was met by large crowds in all of the cities, towns, and villages through which he passed. Often the police had to be called upon to open a path through which he might pass. In Newburyport, Massachusetts, in the early stages of his journey, a plank was dropped on one of his toes, just narrowly missing inflicting a serious injury.

A Boston reporter described the scene as Weston reached Salem: "Mr. Weston's time table would have him arrive in Salem onWednesday evening. Owing to the rainy weather and an accident to his foot, he only reached Ipswich

Wednesday morning. He was expected in Salem during the morning, and every one was watching from an early hour. The whole turnpike was alive with carriages and crowds of people on foot, who manifested the most intense interest. All the horses were in requisition, and the business men made a holiday. What was there to see? A young man of modest manners, of athletic, lithe and graceful movements, clad in close fitting jacket and knee breeches of dark blue cloth, red leggings, a ruffled shirt, shoes laced high up about the ankles, and wearing a broad-brimmed white silk hat, walking at the rate of 120 paces per minute, steady and inexorably, like a machine of steel! I walked at his side for some hundreds of yards. I, too, have been tried in exploring expeditions, and have even ascended to the height of more than three vertical miles above the level of the sea over the eternal snow and ice. But to think of fifty miles daily of this walking! It is only a horrible nightmare! The human organization will not endure such a trial. These 120 long steps per minute are already tiresome. But the mysterious figure at my side moves rapidly, steadily, silently forward. Two or three men follow him on foot, a coach containing the witnesses or judges, and a crowd of carriages with spectators. Not a word is spoken, and the only sounds are from the tramping in the muddy road. Here is serious work. Perhaps he may perform what he has determined to do, and his faith may accomplish what the Scriptures have told an unbelieving world is within its power. These brutes of horses which draw his witnesses have to be changed daily — on the terrible day of one hundred miles they must be changed twice — but their strength is only of the earth."

On Weston strode, through the streets of Boston, hearing the shouts and cheers of the crowds, but striding on and on in rapid paces. He left the Phoenix house at Dedham, Massachusetts, at 12:39 p.m. on November 1, beginning his first attempt to cover 100 miles within twenty-four hours. Providence, Rhode Island, was reached at 8:45 in the evening. Here the crowds in the city of his birth were so great that the police had to strive valiantly to open a passage for him through the streets. Stopping for fifteen minutes at the City Hotel, he proceeded and in response to the cheers of the spectators, he said that he had walked 32 miles of the 100 and was eighteen minutes ahead of schedule. "He was in excellent spirits," a reporter recorded.

On through the night he strode, and the crowds unmindful of the hour were there to cheer him on. In Pawtucket, Rhode Island, the press of the crowd could not be controlled, and they rushed upon him, causing a painful injury to his hip and giving his companion John Grindall a seriously sprained ankle. At Plainfield, Connecticut, at 6:45 a.m. the discomfort caused by his injuries forced him to give up his first attempt at the 100 miles.

Fortunately, the next day was Sunday, so Weston was able to rest in Plainfield. He attended church and relaxed by strolling about town. At a half hour after midnight he set out for Hartford, apparently having recovered from his injuries.

When he reached East Hartford at 4:00 p.m., having walked all day through heavy rains and muddy roads, he was greeted by the cheers of a large crowd which followed him at a trot through the streets of the city, cheering and shouting, until they reached the Allyne House, where Weston was to stop.

He retired to his room to rest and to pose for artists from *Harper's Weekly*. In the evening he appeared in the drawing room, "where he was besieged by as many admirers as though he was military high-cockalorum." He was presented with a handsome Malacca cane "as a memento of the journey, and a token of esteem and friendship." One observer noted that he seemed as little fatigued as though he had just returned from an ordinary walk.

Next day, at 5:00 p.m., after the police had been called to clear a passage through the crowd assembled before the Allyne House, Weston left Hartford determined to cover 100 miles before the next twenty-four hours passed. It was a cold and unpleasant day. After 58 miles Weston, having sprained an ankle, stopped at Chatham, Massachusetts.

At 7:00 a.m. next morning Weston was off again, accompanied as usual by a large number of men, women, and children, cheering and

shouting encouragement to the lithe hero. This day's trek ended at Schenectedy, where his companion, John Grindall, still suffering from the injury incurred in Pawtucket, was forced to retire from the journey and be replaced by another man furnished by Mr. Goodwin.

There still remained three chances for Weston to accomplish the 100 mile feat, but speculation began to grow that his chances of achieving that goal were diminishing. His ankles were beginning to ache, and some observed that he showed signs of fatigue. The excitement and interest in the great walk, however, showed no signs of diminishing.

At midnight on the 9th of November Weston stopped at Oneida, New York, having covered 513 miles. He rested over Sunday and headed toward Syracuse at 2:00 a.m. on the morning of the 11th. At every village and town he was met on the eastern extremities by crowds in carriage and on foot who followed him through town and escorted him for several miles beyond the western limits. At Syracuse, where he stopped to dine and rest, he told a reporter that he had actually gained two and a half pounds since leaving Portand, Maine. That evening he stayed at Weedsport.

The next day he covered 63 miles, six hours of it through a heavy snow storm which rendered the roads exceedingly muddy. Arriving at Congress Hall in Rochester at twenty minutes after midnight, Weston found several thousand people gathered there to greet him in spite of the late hour. The streets had been lined with spectators for hours awaiting anxiously the arrival of the great walker. Earlier in the evening some young wag had provided a diversion. Dressed much like Weston, he had appeared on the highway east of Rochester walking at a brisk pace. Down Main Street he strode with the cheers of the spectators ringing loud and with large numbers following him. Into the Waverly Hotel he walked, and out the back door he went, leaving an angry mob vowing vengeance on him.

On the following morning Weston left for Buffalo and upon arriving at the city limits, he was met by a squad of uniformed police officers who formed a hollow square in which to conduct him into the city. Down Genessee Street they marched followed by a crowd which increased at every block until they reached Main Street where it became a multitude, "one dense mass of human beings, pushing and squeezing each other in their anxiety to get a look at the wearer of the jaunty silk hat."

Eighteen police officers were required to escort him out of Buffalo next morning as he headed for Silver Creek, 32 miles distant, where he would rest in preparation for another try at the 100 mile feat.

At 11:15 that evening after his brief rest and two meals, he set out to walk 100 miles within twenty-four hours. He arrived at Erie, Pennsylvania at twelve noon, remained there for a brief half hour, and strode on over rough roads for nine and a half hours, reaching Conneaut, Ohio, where his ankles were so sore and his feet so swollen that he was once again compelled to abandon his attempt at the 100 miles. He had covered 90 miles and still had an hour and fifty minutes to go.

A Providence newspaper had reported a rumor that Weston was in league with a group of gamblers who had bet against his making the 100 miles in twenty-four hours. This Weston vehemently denied, stating, "If I fail, it will not be because I do not faithfully attempt to accomplish the task."

He had now covered two thirds of the distance, and barring any unforeseen accidents, there was little doubt that he would arrive in

Through cities, towns, and country hamlets, crowds of curious spectators turned out to cheer Weston toward his goal in his walk to Chicago in 1867.

Chicago within the thirty days. He still had two more chances to try for the 100-mile mark.

All across Ohio the crowds increased in size and enthusiasm. The police in the cities had all they could do to prevent the walker from being crushed and injured. Arriving at Toledo at 2:00 a.m. on November 22, he rested for twelve hours preparatory for another attempt at the 100 miles. Again he failed, this time because of confusion over the distance traveled in the first 50 miles.

He had one more try, and this would start from Waterloo, Indiana. Sporting fans were speculating that Weston could have easily made it on the third try had his backers permitted him to go on from Conneaut, Ohio. He had but nine miles to go with nearly two hours remaining. One informer stated that Weston begged with tears in his eyes to be allowed to go on, but his attendants refused to accede to his pleas. Professional athletics at this time were often suspect, as most encounters were accompanied by widespread betting.

After resting in Waterloo over the last Sunday of his journey, Weston started out at twenty minutes after midnight determined to make the 100 miles in spite of the odds. It was raining when he left and it was so dark that a man carrying a lantern walked before him and two men carrying lamps walked on either side of him. The roads were in the worst possible condition; the hills were slippery and the level areas were carpeted with corduroy, logs which had been laid across the road. Through nine hours of darkness over these abominable roads, Weston, clad in rubber coat and overalls, covered 35 miles to Ligonier. After a brief rest and refreshment, he was on his way again.

The knowledge that this was Weston's last chance to make the 100 miles heightened the excitement along the route. One reporter wrote: "It appeared that everybody, young and old, turned out to greet him and wish him God speed. At Goshen he was welcomed by an immense throng, headed by a fine brass band,

Edward Payson Weston combined his walking ability with his talent for promotion to win widespread attention for his walk from Portland, Maine, to Chicago in 1867.

which accompanied the party from the meeting point to Elkhart, a distance of twelve miles, where a similar scene took place. Weston proceeded to the Clifton House, and upon repeated calls appeared upon the balcony and acknowledged the compliment by bowing to the swaying, surging mass of excited humanity below, many of whom had traveled many miles to see him. Weston was in excellent spirits, and conversed cheerily with the ladies and gentlemen who crowded the halls and dining-room. After dinner the tramp was resumed, darkness gradually stealing on as they took up the line of march.

"Bonfires were lighted along the road, and the whole heavens were illuminated with burning barrels and boxes at the next town, Mishawauka. At the place a brass band wheeled into line behind the special police force, and struck up a lively air, but Weston's rapid strides soon took the wind out of their horns. They blowed and ran, and ran and blowed, vainly hoping their discordant music would do some good. If any ridiculous circumstance tending to excite the risibility of the pedestrian served a good purpose, that band earned the first premium. . .

"If possible, the enthusiasm at South Bend exceeded that at the last-named place. The firmament was lurid with the blaze of bonfires, and fifty special policemen kept the crowd at a respectful distance from the little hero, who appeared to be tiring rapidly. He had now traversed nearly 87 miles over slippery clay roads, through rain, sand, and slush, leaving about fourteen miles yet to go, and three hours to do it in. Weston came to a halt here, pleading that he didn't have the strength to finish his task, and further prosecution of it would be but self-inflicted punishment."

His friends and spectators urged him to go on, but he could go no farther. His feet and ankles were swollen, and he was weary and in pain. There was no doubt in his followers' minds and in the opinion of the spectators who had witnessed his remarkable performance under the most trying circumstances that under more favorable weather conditions, he could have made the 100 miles with ease.

He slept here overnight and rose refreshed and ready to continue his trek toward Chicago. Still encountering friendly and excited crowds, he went on to LaPorte, stayed there overnight, and had an easy walk next day to a point a few miles distant from Chicago.

The same reporter described his triumphant entry into Chicago: "The most extensive preparations had been made to accord him a grand reception when he should reach Chicago, and it is a long time since so much excitement was witnessed thereaway. There was an unprecedented demand for vehicles by persons bent on escorting him to the city limits, and the day preceding his arrival scarcely a carriage, buggy, sulky, light wagon or, in fact, anything to which an equine quadruped could be harnessed, could be obtained for love or money. He was met some distance from the metropolis of the West by a tremendous and rather mixed calvacade of mules, horses, donkeys, etc., who received him very enthusiastically, and by the sudden rush to see him might have caused a repetition of the unfortunate accident at Pawtucket, R.I., had not a squad of some fifty blue coats protected him from the eager and thoughtless crowd, marching ahead, abreast and in rear of Weston — and they were compelled to do some tall walking to keep up with their charge. He reached his destination at ten o'clock on the morning of the 28th, and took up his quarters at the Sherman House . . . He had been feted and lionized like a French count since his arrival, and will, perhaps, remain in Chicago for some time."

That afternoon he made an appearance at Crosby's Opera House, probably augmenting his receipts for the walk considerably. For the next few months Weston was kept busy making such appearances and performing exhibitions. Meanwhile, Weston was being badgered by challengers who wished to race against him; but he chose to reap the benefits of his fame before risking his reputation in a man to man contest, a tactic that failed to enhance his popularity in sporting circles.

Weston's great walk had stimulated widespread interest in the sport. Notices in the newspapers frequently announced claims for walking records of various kinds, some rather bizaare, such as the young man in Boston who sought to set a record for walking around the Boston common with a keg of beer on his shoulder. There were also claims of records for one-legged walking, backwards walking, and a number of other variations of the sport. Frank Queen, the editor of the *New York Clipper*, the country's leading newspaper of the entertainment and sporting world, commented on the walking craze, concluding that it would have a healthy effect upon the nation.

In February of 1868 the English walking champion, George Topley, arrived in New York City, prepared to meet all comers. The clamor for a race between Weston and Topley rose; but the American avoided such a confrontation for the time. He was still contemplating that 100 miles within 24 hours. The opportunity to try again came with an invitation from the Buffalo Club, whose members had raised a purse to offer Weston upon the successful completion of the walking feat.

At 5:00 p.m. on April 3 Weston started from Walnut Creek, 10 miles west of Erie, Pennsylvania, in another attempt at the 100 mile mark. A drizzling rain was falling as Weston set out for Buffalo, and the rain continued until he reached Erie, when it turned to snow, rendering the road very slippery. In a few hours, however, the snow stopped, and the weather remained good for the rest of the distance. He arrived at the 100 mile mark on the outskirts of Buffalo with 47 minutes remaining. He had finally achieved that goal that had eluded him thus far.

A newspaper columnist commented: "Now that Weston has proven beyond question his ability to perform such an arduous feat, perhaps his backers may feel inclined to match him against Topley, who has made proposals to that end repeatedly, so far without avail. A contest between these men would be looked upon as an international affair, and would excite a deal of interest on both side of the Atlantic, and at the same time prove beneficial to the pastime in this country."

George Topley in the meantime was winning headlines for his proposed attempt to walk fifty miles within ten hours. His challenges to Weston and other American walkers having been ignored, Topley resolved to walk against time. The date appointed for the attempt was May 4 at the Fashion Track race course. For the first twenty miles Topley looked strong and walked along at a fast pace. Few doubted that he would fail to make the record, and as a consequence the betting was light. At twenty miles he stopped to sponge himself and to eat a lunch of cold fowl and drink a glass of ale. After twelve more miles he appeared in distress as he stopped to rest briefly. He had passed the forty-second mile in seven hours and three seconds when he fell flat on his face in a faint. His failure to walk the distance was credited to his

having consumed a glass of ale during the race.

Weston at this time was on a tour of speaking engagements in New England. Somewhat derisively, the *New York Clipper* commented: "The long distance walker, E. P. Weston, is at present perambulating the New England states, displaying his pedal powers and regaling the credulous people thereof with stories of incidents connected with his tramp from Maine to Illinois, which smack strongly of Munchausenism. On the evening of the 13th inst., Music Hall, Boston, Mass., was filled by masculine and feminine masticators of brown bread and baked beans, desirous of obtaining a view of the famous pedestrian and hearing his narrative. The lecture was very amusing to those who may be classed among the 'knowing ones,' and after its termination he walked a mile, making seventeen circuits of the hall and one hundred and four feet additional, accomplishing the distance, it is said, in eight minutes and thirty-five seconds."

Such taunts from the sports writers may have been the motivating factor that induced Weston to agree finally to meet George Topley in a 100-mile heel-and-toe walking match. Then again, the stalling on Weston's part may have been part of his act, a means of promoting greater interest in the match with the resultant increase in gate receipts when the match would finally take place.

At any rate, Weston's backer, Goodwin, met with Topley's backer, drew up articles of agreement, and placed their deposits in the hands of the stakeholder on May 23. The race would be for $6,000, each side putting up $3,000. The man leading at the 25 mile mark would win $2,000; the walker leading at 50 miles would win $2,000; and the remaining sum would go to the athlete who finished the 100 miles first. If neither walker covered the 100 miles, the purse would go to the one who covered the greater distance.

Before Weston could race Topley, he had to fill a contract to walk 100 miles in 23 hours at the Riverside Park track near Boston. A large crowd gathered to watch Weston in this effort on the afternoon of June 3. Attired in the same outfit that he had worn in the Chicago walk, Weston covered the first half mile at a rather slow pace, then turned about, and walked the second half mile backwards, to the delight of the crowd. His pace picked up after the first mile and he strode around the track in good form until he completed the 27th mile, then he rested for 36 minutes. Before resuming his walk, he poured a pint of whiskey into his shoes and ate a raw egg. On he walked through the night. By morning as he approached the 80th mile, he was showing signs of fatigue and distress. At 90½ miles Weston withdrew from the track and notified the judges that since there was no chance of his making the time, he was withdrawing. He had been walking for 22 hours and 52 minutes.

During this race a young man named Cornelius Payne from Albany, New York, on a wager attempted to follow Weston about the track for seventy miles. Attired in his suit and tall hat, he started to follow Weston during the thirteenth mile, supposedly without any prior training. He won his bet and would appear against Weston in the future.

Had Weston succeeded in this attempt, he would certainly have been the odds-on favorite to win in the match with Topley. Thus the uncertainty of the outcome contributed to the large attendance of spectators who showed up at the Mystic Park race course near Boston on June 19 to witness the big race. Topley started off in the lead. At the end of eight miles Weston paused for refreshments for 17 minutes; at nine miles Topley stopped for a like period of time. At 25 miles Topley was leading. At 75 miles Weston was two miles ahead of Topley when he ascended the steps to the judges' stand to state that he could not go on. Topley continued until he completed 74 miles, then stopped to rest. While the spectators were waiting for Topley to return to the track, Mr. Goodwin made the announcement that the English walker had withdrawn from the race. The judges then declared Weston the winner in 23 hours, 57 minutes, and 4½ seconds, for the 75 miles. The disappointed crowd was astonished at the announcement and voices of suspicion were raised.

Reported the *New York Clipper:* "Thus terminated this curious — to say the least of it — pedestrian match between the leading walkers of the Old and New Worlds, which is not worth even the brief description given, and it will require but few more such palpable frauds to kill pedestrianism as effectually as it ever has been heretofore."

The interest generated by Weston's assaults upon the 100-mile mark spurred others to try also and there were many who claimed that they had walked that distance within 24 hours. Some walkers emerged from among the mass as self-styled champions, and a few won such recognition from the sporting press. These walkers published challenges to Weston, some even offering him a head start in the race, but Weston quietly ignored all of them and continued to race against time. The sports writers began to make unkind remarks about him, although the general press still recognized him as a great walker.

Perhaps smarting under the taunts of the writers, Weston felt in the fall of 1869 that it was time to do something to preserve or regain his reputation as a walker. He announced that he was about to undertake another long distance walk even greater than his walk from Portland, Maine, to Chicago. This time he would start in Bangor, Maine, then walk all the way to St. Paul, Minnesota, by way of Buffalo and Chicago. His journey would then take him to St. Louis, Missouri, thence through the Ohio River towns to West Virginia, Pennsylvania, Baltimore, Philadelphia, and New York City. He would cover a distance of 5,000 miles on foot within 100 consecutive days.

He set out from Bangor on December 1, but within a few days he had given up the walk, due to lameness, he said. Others, however, told that he had encountered financial problems and was not getting along with his backers. The *New York Clipper* commented: "Perhaps he was too closely watched and things didn't work as he anticipated."

Weston had not given up entirely. On January 19, 1869, he started from Bangor again, determined to perform the long walk of 5,000 miles in 100 days. Although Weston's journey this time failed to excite as much interest as his first long walk, he did create excitement locally as he passed through towns en route.

Crossing New York State, he encountered

heavy snows, sometimes having to go through six-foot drifts. His ears were frost-bitten and he suffered from the cold throughout the trip across New York. Arriving in Buffalo on February 19, ten days behind schedule, Weston announced that he was being forced to conclude his walk there because of lack of funds.

Weston remained in Buffalo until spring when he was matched to walk against Cornelius Payne, the young man who had followed him about the track in Brighton, Massachusetts, the year before. They started from Walnut Creek in Pennsylvania on April 1 bound for the finish line in front of the Buffalo post office. The crowd waited at the finish line in vain. The race had been abandoned after about sixty miles. A few weeks later Payne and Weston met again in a contest from which Weston withdrew after eighty-nine miles. Payne went on to finish and win the purse.

Meanwhile, other walkers were claiming records which made Weston's efforts appear puny by comparison. One Joseph McEttrick was credited with having walked 100 miles in the astounding time of 18 hour and 43 minutes. Only the legendary Captain Robert Barclay of England had ever walked the distance faster. Edward Payson Weston took a tour of the midwestern towns to give exhibitions and walk against the clock.

Weston, a showman by instinct, sometimes played a tune on the cornet as he walked around the hall or kept time with the music of the band, waving his walking stick, and he enjoyed giving a speech to the spectators from the judges' stand. He won many influential friends among the newspaper editors, including the venerable Horace Greeley.

After returning from a tour of the Midwest in November 1870, Weston announced that he was going after a new record. He would walk 400 miles within 5 days and he had engaged the Empire Skating rink in New York City for this event. He fell short of this goal, covering 320 miles in 5 days. Some said that he did not extend himself because the attendance was too light. The *New York Clipper* called him an

"arrant humbug" and accused him of trying to "hoodwink" the public.

Nevertheless, in introducing the five-day walk, Weston was starting what would become a mania before the decade was out. He continued his attempts at the 400-mile record and finally in June 1871 was credited with having accomplished that feat against time at the Empire rink in New York City. During the course of that contest against time, Weston succeeded in walking 112 miles within a 24-hour period. Others were soon trying to duplicate or exceed his record; and the challengers for personal encounters continued to be directed toward him without success. Weston was now talking about a trip to England; his walking exhibitions were now being billed as "farewell appearances."

The following year found Weston still in the United States, still trying for records and claiming them. The first man to perform a feat of endurance naturally owns the record for that initial effort, notwithstanding that his tenure as record-holder might be short-lived. Almost as soon as Weston claimed the 400-mile record, others followed suit and made claims that they had exceeded his record, whereupon Weston announced that he was about to walk 500 miles in 6 days.

His first attempt at this distance in May 1874 at the American Institute building, the new name for the Empire rink, was widely publicized. The newspaper stories and a printed notice on the program contained the endorsements of New York's Major Havemeyer and a number of other notables. It was all presented as an altruistic contribution by Weston designed to test the ultimate extent of human endurance. Although Weston fell seventy miles short of his goal in this attempt, he succeeded in taking away $6,000 in gate receipts.

In the first week of March 1875, Weston made a rare appearance against a competitor when he walked against J. R. Judd in a six-day contest at Barnum's Roman Hippodrome in New York City. Judd was quite a way down the list among professional long distance walkers, but Weston agreed to spot him 35 miles in the race. This allowance proved unnecessary as Judd's legs gave out shorty after having completed 200

LITH. OF KELLOGG & BULKELEY, HARTFORD, CONN.

EDWARD PAYSON WESTON.

Walking from Portland to Chicago, Distance 1226 Miles in 26 days.

Edward Payson Weston at Seventy Years

miles. Weston went on to complete 431 miles in the allotted time.

In a rare occasion the *New York Clipper* conceded: "Though we are not disposed to admit the justice of the claims made by Weston concerning alleged wonderful performances, under far less satisfactory circumstances, in the past, we give him credit for the possession of greater stamina than, perhaps, any other pedestrian in the country is endowed with, while his pluck is of the best, and his speed quite good enough to bet upon in a long race."

A dramatic foreshadowing of a rivalry between two men which would last for years was presented before the start of the Weston-Judd race, when a wiry little Irish athlete from Chicago, one Daniel O'Leary, attempted to be permitted to enter the race. Both Judd and Weston declined to acknowledge the overtures of this upstart from the West.

Shortly after the race Daniel O'Leary appeared in New York City for a contest of twenty miles against Wilson Reid, a New York athlete with a first-rate reputation for the shorter distances, if one can consider twenty miles short. O'Leary easily defeated Reid and thus transferred to the East a reputation that he had already earned in his home city of Chicago.

O'Leary was a competitor who thrived upon man-to-man competition. A few weeks later at the American Institute track in New York City he defeated John DeWitt of Auburn, N.Y., in a 100 mile contest, covered in 23 hours, 38 seconds. A week later in Philadelphia O'Leary walked for 24 hours against time. Up until this time Weston's best performance for 24 hours had been 115 miles. O'Leary bettered this mark by a mile, covering the distance in 23 hours, 12 minutes, and 53½ seconds. The public demand for a race between O'Leary and Weston was growing strong, and it was reported that the financial prospects of such an encounter were attractive to Weston.

In May when Daniel O'Leary had returned to Chicago after his triumphant tour of the East, he made a determined effort to walk 500 miles in six days. Before a capacity crowd at the West-side rink, O'Leary walked briskly around the track, often acknowledging the cheers of the 5,000 spectators. With two hours

and 28 minutes still remaining in the allotted time, O'Leary finished the 500 miles. A week earlier Weston had failed again to make the distance but had succeeded in walking 117 miles in 24 hours.

The match between Weston and O'Leary was now inevitable, and negotiations between the two were started. The race would be in Chicago in November at the Exhibition building; the distance would be 500 miles. Weston was offered $500 for coming to Chicago, and he would receive one-half of the gate receipts. He had been prospering of late as a professional athlete and with good reason could anticipate a lucrative purse, win or lose. O'Leary, as with most Irish athletes, enjoyed immense popularity in Chicago, a factor which alone would insure a large gate. Weston's fame in the city for his celebrated walk from Portland, Maine, to Chicago had not diminished either.

The *Chicago Evening Journal* on November 11 reported that Weston had arrived in town. "He travels in style, being attended by two negro servants," it stated.

When the race started at 12:08 a.m. on November 15, O'Leary set a brisk pace, piling up a lead of 20 miles on the first day. Some expressed apprehension that he was moving too fast and would be overtaken by Weston; but he continued on adding to his lead until the last day when he completed the 500 miles at about 11 o'clock Saturday night, finally withdrawing from the track at 11:20, having walked 503 miles. Weston left the track at the same time with 451½ miles to his credit.

America was for O'Leary now. He could reap a small fortune in personal appearances and in walking contests. His triumph over Weston, coupled with his Irish origin, made him much in demand. He was already receiving invitations and challenges from England, but America had to be covered first.

The situation was entirely different for Weston. There were not many more records that he could invent and O'Leary had clearly pushed him aside as a gate attraction in the walking arenas of the United States. Probably recognizing this situation, Weston left for England, where in a short period of time he was repeating the walking exploits which he had performed in the United States over the last seven or eight years.

Weston's initial encounter was with William Perkins, who was billed the English champion walker. Meeting in a 24 hour race, an event unfamiliar to the Englishman, Weston was the winner. After this he began his series of races against time, attracting large crowds, one of which was reported to be over 16,000. Efforts to induce him to respond to challenges from other walkers fell on deaf ears. Weston responded to some that his schedule was full, and to those who offered to bet on their skill against his, he responded that he never bet or walked for stakes.

When Harold Vaughn, the English pedestrian, walked 120 miles in slightly under 24 hours, Weston was harried for match races. He carefully avoided all challenges and continued his races against time. In spite of his failure to respond to challengers, Weston was well received by the public. In one six-day walk he was credited with having covered 500 miles.

In October his American conqueror, Daniel O'Leary, sailed for England. Upon landing, he issued challenges to all comers and especially to Weston, to whom he offered a 25 mile start in a 500 mile race. The little Irishman had to content himself with waking the 500 miles by himself in Liverpool, successfully covering the distance on his first try and going on for 2 more miles within the allotted time.

The clamor which was raised for a match between the two Americans could not be stilled. English promoters offered a $5,000 purse for the winner of a six-day walking race, an inducement that Weston could not refuse. It was considered the first bona-fide match that Weston engaged in since his arrival in England a year before. The two men toed the mark in Agricultural Hall in London on April 7, 1877, in a contest which had created more excitement than any event within the memory of any member of the sporting fraternity. One night's attendance was reported in excess of 20,000.

O'Leary's walking form was regarded as the better of the two. He walked erect in good upright form holding in each hand a piece of wood, at no time his feet losing contact with the ground. Weston walked with a jaunty air,

jesting with his friends in the arena, and keeping time with the music, strutting at times. During the race O'Leary abstained from solid foods, his bill of fare for the week consisting of chicken broth, tea, jellies, oatmeal gruel, yolk of eggs with tea, grapes, strawberries, and oranges. Weston chose more solid fare — steaks and mutton chops, mutton broth, bread and butter, rice pudding, red currant and calves-foot jellies, biscuit and cheese, grapes, oranges, prunes and figs. He drank tea, coffee, ginger ale, soda, milk, and seltzer water. Weston weighed 12 ounces less at the finish than at the start, while O'Leary lost more than 8 pounds. During the six days O'Leary rested 26 hours, 23 minutes, and 6 seconds; Weston's stoppages totaled 23 hours, 12 minutes, and 37 seconds.

O'Leary, in the lead on the sixth day of the race, passed the 500 mile mark at 2:37 in the afternoon, with Weston trailing him by 23 miles. At this point O'Leary appeared much fatigued, and Weston seemed fresh and well rested. At four in the afternoon O'Leary left the track to rest, but he appeared in such bad condition that some felt that he might not be able to return and would thus lose the match in spite of his lead at this point. He re-appeared, however, after a 35 minute rest. Both men went on until nine o'clock, at which point O'Leary had covered 519 miles. Weston rested briefly, then resumed the walk, although he knew at this point that he could not overtake O'Leary, who had now gone to his tent to rest. The crowd cheered Weston loudly, giving him an ovation such as he had seldom heard. O'Leary in his tent felt that the cheering belonged to him, so he emerged and walked around the track with the assistance of friends, acknowledging the tribute of the crowd. The final score showed O'Leary had covered 520 miles to Weston's 510. Both men won the accolades of the spectators.

There was nothing but praise for Weston's performance, in spite of the fact that he had trailed his opponent by ten miles in the contest. O'Leary in his remarks after the race paid high compliments to Weston for his courage and ability. English sports writers in their reports thought that Weston could have won if the contest had gone on for three more hours. While O'Leary was near total exhaustion at the conclusion of the contest, Weston looked as fresh at that point as he had early in the race. Some still considered him the better of the two walkers. Defeat had not diminished his fame.

O'Leary returned to America for a succession of appearances on tracks throughout the United States, while Weston remained in England reaping the benefits of his fame.

The six-day race was an innovation to the sporting scene that was largely credited to Weston for its introduction. Its popularity as a spectator sport spread rapidly, reaching the "mania" stage in 1879 and 1880. An English nobleman, Lord Astley, added interest to the event by offering a large silver and gold international championship belt. The first competition for the belt was scheduled for March 1878 at the Agricultural Hall in London. For 142 hours the athletes would endeavor to cover as many miles as they could by either running or walking. For this reason they became known as "Six-day go-as-you-please" races. A track made of a combination of loam and sawdust was laid out around the hall. Elaborate tents in which the contestants could rest were erected within the circle. At the first race for the Astley belt two tracks were built, running concentrically, one for the Englishmen and one for the foreigners.

Weston was among the twenty runners scheduled to compete. O'Leary, back in Chicago, learned about the big race and took off for England to vie for the honor. Although he arrived in England after the entry deadline, O'Leary was still permitted to enter the race. When the athletes toed the mark, it was found that Weston had withdrawn from the contest because of illness. O'Leary won the race with a record of 520¼ miles.

The competition for the Astley belt for the next few years would be one of the top sporting events of the era. Shortly after Daniel O'Leary's victory. Lord Astley offered to back Weston in a match for the championship belt, but O'Leary surprised the English by agreeing to such a match provided it were held in Chicago. There was some discussion as to whether the belt should be permitted to leave England, a question which Lord Astley settled by saying there was nothing in the rules to prevent such a course.

O'Leary returned to the United States, where he made a rather disappointing defense against a challenger at Gilmore's Garden in New York City. It was a financial success, however, as large crowds attended the performance every day to see the champion walk. Without much competition he covered slightly more than 400 miles. Weston in the meantime with the backing of Lord Astley was resuming his Portland, Maine, to Chicago routine. In January 1879, he had undertaken to walk 2,000 miles over the English roads in a thousand hours. He would deliver a lecture in each of the principal towns through which he passed.

The six-day contests which Weston had popularized were being held both in England and the United States at frequent intervals and without his participation. Several athletes were developing into championship caliber, and the competition was becoming keen.

In February Charles Rowell, a leading English pedestrian, issued a challenge to O'Leary to race for the Astley belt. Papers were signed, and the race was set for March 10, 1879 at Gilmore's Garden in New York City, with four contestants taking part in the race. O'Leary, apparently suffering from over-indulgence, lasted only three days. Rowell took the title, the Astley belt, and $20,000 back across the Atlantic. This was all prelude to Weston's next exploit as a walker.

Rowell wasted little time in responding to challenges for the belt, agreeing to compete against four pedestrians in the Agricultural Hall in London on June 16. Weston appeared among the challengers. A few days before the contest, Rowell sprained his ankle and upon the advice of his physician was forced to withdraw from the race.

The four contestants remaining in the race were two Englishmen, "Blower" Brown and R. Harding, John Ennis of Chicago, and Edward P. Weston. Betting odds at the start were 6 to 4 on Brown, 5 to 1 against Ennis, 6 to 1 against Harding, and 10 to 1 against Weston. At one a.m. on Monday the four athletes took off and traveled around the circuit with Brown in the early lead. By noon Brown, still in the lead, had covered 68 miles, followed within a mile by Weston. The other two contestants were far behind. Brown continued a fast pace, leading the spectators to expect a repetition of his performance when he recently covered the largest number of miles in six days. Weston stayed always within a few miles of the leader; Ennis and Harding, both suffering, following far behind. At the 50 hour mark Brown had covered 227 miles to Weston's 220. Both Brown and Weston appeared in good condition, but Harding and Ennis were struggling to keep on circling the track. Harding withdrew first, and not long after, Ennis gave up.

Brown lengthened his lead over Weston to ten miles at times; but Weston kept running and walking without showing any signs of distress. At three a.m. on the 19th the score was Brown 318 miles; Weston, 313 miles. At 346 miles Brown, appearing much fatigued, retired to his tent to rest at 10:14 a.m. Weston, taking advantage of his opponent's absence, stepped up his pace and by 11:00 a.m., Weston had equaled Brown's score of 346 miles. A great shout rose from the spectators and when Brown returned to the track, he was no longer leading. Brown was now limping, while Weston looked stronger than ever. The bookmakers were now offering ten to one odds on Weston to win.

At the 88 hour mark, Weston, with a score of 368 miles, was leading Brown by 8 miles, a lead that within a few hours he had increased to 14 miles, and each hour added to it, until at 112 hours Weston was 438 to 400 for Brown.

At 3:00 a.m., on the last day of the race, Weston had stretched his lead to 53 miles, having made 473 miles. There was no hope for Brown at this point, but he kept on in an effort to cover 450 miles, a condition necessary for him to share in the gate receipts. Suspicions were being voiced that Weston was being allowed to win the race so that the belt would go back to New York City where the gate would be much more lucrative for the participants. After all, Brown had set a record of 542¼ miles, and the best that Weston had ever done was 510 miles for a second place behind O'Leary.

"The American seemed on springs, always fresh and in splendid spirits. When the music played he walked faster than ever," wrote a New York reporter. He did his 526th mile in 7 minutes, 37 seconds, the fastest mile of the match.

As Weston passed his tent for the final lap, he was given a British and an American flag, which he carried around the track, waving them amidst the shouting and cheering, as the band played "Yankee Doodle," followed by "Rule Britannia." At the end of that lap he had completed 550 miles, a new record and a remarkable feat, sufficient to dispell all rumors that there had been any pre-arranged outcome.

The excitement in America over the victory was described by the *New York Clipper:* "In this city a lively interest was taken in the result, dating from the period at which the American assumed the lead, on the 19th, and increasing after the announcement was made that he was to attempt to cover 550 miles in the allotted 142 hours, while on the afternoon of the last day, when it was even betting that he would succeed in the unexampled effort, the interest took the form of excitement, and the bulletin boards displayed in front of the newspaper offices down town were anxiously scanned by thousands, many of whom stood their ground for hours. After nightfall, when the end was fast approaching, the interest greatly deepened, and while the crowds anchored before the canvas indicators in Printing House Square were doubled and trebled in dimensions, thousands gathered in front of the illuminated bulletin boards opposite the Fifth Avenue Hotel, at the Standard Theatre and other points in the upper part of the city, and when the announcement came that Weston, the first native American who has won the coveted trophy, had accomplished the task he had undertaken, and thrown in the shade all previous records, the enthusiasm was intense. The great majority were astonished that he should have succeeded in accomplishing so magnificent a performance, but those who were aware of the wonderful staying powers of the man, and remembered that in his match with O'Leary he had covered 510 miles by walking alone, were not greatly surprised to know that he had done forty miles better when allowed to run and walk at will. It is certain that a flattering reception is in store for Weston when he again makes his public appearance in New York, which will probably be before the lapse of many days. In the past we have had occasion to speak of him in by no means complimentary terms, because of the objectionable way in which many of his exhibitions were carried out, but we have never withheld credit when it was deserved by him, and we now cheerfully accord to Weston the praise to which this achievement fairly entitles him."

The *Clipper* ordered a poem written in honor of Weston and he was praised in editorial comment in the columns of the paper which had so often treated him with scorn and derision.

After his amazing feat, Weston did not return to his native country immediately but remained in England until August, during which time arrangements were being made for a defense of the Astley Belt in the United States. It was finally decided that the defense of the title would take place in Madison Square Garden on September 22. Complications had arisen over the use of this arena since Daniel O'Leary, now a promoter of six-day races, had entered into a contract for the use of the hall which stipulated that no walking matches would be held prior to his. The sponsors of the Astley Belt contest got around this by presenting the race as an adjunct to a concert. Since bands were an important part of the six-day scene, their performance would be regarded as a concert.

Weston finally sailed from Liverpool, England, accompanied by his wife and three children on the steamer *Nevada* August 16, arriving in New York City on August 27. A welcoming group chartered a small steamboat which took them out into the harbor to greet the returning hero. They met the *Nevada* with a volley of cheers. A ladder lowered from the ship enabled them to come aboard to greet the champion.

Weston's propensity to talk soon got him into difficulty. He told his welcoming delegation, among whom were newspaper reporters, that it was against his wish that the defense of the Astley Belt was to take place in New York City. He complained that he had never received the treatment which he had deserved, or the credit to which he was justly entitled, at the hands of the New Yorkers. If it had not been for the persuasive arguments of his wife, and Lord Ast-

ley, he would have defended his title in Australia or some country far removed from America. These remarks, which were almost immediately echoed in the press, tended to put a damper on the reception which had been planned for him on August 29 at Madison Square Garden.

At the reception Weston attempted to explain away his remarks but in the viewpoint of the newspaper reporters he was not very successful. The *New York Clipper* commented: "The reception was not a very brilliant nor a very enthusiastic affair, and his rather lengthy speech contained sentences which were not prompted by modesty, and were better unuttered."

Next day he and his family left for Providence, Rhode Island, where a full-scale public reception had been planned by his fellow townsmen. A mammoth tent had been erected in Park Garden for the affair. After the celebration Weston left for a home in the country where he could train seriously for the defense of his title.

The controversy over the use of the Madison Square Garden was still raging, and an injunction to prevent the race from taking place there was being threatened. Weston, a teetotaler and a non-smoker, was demanding that all smoking be banned in Madison Square Garden during the race, thus further complicating the affair. He threatened to withdraw from the race if his demand for a ban on smoking was not met. Odds makers were beginning to offer two to one that Weston would not be among the starters. While it was conceded that smoking on the ground floor might be harmful to the contestants and might justly be banned, it would be almost impossible to ban smoking throughout the building. Besides, the sale of cigars in the Gardens was a profitable concession.

Eventually all of the obstacles were overcome, and the race was scheduled to go ahead as planned. Workmen were laboring day and night to have everything in readiness for the race. A track eight feet wide composed of sifted loam and tanbark, with a light top dressing of sawdust had been prepared. It had been decided that for the benefit of the athletes smoking would be banned on the main floor. Another rule which was adopted provided that the entire hall would be cleared of spectators between the hours of five and six a.m. to give the custodians time to clean up the place. This was the explanation given by the management; the reason understood by the spectators and press was to prevent individuals from remaining in the building the greater part of the week for the price of one admission. The price was set at one dollar, twice the amount required at previous contests.

Thirteen athletes were signed up for the race. All the sports followers were becoming excited over the event, and the daily press was giving space to it. The *New York Times* was one exception. In an editorial the *Times* belittled the contest and referred to Weston as "a tedious and wholly unnecessary person." The editorial went on to say, "If Mr. Weston would pledge himself to die in the course of his next match, there are thousands of people who would be ready to witness the performance, and to show their appreciation of his good taste, but we all know that neither he nor his companions will do anything of the sort. They will become exhausted, giddy, and faint. They will suffer a degree of physical anguish that a heathen Roman audience would recognize as being not out of place in a first-class gladiatorial show, but they will stoutly refuse to die and so put a stop to the match. Mr. Weston, in particular, will survive the international walking match, and will live to make a dozen more pedestrian failures before he retires from public life . . ."

The editorial suggested that the only form of pedestrianism that it would recommend for Weston would be for him to walk the plank "which so many involuntary pedestrians successfully performed in the days when piracy was one of the most popular of athletic sports." He should walk a thousand miles away from civilization and never come back, the editor wrote. The *Times* was not at all kind to Weston.

When the thirteen athletes toed the mark at one a.m. on Monday, September 22, 1879, Madison Square Garden was crowded with excited spectators. Many of them had been gathered on the sidewalks about the building all afternoon to get a first glimpse of the contestants. Just before the start of the race, Charles Rowell, the English champion, made a presentation in behalf of the English contingent of a

gold-headed riding whip to Edward Payson Weston for his contribution to the sport of long distance walking.

As each contestant emerged from his tent, he was greeted with loud applause and cheering, except in the case of Weston, who made his appearance attended by his English butler Charley. The reporter for *The National Police Gazette* wrote, "When Weston appeared he did not receive a single cheer. No demonstration of ill-feeling was made, but he was studiously slighted by unanimous consent."

George Hazael, the English champion at 50 miles, went out to an early lead which he held for the first 50 miles when Charles Rowell took over. At 11:30 that evening, Rowell, still in the lead, had covered 115 miles. Weston was well back in the field with 95 miles.

Throughout the next few days a spirited contest was waged between Rowell and the leaders, but Weston did not seem to be taking the race seriously. He spent much of his time clowning. When the band struck up a lively air, Weston kept step with the music, waving his riding whip, and at times dancing to the music. He would fling his whip into the air and catch it. At one time he balanced a cup on the end of his whip and carried it around the track. Whenever he spied anyone smoking near the track, he called the attention of the police to it. He made faces at the spectators, mimicked the other contestants, and played the role of clown. *The National Police Gazette* reporter wrote, "To judge from his playfulness, one would think that a six-day walk is a holiday with him, and the tan bark a delightful playground."

Charles Rowell won the race with 530 miles, 15 miles in front of a young athlete, Samuel Merritt, from Bridgeport, Connecticut. Weston came in sixth place with 455 miles, just enough by five miles to qualify for a share in the gate receipts. In the final division of the funds Rowell received $27,721; Weston's share $1,663.

After what the *New York Clipper* described as a "miserable performance," Weston rested then took to the road for a series of exhibitions and lectures. By winter he was performing on the West Coast and up to his old game of racing against time, seldom overtaking it. In March he was matched for a six-day walking race against his old opponent Daniel O'Leary. Weston trailed in this race, but remained in California performing before audiences which grew smaller with each failure.

His return to the East was noted in the *New York Clipper* in an item which was not at all complimentary: "E. P. Weston after making a dismal failure in San Francisco, Cal., has returned East. A reporter of a Rochester, N.Y., paper who interviewed him en route home states that Weston expressed himself as 'disgusted with pedestrianism, which has descended to hippodroming.' After the late contests in San Francisco, the first of which was for an imaginary stake of $10,000, this is a curious remark for E.P.W. to make, although quite in keeping with the character of the man. He also says he will do no more prize-walking, 'unless the English managers pay enough to entice him' — in other words, guarantee him a reasonable sum, win or lose. Considering the sorry exhibitions the poor fellow had given since he returned to America, it is difficult to understand why they should offer inducements for him to 'perform' in England. He also expressed the opinion that Hart's record of 565 miles 165 yards was made only on paper — a statement which is likely to have a boomerang effect, by throwing suspicion on the honesty of his reported performance of 550 miles 110 yds. in London, for which we have always given him credit. However, Weston must feel very badly over the events of the past nine months, and we presume too much attention should not be paid to the utterances of a disappointed man."

In February 1881 when Charles Rowell was visiting the United States, Weston made arrangements with the English champion for a contest in London for the Astley belt. No definite date was set until after a meeting in March when it was agreed that the two would meet in London on June 20. The match between Rowell and Weston excited little interest since it was a foregone conclusion that Rowell would win. On the third day, trailing by seventy-seven miles, Weston dropped out, pleading illness.

Weston remained in England for the next few years, lecturing and giving exhibitions under the sponsorship of a temperance society. In 1883 he was planning to walk 50 miles a day for 100 days, for a distance of 5,000 miles, Sundays, of course, excluded. The announced purpose of this demonstration of physical endurance was "to demonstrate the superiority of tea over beer and alcoholic drinks in general during periods of prolonged muscular exertion." At the close of each day he would deliver in the town where his day's journey ended a lecture entitled "Tea vs. Beer."

Weston set out from London on November 21, 1883, on this long walk which would take him through much of southern England and Wales. As he approached the end of this arduous task, a great deal of interest in its outcome was stimulated. Walking from Brighton to London, a distance of 53 miles, Weston arrived in the city on March 8, 1884, with 300 miles yet remaining. These miles would be finished on a track which had been constructed at the Victoria Palace on the Waterloo Road. When he arrived at that hall he took to the stage to deliver his lecture, "Tea vs. Beer."

Throughout the following week he walked around the track before the spectators. Saturday evening as he neared the 5,000 mile mark, every seat in the hall was filled and the crowd cheered him on enthusiastically. At the completion of the walk Weston was examined by a team of physicians who pronounced him in as fit a condition as when he started 100 days earlier. The platform was crowded with clergymen, doctors, and others associated with the temperance cause.

In walking the 5,000 miles, Weston had covered 1,699¼ miles on the roads and the balance of the distances in halls and inclosures. The feat must have had its financial rewards for Weston, especially when the temperance movement leaders undertook a fund-raising campaign to show their appreciation for his demonstration of the effectiveness of abstinence from alcoholic beverages.

Weston returned quietly to the United States in August of 1884. By this time professional walking and running were on the decline in this country. Suspicions of dishonesty in fixed races, the growth of interest in amateur athletics, and the introduction of the new sports of cycling and roller skating all helped to bring on the demise of the long distance professional

Having won the Astley Belt in London, covering 520¼ miles in 142 hours to defeat Weston, Daniel O'Leary, returned to the United States, where he defended his title at Gilmore's Garden in New York City in a rather disappointing performance, won by O'Leary in slightly more than 400 miles.

THE O'LEARY-CAMPANA PEDESTRIAN CONTEST, AT GILMORE'S GARDEN, NEW YORK CITY.—1.—THE START, AT ONE O'CLOCK, ON THE MORNING OF THE 23RD. 2.—O'LEARY TAKING HIS NOURISHMENT ON THE TRACK. 3.—SPORT TAKING REST AND REFRESHMENT AT HIS QUARTERS. 4.—THE CHAMPION LETTING HIMSELF OUT. 5.—SPORT MAKING ONE OF HIS FAMOUS SPURTS.—See Page 7.

95

races. The performers continue to run throughout the 1880's but to ever decreasing crowds.

In 1884 it was no longer profitable for Daniel O'Leary to promote and sponsor long distance races. He traveled around the country giving exhibitions in halls and skating rinks. Weston upon his return to the United States renewed his rivalry with the little Irishman in rather pathetic performances. In a twelve-hour-a-day race for six-days in Newark, New Jersey, O'Leary beat Weston by four miles, 284 to 280 miles. A reporter commented, "At that rate of traveling they can hardly keep themselves warm."

The two old athletes now approaching fifty continued these matches until lack of interest no longer attracted spectators. Weston continued his lectures and exhibitions, but the days of big crowds and excitement seemed to have passed. In the 1890's he and Daniel O'Leary under the sponsorship of temperance groups engaged in a series of "contests" designed to demonstrate the effects of alcohol upon the human body. Of course, Weston was allowed to win in such meetings. He lapsed into relative obscurity in spite of his efforts to maintain his fame.

Had Weston's career terminated at the close of the nineteenth century there would be little cause to remember him today. Other pedestrians like Charles Rowell, Daniel O'Leary, George Littlewood, and a number of others established records and enjoyed careers that were far more successful than anything that Weston ever accomplished; yet they are completely forgotten while Weston from time to time still receives notice as "Weston the great walker."

In 1906 Weston, at the age of sixty-seven and still walking and talking, was discovered by the *New York Times*. A new generation of reporters and writers, whose memories did not go back to the day when the *Times* called Weston "The Great Failer" and suggested that he walk the plank, found the aged walker and made him a celebrity, adorning him with laurels of praise far beyond any notice that he had ever received in his younger days. In May of this year he had undertaken to walk from Philadelphia to New York City in an effort to improve the time he

had made for that route in his initial walking feat of 43 years before when he had walked to President Lincoln's inauguration.

This time Weston, accompanied by two physicians, was walking in the interest of science. His food was carefully chosen, measured, and given to him by the doctors, and he was examined periodically in order to study the effects of the walk on the old man. He arrived at the City Hall in New York City at midnight on May 6, having walked the distance faster by twenty-five minutes than he had as a young man.

In the following year he announced that he was going to repeat his famous walk from Portland, Maine, to Chicago. Amid the cheers of a thousand people gathered in front of the Portland post office, among whom were some who had been there forty years before, Weston started out on October 29. He arrived in Chicago forty hours ahead of his previous record.

Having arrived at the outskirts of Chicago shortly after midnight, Weston was greeted by a large crowd, a squad of police officers, and a delegation of members from the Illinois Athletic Club. Rather than enter Chicago at this late hour it was decided that Weston would stay at Chicago beach for the night. Next morning he made his triumphant entry into Chicago followed by a procession of automobiles and a large number of people on foot, the latter being forced to run to keep pace with the brisk walker. The journey was scheduled to terminate at the federal building, where the mayor and other city notables were waiting to greet him. Upon arrival there, Weston approached the employees' entrance where he was denied admission by a uniform guard who directed him to another entrance. Miffed by such a reception, he turned without asking for any explanation and asked the way to the Illinois Athletic Club, leaving the mayor and dignitaries waiting. When a custodian informed the reception committee what had happened, they quietly decided to dispense with the reception. At the Illinois Athletic Club, Weston received an enthusiastic reception. So dense was the crowd that the police had great difficulty opening a passage through which Weston could reach the building. Addressing the crowd from the steps of the building, he thanked them for their in-

WESTON
AND HIS
WALKS

Souvenír Programme

OF THE GREAT

TRANSCONTINENTAL WALK

Ocean to Ocean in Ninety Days

Starting from City Hall, Los Angeles, Cal., at 4 o'clock
P. M., Tuesday, February 1, 1910, near the
Seventy-second Anniversary of His Birth

Life and Record of Edward Payson Weston
The Great American Pedestrian

Price, Ten Cents

terest in him and issued a challenge to the world for a walking race.

As a correspondent of the *New York Times*, Weston wrote a description of his reception in Chicago: "It has been ended by a demonstration greater than I ever imagined could be given any man, much less my humble self. Chicago afforded me a welcome which will be a treasure to my memory for the rest of my life."

At the approach of his seventieth birthday, Weston announced that he was planning to undertake the greatest walking attempt of his long career, a hike from New York to San Francisco. His goal in this great walk would be to cover the distance in 100 days, resting on Sundays. His route was not to be a direct one. From New York City to Buffalo, he would then proceed to Chicago, St. Louis, across Kansas, through Colorado, to Wyoming into Utah and Nevada. To avoid the alkali deserts, he had mapped his route to take him from Reno to Los Angeles, then on to San Francisco. Some of the detours in his route were admittedly made to accommodate speaking engagements which had been arranged for him in advance. Other income would come from his exclusive reports which he was under contract with the *New York Times* to cable each day. The interest generated by the walking exploits of the re-discovered Weston was enough to induce a promoter to offer a six-day race at Madison Square Garden, although it proved to be no great success. The physicians and health educators, however, were lavish in their praise of Weston's role in promoting a general interest in walking and exercise.

Other pedestrians in the past had made claims for trans-continental walks, but most, if not all of them, were held in suspect. The *New York Times* reviewed the history of the trek across the country from the days of the prairie schooners to the recent record run of the Harriman special from San Francisco to New York in three days. The record for an automobile, made by a six-cylinder Franklin from Stockton, California, to New York was fifteen days, two hours, and ten minutes; while the record from New York to San Francisco, made by a Buick, was twenty-four days, eight hours, and forty-five minutes.

Weston celebrated his seventieth birthday on Monday, March 15, 1909, by starting from the front of the general post office in New York City on his trans-continental hike. A large crowd had gathered to see him off as he departed with his police escort and an honor guard of about thirty of his Civil War comrades from the Seventh Regiment. Weston was to be followed by an automobile driven by an attendant. In the automobile were his changes of clothing and other supplies which he might need along the way. He would pick up judges to cover the various stages of the journey en route. A number of reporters filled out the entourage. The Civil War comrades soon stopped and bid him goodbye and good luck, and he was on his way.

Encountering the usual friendly crowds, walking through rain, snow, and sleet, over muddy roads, Weston crossed New York State where he was beginning to become a familiar figure, for there were still people standing by the side of the road who had cheered the young Weston on his way to Chicago years before. Regular accounts under Weston's by-line appeared in the *Times*, accompanied by a time schedule and a map. These reports were supplemented by more lengthy articles written by the reporters. Weston must have relished the attention; he was finally winning the appreciation which he felt he deserved.

In Chicago, St. Louis, and every city and town through which he passed, he was given a reception. He tramped through heavy rains in the midwest, endured high winds in Wyoming, extreme heat in Nevada and California. He finally arrived in San Francisco on July 14, 1909, having successfully walked across the United States, but much to his disappointment, he had exceeded the time goal by five days. In an earlier generation, this would have been labeled a failure and would have been greeted with scorn, but now he was praised throughout the press and was the subject of a highly complimentary editorial in the newspaper that had once written, "If Mr. Weston would pledge himself to die in the course of his next match, there are thousands of people who would be ready to witness the performance, and to show their appreciation of his good taste . . ."

Weston said that his failure to complete his walk on time was the worst failure of his career and that he would be sufficiently rested in ninety days to walk back to New York City. He remained on the West Coast, however, until the following year. Then he walked across the country by a different route in seventy-six days, 23 hours, and 10 minutes, a record which is held in suspect, since Weston's return trip was not carefully supervised.

Weston's last great walk was performed in 1913 when he was 74 years old. He left New York City on June 2 on a 1,500 mile walk to Minneapolis, Minnesota, where he was to lay the cornerstone for the new building of the Minneapolis Athletic Club, on August 2. Upon his arrival in St. Paul, he was met by Governor Eberhart, who walked with him to the city limits, where he was greeted by the mayor of Minneapolis. He laid the cornerstone of the new building a few minutes after noon on August 2.

In 1927 Weston was found in a dazed and helpless condition walking about the streets of New York City. Anne Nichols, the author of *Abie's Irish Rose*, out of concern for the aged athlete, set up a trust fund which yielded $150 a month for the rest of his life. Shortly after this he was struck by a taxi cab and was forced to spend the rest of his life in a wheel chair. He died in New York City on May 13, 1929, at the age of ninety. According to the *New York Times*, ninety years was the goal which he had set for himself.

Although Edward Payson Weston may not have outlasted such competitors as Charles Rowell and Daniel O'Leary in competition, he did outlast them in years and was able without

Newspaper reporters in a Peerless automobile follow the ancient Weston on his way through Indiana en route to California.

challenge to establish a reputation as a great walker which persists to this day. In the 1920's and '30's there were still living sports fans and old-time athletes whose memories carried them back to the golden age of long distance walking and running. At the mention of Weston's name, these old-timers bristled with indignation and hurled the most uncomplimentary epithets at him. With the younger generation of reporters he enjoyed total immunity from the old charges and was able to bask in the limelight all by himself. He was not only a protégé of the *New York Times,* he was lauded by the *Nation, Harper's Weekly, Saturday Evening Post,* and a list of other publications.

In retrospect, Weston was not a great athlete. He was an industrious and persistent one. He was able to parlay an ability which probably exceeded mediocrity by a comfortable margin, but failed to achieve excellence by an equally generous margin, into fame and a modest living through his talent for winning headlines. His records were set at tasks that had not been tried before, but once set, they were soon exceeded by others. He lived to see his 100 miles in 24 hours relegated to a common performance, and had he lived to the age attributed to the Georgians, he would have seen a runner cover 160 miles in 24 hours in 1973. His great walks from city to city and across the country were promotional affairs which were never tested in competition with others.

Had he failed to maintain his vigor into old age he might have slipped off into the obscurity of those who humbled him in competition. However, he was a neat, well-groomed, picturesque old gentleman who captivated the press and made good news copy.

Six-Days Go-As-You-Please

When the English long distance runners presented a gold-headed riding whip to Edward Payson Weston before the start of the Astley Belt race in Madison Square Garden on Monday, September 22, 1879, they were acknowledging the contribution he had made to the sport of long distance walking. Although many would cast aspersions upon Weston's true athletic ability, few would deny that he was the principal popularizer of the sport of long distance pedestrianism. While Weston earned the credit for initiating the sport, Lord J. D. Astley shared the credit for increasing the popularity of the activity. His presentation of a handsome belt emblematic of the international championship added a competitive interest in the sport which would endure for twenty years.

Distance walking and running achieved a popularity during the 1870's and 1880's that would not be equaled again, unless the present interest in the sport continues to grow. Besides the six-day races, there were 24-hour races, 48-hour, and 72-hour races. There were 25-mile, 50-mile, and 100-mile races. Madison Square Garden enjoyed the distinction of staging the big international matches; but in nearly every city and town throughout the country, there were races, some for local pedestrians and some for the traveling pro's. The introduction of roller skating at this time provided rinks which could be used for these long distance spectacles, but few halls were considered too small for races. Some had 42 laps to the mile, or even as many as 50, as contrasted with the large eighth of a mile track at Madison Square Garden.

Not to be outdone by Lord Astley, Daniel O'Leary had a handsome silver championship belt made. This he offered as a prize for the winner of a six-day race and the long distance championship of America. The first contest for the O'Leary Belt was set for September of 1879 but had to be deferred until October because of the race for the Astley Belt.

Many felt that O'Leary's race, coming so close on the heels of the Astley competition, was doomed for failure; but the sponsors were pleasantly surprised when a capacity crowd showed up for the opening night. Thirty-five contestants started out on the long trek, and twenty-four of them dropped out before the sixth day. The leading star among the pedestrians entered was the Englishman "Blower" Brown. However, after covering 25 miles, Brown took to his resting quarters and remained there for five hours. He had developed stomach cramps which soon forced him to give up after covering but 32 miles. The other imports, Peter Crossland of England, and James McLeavy of Scotland did not fare much better. They left the race in the early stages. A tall, impressive-looking athlete from California who billed himself as "Cromwell, the Indian Scout," led the field around the first lap; but after 25 miles he took to his tent, never to return. A young lad of 18 years, one Nicholas Murphy, of Haverstraw, N.Y., was questioned about his entry. It was thought that he was really too young for such a gruelling contest against mature and seasoned professionals. After 31 miles and 3 laps, Murphy went into the lead, but yielded to Curran after 65 miles. Three miles later the youthful Murphy strode into the lead once more and held the lead through mile 110. At this point Walker moved ahead for a mile, then fell back as Murphy took over again. From this point on Murphy was never headed. At the end of 142 hours he had covered 505⅛ miles and had won the O'Leary Belt and $5,000.

In December, between Christmas and New Year's in a six-day race at Madison Square Garden, Frank Hart, a Negro athlete, won with 540⅛ miles. What astounded the fans in this race was the fact that eight contestants succeeded in covering 500 miles or more. Prior to this race the largest number to break 500 miles in a race was three. Up until this time 450 miles had been used as a breaking point for picking those who would share in the gate receipts. Henceforth, the limit would be placed at 500 miles.

During the year 1879 there had been six-day races from coast to coast. Frank Keogh had covered 410 miles to win one in Milwaukee, Peter J. Panchot won one in New York at 480⅛ miles; Guyon took the next one at 480¼; Cy Walker was the winner in Toronto in 434; R. Lacouse won in Boston with 427; Frank Edwards won in San Francisco in 371; and Peter McIntyre, the West Coast champion, covered 500 miles to win in San Francisco. The differences in the size and quality of the tracks would in some degree account for the variations in scores.

Women were also competing for long distance laurels. Early in the year Madame Anderson walked 2,700 quarter miles in 2,700 hours on a track set up in the Mozart Gardens in Brooklyn. Soon after, Madame Exilde La Chapelle covered 3,000 quarter miles in 3,000 hours in Chicago. In six-day races Bertha von Burg did 372 miles in New York City; Mae Belle Sherman covered 337 miles to win in San Francisco; and in another San Francisco race Madame Exilde La Chapelle was the winner in 306 miles. *The National Police Gazette* depicted

American Antiquarian Society

102

the ladies as glamorous, attractive, buxom beauties and described the affairs from the erotic viewpoint, rather than athletic.

The ladies closed the year with a grand six-day race at Madison Square Garden just before Christmas. Twenty-five starters took off at 12:01, December 20. At the end of the six days Amy Howard was the winner with a new record of 393⅛ miles. She was followed by Madame Tobias with 387¼. Fanny Edwards received a gold medal for neatness and best appearance.

There were many other long distance contests besides the six-day races. The 72-hour race enjoyed popularity. This was usually run for 12 hours each day, from 11:00 a.m. to 11:00 p.m. There were also many 48-hour races, as well as races at stipulated distances, frequently 50 or 100 miles. The celebrated professional sculler George Hosmer spent his winter months competing in walking races at distances from 10 to 50 miles.

The men, and women, too, were running for a living. How well did they do? For Charles Rowell, the winner of the Astley Belt race in September, it was a very profitable profession. He won $19,500 in this race and collected $6,000 in sweepstakes money. In addition he probably made a few more dollars in exhibitions and public appearances. The champion would be invited to appear in one of the local theatres or burlesque houses as an added attraction. Saloons would also pay such a champion for making an appearance.

In many of the races a large entrance fee was required, in this instance $500 per contestant. Since few professional athletes could come up with such an amount of money, they had to find backers, people with money who had confidence in the athlete's ability. Thus, any winnings had to be divided with the backer. John Hughes was more fortunate than most. He was backed by the *Police Gazette* and in return wore a jersey with the title of that publication emblazoned upon it.

The Astley Belt race was an exceptionally lucrative one. Nicholas Murphy received only $5,000 for winning the O'Leary Belt; but this, too, was a substantial amount of money for the time. In the race at Madison Square Garden in December, the purse was smaller. The gross receipts were $13,500, of which half was retained by the manager for expenses. The other half was to go to the contestants after the $200 entrance fee had been returned to those who had covered the required minimum number of miles. This left but $4,950 to be divided among the first seven winners, 50 percent, or $2,475, to Frank Hart; 20 percent to the second place winner; 10 percent to the third; 7½ percent to fourth; 5 percent to fifth; 4 percent to sixth; and 3½ percent to 7th.

The New York races were the most profitable contests. When the runners competed elsewhere, they had to content themselves with smaller purses. Daniel O'Leary, in collaboration with Fred Englehart, traveled about the country sponsoring distance races. In their 75-hour go-as-you-please contest in Boston, they awarded $250 to first place, $150 to second, $100 to third, and $50 to fourth. Since the seating capacity of the hall was limited to 600, it is not likely that the sponsors profited a great deal from the venture.

Two weeks later O'Leary and Englehart sponsored a 75-hour race in Providence, Rhode Island, under a mammoth tent in which several thousand could be seated. Forty-three runners and walkers entered, causing difficulty in scorekeeping. The prizes were the same as offered in Boston. A special award of $25 was given to G. R. Daniels, a sixteen-year old boy from Woonsocket, who stayed in the race to the end, covering 200 miles.

In shorter races purses of $50 and lower were offered. These races often attracted beginners and novices for whom such prizes would be attractive inducements. Some of the regular pro's like Frank Hart, Daniel Herty, Pete Hegelman, and George Noremac, would compete in a score or more contests in a year, covering as many as 5,000 miles in competition in races from 24-hours to six days. It must have been profitable at times for these men, for they remained at it for a dozen years, performing in cities and towns throughout the nation.

The women pedestrians did not fare as well as the men. In the grand sweepstakes at Madison Square Garden which was won by Amy Howard, she received $975 for first place. Madame Tobias earned $725 for her second place.

In their races outside of New York City where the halls were smaller and the attendance lighter, the prizes were considerably smaller.

Eighteen athletes went to the mark in the second contest for the O'Leary Belt at Madison Square Garden on April 5, 1880. The odds were on Frank Hart to win. His performance in December plus the fact that he was training under "Happy Jack" Smith made him a solid favorite. At the end of the first day Hart had covered 131 miles, a fast pace that made some doubt that he would last through the week. At the 145th mile Hart was overtaken by John Dobler, trained by Daniel O'Leary. From this point on until the 360th mile, the lead alternated between Dobler and Hart. At this point Hart took the lead which he held to the finish. Dobler fell back and was passed by William Pegram, another Negro from Boston, and Harry Howard, of Glen Cove, Long Island. Hart set a new record of 565 miles for six days.

His winnings for the race were considerably better than the purse which he won on the same track in December. This time he won $6,970.

Frank Hart, a resident of Boston for 17 years, was born Fred Hichborn in Haiti in 1857 of

Women had their own six-day races. In a contest at Madison Square Garden just before Christmas in 1879, Amy Howard was the winner with a new record of 387¼ miles. Fanny Edwards received a gold medal for neatness and best appearance.

mixed parentage. He was 5 feet 7 inches in height and weighed 145 pounds. He had started competition at long distance running a year earlier when he had won a 30-hour race in April 1879. A month later he finished second in his first six-day race in Boston.

In the six-day go-as-you-please races, the contestants could do just that. They could run or walk and stop to rest whenever they pleased. Each man had three score-keepers assigned to him to keep a record of the number of laps traveled. To convey an impression of integrity, the Madison Square Garden sponsors employed men from the various amateur clubs in the area. There were standard rules to be observed in respect to passing and other action on the track. The runners or walkers could reverse their direction when they wished; but they had to notify their score-keepers one lap in advance of their change. The score-keepers relayed the number of laps to men who stood on a platform before a huge blackboard. This way the spectators were kept informed of the progress of the contestants. One of the marvels announced at this race was that telephones were being used for the first time to relay the scores to the blackboards. The sponsors of the race had reverted to gas light. The new electric lights which had been installed were too bright for the contestants.

The runners could leave the track to rest whenever they pleased. Each contestant had a tent at one end of the building to which he

WOMEN ON THE SAWDUST TRACK.

END OF THE SIX DAYS' WALKING CONTEST BETWEEN PETTICOATED PEDESTRIANS AT BALTIMORE, MD., IN WHICH MISS KILBURY WON.

could retire to rest. In other races the tents had been set in the center of the track, but spectators complained that they obstructed their view. Now the contestants were complaining. The tents were too close together, preventing secrecy in planning and strategy. In this race Frank Hart had rested but 23 hours, 23 minutes, and 19 seconds. The remainder of the 142 hours he had spent in motion. Second place winner William Pegram had rested 32 hours, 18 minutes; Howard, 31 hours, 23 minutes; and Dobler 23 hours, 7 minutes.

A few months after this race William Pegram issued a challenge to Charley Rowell to race for

In the six-day race for women won by Amy Howard at Madison Square Garden, one of the contestants was removed from the race when it was discovered that the contestant was a man in woman's attire.

the Astley Belt. Rowell had won the belt twice and needed one more victory to gain permanent possession of it. When he heard of Pegram's challenge, Rowell sent a cablegram to the *New York Clipper* announcing that as soon as Pegram deposited his money with *The Sporting Life*, the official stake-holder, he would be ready to make arrangements for the race. The sporting journals not only served as clearing houses for challenges but also held stakes and served as arbitrators in disputes.

The defense of the Astley Belt was held on November 6, 1880, in the Agricultural Hall in London, with two Americans, William Pegram and John Dobler, contesting Charley Rowell's title. Rowell not only succeeded in defending the belt but set a new record of 566 miles. Had he been pressed, it was felt, he would have been able to have turned in an even larger total. His closest rival was an Englishman, George Littlewood, who trailed him by nearly 100 miles,

BOUND TO BE A WALKIST—JOHN DERMODY IS DRESSED UP IN FEMALE APPAREL AND ENTERED BY HIS BACKERS FOR THE FEMALE WALKING TOURNAMENT AT THE MADISON SQUARE GARDEN; NEW YORK, DEC. 14. SEE PAGE 11.

In a six-day race at Gilmore's Garden in New York City in March 1879, Charles Rowell of England easily defeated Daniel O'Leary to capture the Astley Belt and return it to its land of origin. Here he leads James Albert in a special match race.

finishing with 470 miles. John Dobler ended third with 450 miles. Just a few years earlier the sporting fans had been electrified with the announcement that Dan O'Leary had performed the incredible feat of running or walking 500 miles in six days. Now that mark had been exceeded by 66 miles.

Rowell's victory did not win for him permanent possession of the belt after all. It was found that the rules called for three consecutive victories; this win made it two in a row. Rowell would have to win the next one in order to retire the belt. He announced that he would accept the challenge issued to him by Daniel O'Leary in behalf of a runner whose identity was withheld. Until race time he would be referred to as "O'Leary's Unknown." This was not an uncommon practice in professional sports circles. It added an element of mystery and uncertainty to an event.

The record inched its way upward once more in January 1881, when John Hughes, the pride of the *Police Gazette*, ran and walked 568 miles, 825 yards, in six days in the competition for the O'Leary International Belt. Because Madison Square Garden was undergoing repairs, the race had to be held at the American Institute building, the only other available site large enough to accommodate an eighth of a mile track. This belt was the second offered by Daniel O'Leary and was distinguished from the American belt by its international designation. James Albert of Philadelphia finished second with 558 miles; and Robert Vint of Brooklyn took third with 550 miles. Of the thirty contestants who started, five completed more than 500 miles.

The next big six-days event was Frank Hart's defense of the O'Leary Belt for the American championship. This took place at Madison Square Garden starting on February 25, 1881. Hart, who had suffered sunstroke during the summer, had been out of competition for some time but was now fully recovered. The race was

John Hughes in winning the six-day race for the O'Leary Belt in January 1881 pushed the record upwards to 568 miles. Throughout most of his pedestrian career, Hughes ran with the backing of the Police Gazette.

different in that the record for six-days was not broken. During the first day's competition, two of the top favorites, Frank Hart and John Hughes, dropped out. The surprise was in the performance of one referred to as the "old-time letter carrier," Peter Panchot, of Hastings, Minnesota, formerly of Buffalo. Thirty-nine years old, five feet five, and weighing 128 pounds, Panchot went into the lead at the end of 16 hours and moved so fast that he set a new record for 24 hours, covering 135 miles in that time. He continued on at that pace, bettering the existing record for 48 hours by seven miles and for 72 hours by a mile and a quarter. After this he fell behind but went on to win with 541 miles. The large attendance at the start of the race dropped off with the removal of Hart and Hughes, so perhaps the incentive for going any faster was not there. Three of the runners exceeded 500 miles, Fred Krohne finishing second with 523 miles and Tom Curran third with 508 miles. Because of the sparse attendance, there was less than $1,000 to be distributed among the winners; but Panchot collected $1,900 in the sweepstakes made up from the entry fees.

The very next week the international contest for the Astley Belt between Charley Rowell and "O'Leary's Unknown" took place. The "Unknown" turned out to be James Albert, the Philadelphian who had finished second to Hughes in the race for the O'Leary International Belt in January. As an added attraction Daniel O'Leary, himself, engaged in a challenge race, six days heel and toe walking, with Harry Vaughn, the English champion walker.

The crowd began to gather at the entrances to the Madison Square Garden on Sunday afternoon. By evening the crowd had become immense. When the ticket offices opened at nine p.m., the lines extended up and down Madison and Fourth avenues and around into Twenty-six and Twenty-seventh Streets. There was quite an uproar when the people learned that the management had doubled the price of

Charles Rowell, the English runner and winner of the Astley Belt, was a popular athlete on both sides of the Atlantic. He became quite wealthy from his winnings in six-day races.

THE NATIONAL POLICE GAZETTE

THE GREAT WALKING MATCH

THE OLDEST ILLUSTRATED WEEKLY. ESTABLISHED 1846

Entered according to Act of Congress, in the Year 1879, by the Publisher of THE NATIONAL POLICE GAZETTE, in the Office of the Librarian of Congress at Washington.

Vol. XXXV.---No. 106.   NEW YORK, SATURDAY, OCTOBER 4, 1879.   Price Ten Cents.

THE GREAT WALK FOR THE ASTLEY BELT, AT MADISON SQUARE GARDEN, NEW YORK CITY. EXCITING SCENE OF THE START OF THE THIRTEEN ASPIRANTS TO PEDESTRIAN HONORS AND EMOLUMENTS, AT ONE O'CLOCK ON MONDAY MORNING, SEPTEMBER 22.—[SKETCHED BY GAZETTE ARTISTS. SEE PAGE 6.

admission from the fifty cents which they expected to pay. There was a loud chorus of jeers and hisses, but most of the people paid and the hall was filled to capacity at starting time.

In the race between Rowell and Albert the pace was fast, at least on Rowell's part. At the end of 24 hours he had covered 144 miles for a new record. Albert trailed far behind with 102 miles. He complained of an injury to his foot suffered when he stepped on a stone during the early hours of the race. At the end of the 25th hour, Albert withdrew from the race, despite efforts on O'Leary's part to persuade him to continue. Rowell went on through the 72-hour mark before retiring from the race. The moment Albert left the race Rowell was the winner, so there was not much point in continuing.

O'Leary in the meantime had lost many miles in leaving the track to talk with Albert and also from stomach sickness. Vaughn walked on at a fast clip, eclipsing all previous walking records up to 48 hours. He finished the six days with 461 miles to O'Leary's 450.

In spite of the disappointment over Albert's withdrawal, the attendance was fairly good throughout the week. When Albert dropped out, the management lowered the price of admission to fifty cents. Nevertheless, after expenses were met there were $14,000 left for division among the participants.

The O'Leary International Belt, competed for again in May 1881, was a greater success than earlier six-day races during the year had been. Although only fourteen men started, the smallest in a major race since 1878, eleven of the contestants were still in the race at the close of the fifth day. The entries included George Littlewood and George Hazael, two of the leading long-distance stars, as well as the defender John Hughes and Robert Vint, who had finished third behind Hughes in January.

Vint, born in Ireland in 1846, was a bootmaker and a resident of Brooklyn, who took up professional running three years earlier in an effort to improve living conditions for his family. The smallest man in the field, only 5 feet 2 inches in height and 127 pounds in weight, Vint won the attention of the crowd. He went on to win in a new record of 578 miles 610

yards. Eight of the men covered 500 miles or more. John Sullivan finished second with 569 miles, and John Hughes was third with 552 miles.

One more major race in 1881 was held when John Ennis, a competitor in the first Astley Belt races, decided to become a promoter. He made arrangements to engage Madison Square Garden for the week of October 24-29 and announced that he would award firm prizes of $1,500 for first place, $800 for second, $400 for third, $200 for fourth, and $100 for fifth. Charley Rowell and his manager were in New York City for a visit and Ennis hoped to lure him into the race. Rowell, interested in making big money, advertised for a match of his own, offering to race any man for $1,000 a side. He declined to participate in Ennis's race. Further problems beset Ennis as Madison Square Garden declined to rent its building because the owners were planning to sell the property. Ennis then made arrangements to rent the American Institute Building.

The race finally started with fifteen men, including such headliners as Frank Hart, Fred Krohne, Harry Howard, and Patrick Fitzgerald, all of whom had exceeded 500 miles in previous contests. In addition, there were some contestants who had won 72-hour races, among whom were George Noremac, whose name was really Cameron, and Daniel Herty. Midway through the second day of the race Patrick Fitzgerald moved into the lead and held it to the end. As the miles piled up, it became apparent that Fitzgerald was moving at a record-breaking pace. At the end of the six days Fitzgerald had covered 582 miles 55 yards. George Noremac finished far behind in second place with 565 miles.

Financially the race was a disaster. Although Ennis had promised set prizes, he failed to take in enough from gate receipts to pay the runners. Fitzgerald for all his labors received only $500.

Among six-day runners, Patrick Fitzgerald stood out. Born in 1846 in Ireland, as most of the athletes were, he came as a child with his parents first to Canada. Here at the very early age of 12 he won his first race. While still a teen-ager, he established a reputation for his speed at the mile and two-mile distances, numbering among his victories a win over the famous Indian Daillebout. In 1865 he came to New York City, where he became the leading ten-mile runner. His first effort at the six-day race was in October 1879 in Madison Square Garden. He retired from this race with a swollen knee after 85 miles. In December 1879, he tried again, finishing fifth behind Frank Hart with 520 miles. In his next try he gave out after 113 miles but came back a couple of months later with a creditable 546 miles behind Robert Vint, in fourth place. His ascendancy to the record was no fluke.

Before the Ennis tournament there was talk of a grand international sweepstakes in which each contestant would be required to put up stakes of $1,000. Gradually the talk settled down to specific announcements. Such a race was to be held at Madison Square Garden starting on February 27. Already in December it was

known that Charley Rowell would be among the contestants. With stakes as high as $1,000 it was certain that only the best would be among the entries. The conditions of the race stipulated that the winner would take all of the stake money. If there were more than five in the race, the second place finisher would receive $1,000 from the stakes. The gate receipts after expenses were to be divided among the contestants who covered 525 miles or more.

Raising the money for the stakes was a problem for some. Frank Hart had to scurry about for a backer and he arrived too late with his entry fee, but those who had already put up their stakes voted to permit Hart to enter. John Hughes had no problem, since he was backed by the *Police Gazette*. James Albert, the Philadelphian, had sold a house in Atlantic City to raise his stake but he came down with "inflammation of the bowels" and could not participate.

The winner of the race would also receive an unusual trophy shaped in the form of a riding whip, emblematic of the six-day race. It was described in this manner: "The handle is richly

GEORGE D. NOREMAC.

George Noremac, a Scotsman by birth whose professional name was his real name, Cameron, spelled backwards, was one of the regulars who stayed with the sport to the end.

FRANK HART.

A native of Haiti, Frank Hart came to Boston with his parents as a child. There he established a reputation as a top runner before entering the six-day races. He held the record briefly in 1880.

mounted in gold and studded with precious stones, while a diminutive figure of E. P. Weston, 'the father of long-distance pedestrianism,' and for whose benefit this particular style of traveling was inaugurated by Sir John Astley, carrying a whip in his hand, adorns it, and surmounting the whole is a pedestrian cap, formed of valuable gems, combining the national colors. It is at once a novel and costly trophy . . ."

The final entries for the tournament were Charles Rowell, Patrick Fitzgerald, Robert Vint, John Hughes, John Sullivan, George Noremac, Peter Panchot, George Hazael, William Scott, and Frank Hart. Of these entries, Scott was relatively unknown. His reputation had been made on the West Coast, where he had been a winner in six-day races in California. Rowell stood out as the clear favorite among the bookmakers. Betting was heavy on the other places in the race, however. "This may indeed be termed a race between champions, as well as truly international in character, and the winner of a fair contest will assuredly be entitled to style himself the champion of the world," commented one sports writer.

The advance publicity, combined with the presence of the popular Charley Rowell, assured the sponsors of a large gate. A Mr. Kearns was confident enough of the prospects of a good gate to pay $6,000 for the bar and lunch privileges. Gilmore's celebrated band had been engaged, and everything was ready for a grand affair. The admission price had been set at one dollar.

As soon as the doors were open, the crowd began to assemble. At 11:30 Sunday evening the doors were closed and hundreds of disappointed fans were left standing in the streets. The hall was filled. People were standing in the stairways, around the track, and within the track. The bookmakers circulated among the spectators taking bets. Rowell was still the heavy favorite. Fitzgerald's odds were 4 to 1; Noremac, 6 to 1; Hart and Panchot, 7 to 1; Hazael and Sullivan, 8 to 1; Hughes, 12 to 1; Scott, 20 to 1; and Vint, 25 to 1. Robert Vint had fallen in the odds when it became known that just before the race he had presented two letters from doctors attesting that he was suffering from rheumatism in the left hip joint. To

PATRICK FITZGERALD.

Among six-day runners Patrick Fitzgerald stood out. Born in 1846 in Ireland, he emigrated first to Canada, where he won his first race at the age of 12. He came to New York City as a ten-mile runner in 1865.

ROBERT VINT.

Born in Ireland in 1846, Robert Vint became a bootmaker in Brooklyn. He took up professional running in order to improve living conditions for his family. In May 1881 he upped the six-day record to 578 miles.

compete would be dangerous to his health, the doctors said. Vint presented the letters from his doctors and requested that his stake be returned to him. The other entries expressed their sympathy for Vint's predicament but declined to return his money. Vint then decided that he would run and do his best to win back his money.

At five minutes after midnight the referee gave the signal which sent the runners on their long trek. John Hughes led off at a fast pace followed closely by Charley Rowell. After two hours, Rowell moved into the lead, running in his mechanical gate, at about seven and a half miles per hour. At this point Robert Vint, suffering great pain, was forced to withdraw. On and on Rowell strode without varying his pace. At nine o'clock in the morning Rowell had built up a lead of seven miles. By ten o'clock George Hazael had moved past Hughes into second place. The crowd shouted encouragement throughout the night, and most of them remained there until after daylight, when they began to leave. By nine o'clock there were only a few hundred of the faithful left.

Rowell plodded on and on, never faltering nor slackening his pace. At 1:26 p.m. he had completed the first 100 miles in the unprecedented time of 13 hours 21 minutes. At the announcement of this achievement the crowd cheered enthusiastically. Rowell took one more spin around the track before retiring for food and rest. He was at this time 11 miles ahead of the field. Hazael running in second place was 8 miles in front of Hughes.

Just before two o'clock Rowell returned from his shelter and resumed his trot at the same pace which he held throughout the afternoon. Several of the runners were suffering from stomach ailments, but this was not considered serious since such derangements afflicted most pedestrians during the first 24 or 48 hours of a race. The score at six o'clock — eighteen hours into the race — was: Rowell, 125 miles 7 laps; Hazael, 113 miles; Hughes, 104; Sullivan, 100; Hart, 94 miles 6 laps; Fitzgerald, 94 miles 6 laps; Noremac, 88; Panchot, 85; and Scott, 77 miles.

By nine o'clock in the evening about 5,000 spectators had gathered, not as many as on the

DANIEL J. HERTY.

Daniel Herty was one of the old troupers who followed the sawdust trail to the end, competing and winning purses in races from Madison Square to California.

PETER J. PANCHOT,

Peter Panchot, a 39-year-old letter carrier from Hastings, Minnesota, upset the odds-makers by taking a surprise victory in the six-day race for the O'Leary Belt at Madison Square Garden in February 1881.

previous night, but a good crowd for a Monday evening. At 28 minutes after 10, Rowell had covered 150 miles, which when announced, was a signal for a tumult of applause and a shower of floral tributes for the great pedestrian, who after one more lap retired to rest. He was leading Hazael, who had left the track to rest, by fifteen miles. Hughes remained on the track until he had completed 140 miles which moved him into a lead of five miles over Hazael. Rowell returned to the track after a three hour rest. Hazael also returned and began to regain the miles lost to Hughes. After an hour Hughes returned from his rest, and the close contest between him and Hazael resumed.

Throughout the second day Rowell held his lead but Hazael and Hughes kept on running at a fast pace, thus preventing Rowell from taking his rests. On through the third day he trotted, maintaining his lead and eclipsing all previous marks for the distance covered. At 6:00 a.m. of the fourth day, Rowell had traveled 374 miles; Hazael, 356 miles 7 laps; Hughes, 352 miles; Fitzgerald, 336 miles; Sullivan, 330 miles; Hart, 325 miles; Noremac, 308 miles. At 8:20 a.m. Rowell left the track to rest. This surprised the people in the building; but it surprised them even more when he remained in his house a full two hours. This was very unusual for this time of day. When he came back to the track, he was only 5 miles ahead of Hazael, who had been running strongly during Rowell's absence. Rowell "looked hagard and drowsy, there were dark circles about his eyes, his face was pinched-looking, and his movements lacked the dash so characteristic of Rowell at his best. There was a wan expression on his countenance, and a dullness about the eyes which boded his backers no good," wrote a reporter.

To the surprise of the spectators Rowell again left the track to rest shortly after noon, despite the fact that Hazael had been gaining rapidly on him. During this rest period Hazael not only overtook Rowell in the scoring but began to build up a lead over his countryman. Rumors

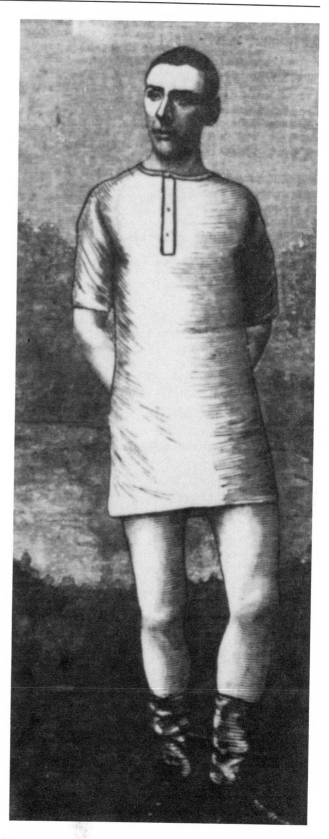

George Haezel, English runner, became the first man to exceed 600 miles in a six-day race at Madison Square Garden in February 1882.

began to circulate that all sorts of things were wrong with Rowell. One story was that he had drunk a cup of strong vinegar, thinking it was beef tea, and as a result was suffering from nausea and diarrhea. The physician in attendance denied this and stated that all he needed was sleep and rest. Not a few believed the rumor that he had fallen back deliberately in order to influence the betting and that he was well enough to recover the lost ground and win handily. By the time that he returned to the track at ten minutes to four, news that he was in trouble had circulated throughout the city, and as a result the crowd began to assemble early in the afternoon.

After adding a little more than 6 miles to his total, Rowell again retired to his resting quarters at 5:57. At 6:20 Fitzgerald who had passed the tiring Hughes, moved into second place behind Hazael. By early evening the crowd in the garden had built up to over nine thousand, so great was the excitement in the city. Although Hazael was well ahead of Fitzgerald, many of the fans believed that he, too, would falter. He had only succeeded in surpassing 500 miles on one occasion. It was believed that Fitzgerald, Sullivan, or Hart was capable of overtaking him yet. Not all had given up on Rowell, however, for when he appeared on the track again at nine o'clock, he was greeted with a warm and enthusiastic reception.

Rowell added 4 miles to his score during the next hour and did about the same for the following hour, then he returned to his rest house. Back again at midnight, he ran until 1:08, when he went off to rest. By this time he had been passed by Hart, Sullivan, and Noremac, and was running sixth. Hazael and Fitzgerald kept piling up the lead, running nearly all the time; the former now had 46 miles lead over Rowell and was 22 miles ahead of Fitzgerald. Rowell was back on the track at 3:30 and kept on walking until 5:11 a.m. This time when he went into his rest house, he did not come out in two hours, or even three. Anxious eyes watched the door of his hut, expecting him to come out for another try. There was no hope of his winning now, but some expected that he might still try to win a share of the gate. His absence from the track had stretched to five hours. At 10:00 a.m.

the door of the hut opened and the former world's champion emerged attired in his street clothes.

The outcome of the race on the fifth day was still uncertain. Although Hazael enjoyed a comfortable lead over Fitzgerald and the other contestants, his reputation for fading toward the finish made Fitzgerald's chances of victory look good. Also looking stronger and improving with each mile was the little Scotsman Noremac. At the end of the fifth day Hazael had piled up a day's total of 106 miles; Fitzgerald, 100; Noremac, 104; Hart, 78; Hughes, 89; and Sullivan, 53. At 2:52 a.m. of the sixth day Fitzgerald had completed 525 miles and was going strong; but he was still 22 miles behind the leader, who passed the 550 mile mark at 3:24 a.m. No one doubted at this point that the old record would fall before the day was over. By daylight it was also concluded by most that the order of finish was established and that Hazael would emerge the winner. The excitement of the contest was over, as the men took more frequent rest periods and contented themselves only in holding their places.

Aided substantially by the fast pace set in the early stages of the race, Hazael in winning set a new record and became the first man to exceed 600 miles, having gone one lap, an eighth of a mile, beyond that mark. Fitzgerald in second place finished with 577⅛ miles, and George Noremac took third with 555 miles. Hart, Hughes, and Sullivan followed in order, all finishing above the 525 mile mark. Rowell, Panchot, Scott, and Vint failed to finish.

For the successful contestants the race was a profitable affair. In addition to his $9,000 sweepstakes money, Hazael's share of the gate receipts was $9,380.81. Fitzgerald's share, with his $1,000 sweepstakes money, amounted to $4,742.39. The other finishers received smaller amounts. The contestants had anticipated a larger purse from the gate receipts than those received; but the sponsors submitted a list of expenses which exceeded by far the amount left for division among the contestants. Some of the officials made more than the contestants.

In October 1882, there was a replay of the same contest with different results. At Madison Square Garden, Rowell, Hazael, Fitzgerald, Noremac, Hughes, Hart, Vint, Herty, and Panchot met in what was billed as the Champion's Race. From the start, attendance was light and interest failed to develop. On Thursday both Hazael and Rowell were forced to withdraw from the contest, causing a further decline in interest. Fitzgerald took the race with 577¼ miles. He was followed by Noremac with 566½ miles; Daniel Herty, 544; and Hughes, 525. The other two finishers, Hart and Vint, failed to make 500 miles.

The failure of this race to attract spectators discouraged the prospects of any further races for the foreseeable future. "What will in all probability be the final important six-day race that will ever be gotten up in this vicinity closed at Madison Square Garden on Saturday evening, Oct. 28," commented the *New York Clipper* in a premature prophecy. The sport was not completely dead, however. There were no big races in 1883; but in April, 1884, the principal contenders, with the exception of George Hazael, were back in Madison Square Garden again for another tournament.

The pace at the start of this race was not so torrid as that set by Rowell in the record-breaking race of 1882. The lead alternated between several contestants until after the 19th hour, when Rowell moved into the lead. He continued to head the pack through the second and third days but could not build up much of a lead over Patrick Fitzgerald. Neither runner rested much during the first few days. On the first day Rowell rested 2 hours 41 minutes; Fitzgerald, 3 hours 22 minutes; second day — Rowell, 4 hours 57 minutes; Fitzgerald, 4 hours 16 minutes; third day — Rowell, 3 hours 3 minutes; Fitzgerald, 4 hours 5 minutes.

On Thursday Fitzgerald rested only 2 hours 36 minutes to Rowell's 5 hours 19 minutes. After the 78th hour Fitzgerald overtook Rowell and soon passed him. He began to build up a lead over his English opponent but the former world's champion was not done yet. He con-

A native of Scotland, William Steele came to America for a series of distance races in 1882. He returned home, but a year later he was back in the United States as an immigrant and "Champion of America."

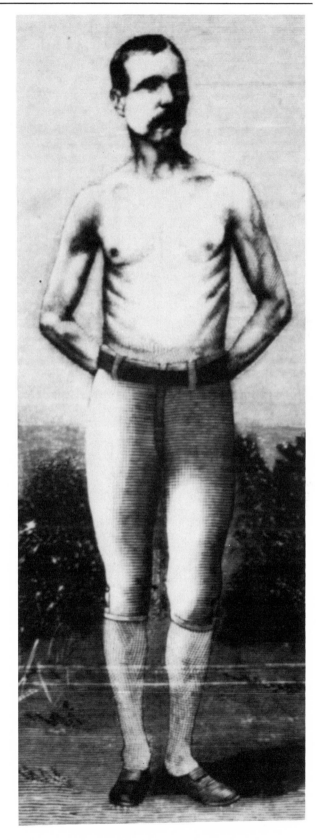

117

tinued to dog his opponent until the last evening when but five miles separated them. Finally, as the race drew toward the end, it became apparent that the race was to be Fitzgerald's. He and Rowell walked around the track together amid loud applause which grew deafening when the two men ran a lap with Fitzgerald carrying the Stars and Stripes and Rowell the Irish banner. Fitzgerald was credited with 610 miles, a new record, and Rowell with 602 miles. In third place far behind was Panchot with 566 miles and Noremac fourth with 545 miles.

Fitzgerald collected $9,456.15 from gate receipts and $9,000 from the sweepstakes, faring far better than in his last victory. He was honored in a formal reception by the people of Long Island City, where he lived, and soon would be alderman.

In spite of the success of this race the interest in the sport seemed to be on the wane. No major contest was held in New York City until four years later. A six-day roller skating race in March 1855 in which the winner piled up a total of 1,091 miles failed to generate much interest. Frank Hart tried his hands, or rather his legs, at it and gave up on the second day. In England in 1885 a 72-hour race won by George Littlewood attracted a record number of spectators and prompted the winner to issue a challenge to Patrick Fitzgerald. However, Littlewood wanted the race to be held in London; and Fitzgerald was reluctant to meet him there, feeling that a race in New York City would be more profitable.

The next few years were lean years for the long distance pedestrians. The sport seemed all but dead in New York City and was struggling for survival in the rest of the country. The old troopers, Frank Hart, George Noremac, Robert Vint, and Peter Hegelman, took the show on the road, performing in 72-hour races and six-day races wherever they could generate enough in-

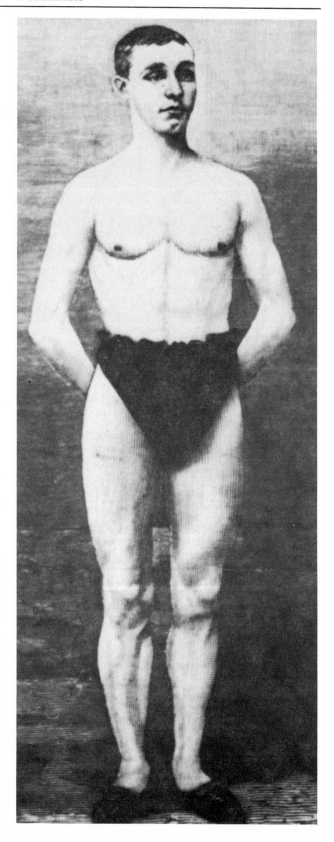

William Cummings, Scottish professional who was credited with running records at distances from one to fifteen miles, visited America in the 1880's for a series of races.

terest for one. In Paterson, New Jersey, in September 1885, Noremac, Hart, and Hegelman trailed Wright in a 72-hour race. In December of the same year in the Apollo Hall at Paterson in a 72-hour race, Noremac and his traveling companions dropped out of a race in mid-week because the attendance was so poor. The management failed to take in enough to pay the runners for their efforts.

In December at Easton, Pennsylvania, Peter Golden led Frank Hart to the finish in a 72-hour race with 243 miles. The prizes were not awarded because no contestant had covered 300 miles within the time limit. The newspapers used quotation marks around the word contest in referring to this race.

The second grand six-day race for the O'Leary Belt at Madison Square Garden in April 1880, won by Frank Hart with a record of 565 miles.

The long distance pedestrians picked up three notable recruits during these lean years. Peter Golden, an amateur star, had turned pro and was beginning to show up among the winners. Gus Guerrero, who had become a reigning professional in California, joined the troup in 1884. He had come to the East in a most unusual fashion. Having accepted a challenge from L. P. Federmeyer to push a wheel barrow from San Francisco in 1883, Guerrero won, claiming to have performed the journey in five months and twenty-five days. The third recruit of note was Anton Strokel, an Austrian immigrant lad, who had worked on the docks at Saginaw and Bay City, Michigan, loading lumber on ships and barges. When the ship left Bay City to go up the river to Saginaw, Strokel, instead of accompanying the other dock wollopers on the deck, chose to walk, a distance of about fifteen miles. He would be seated upon a pile of lumber waiting when the boat arrived.

THE SECOND GRAND PEDESTRIAN MATCH FOR THE CHAMPIONSHIP OF AMERICA AND THE O'LEARY BELT; SIX DAYS GO-AS-YOU-PLEASE—BEGAN AT MADISON SQUARE GARDEN SUNDAY NIGHT, APRIL 4, ENDING SATURDAY NIGHT, APRIL 10—SCENE DURING THE RACE. [SKETCHED BY GAZETTE SPECIAL ARTISTS.—SEE PAGE 7.

Strokel first participated in a 72-hour go-as-you-please race in his hometown of Saginaw in April 1885. Competing for a prize of $100 and the State Championship medal, Strokel won with ease, covering 309 miles, 42 miles ahead of the second place finisher. Encouraged by his easy victory, Strokel found local backers to finance his trip to Denver for a 72-hour race. He won this by a comfortable margin over a field which included George Noremac.

A year later he won a 72-hour race in Philadelphia, leading Peter Hegelman, Robert Vint, and John Hughes, with 386 miles. In May 1887, he won a full six-day race at Philadelphia, beating Albert, Noremac, and Hart, in that order.

The long distance performers during these years appeared in many places considered remote, lumbering towns and mining communities. They traveled to Carson City, Nevada; Manistee, Michigan; Oshkosh, Wisconsin; Kansas City, St. Louis, Cincinnati, Easton, Pennsylvania; New Bedford, Massachusetts; Denver and Leadville, Colorado; Detroit, and a host of other towns. Attendance was not always good; and more than once the tired "peds" found an empty purse at the end. When they could not find a 72-hour or six-day race, they promoted a shorter race of twenty-five or fifty miles. They competed in opera houses, skating rinks, halls, and armories, on small tracks and large.

The six-day spectacle might have withered away and disappeared if a confident promoter in February 1888 had not decided to stage another such affair at Madison Square Garden. Perhaps because there had been no race of importance for a long time, the crowd that turned out on the first night was fully as large as in the earlier races. Although the tournament failed to attract such "shining lights" as Fitzgerald, Rowell, Hazael, or Littlewood, it did have among the entries the wandering "peds," George Noremac, Dan Herty, Frank Hart, Peter Hegelman, Peter Panchot, and John Sullivan, as well as the three new recruits, Gus Guerrero, Peter Golden, and Anton Strokel. Only the presence of George Cartwright of England gave the contest an international aspect, but he dropped out soon after the start. So many contestants started in the race that a rule was adopted which stipulated that any runner failing to make 100 miles during the first 24 hours would be eliminated from the contest.

James Albert, the Philadelphian, won the race with a new record of 621 miles and 1,350 yards, nearly forty miles over his closest rival, Dan Herty of Boston. Gus Guerrero, the Californian, finished third. Eight men covered 525 miles or more, Hart, Moore, Strokel, and Noremac following in that order.

James Albert in winning announced that he was retiring from competition. He had won more than $9,000 in the tournament and had supplemented that figure with $500 for appearing in Dockstader's Minstrels in a burlesque skit on walking. In his acceptance speech at Madison Square Garden, Albert stated, "I am thirty-six years old and will retire on my laurels. It is my last race. I thank you for the demonstration, and will say goodnight."

He returned a hero to Philadelphia and Atlantic City, where he also had a home. In Atlantic City he was the recipient of a public reception followed by a banquet and fireworks in the evening. At Philadelphia the citizens presented him with a gold medal.

George Littlewood, the English champion who had defeated James Albert in a 72-hour race in Philadelphia in 1887, returned to New York City to compete in a six-day race at the Garden in May 1888. Littlewood won but failed to improve upon Albert's record, although he did cover 611 miles, 570 yards, thus exceeding Fitzgerald's mark. In this race Gus Guerrero finished second followed by Dan Herty, George Noremac, Peter Golden, and John Hughes.

In the fall of 1888 an unusual six-day race was held at Madison Square Garden. The inventor and manufacturer of the "road-sculler," a tricycle which was moved forward by rowing, offered attractive purses to the scullers. Most of the leading professional oarsmen were entered. They were to row for ten hours a day for six days. Jacob Gaudaur, the Canadian pro, who rowed out of St. Louis, Missouri, won the grand prize of $1,500. In spite of the array of stars entered in the race, the affair was a failure. Blistered hands forced some of the contestants to retire early in the race, and as a result the attendance fell off. The race does not seem to have succeeded in promoting the pop-

AFOOT FOR SIX DAYS.

EPISODES OF THE PEDESTRIAN CONTEST AT MADISON SQUARE GARDEN. NO. I—A RACE ON THE ROOF. NO. II COLORED SISTERS CHEERING BURRELL. NO. III—RUBBING CHARMS ON THE INDIAN. NO. IV—NOREMAC IN TENDER HANDS. NO. V—GIVING ROWELL A BATH. NO. VI—WAKING UP A WALKER. NO. VII—PETER DURYEA, THE MANAGER.

[From Sketches by "Police Gazette" Special Artists.]

ularity of the "road-sculler," at least, there is no record of highway congestion caused by them.

Promoter William O'Brien sailed to England in the fall of 1888 to attempt to persuade a bevy of English stars to come over for a grand international six-day race. He returned late in October with the news that he had obtained promises of attendance from George Littlewood, George Hazael, Archibald Sinclair, and George Mason. In addition, the old, well-tested regulars, Dan Herty, John Hughes, Frank Hart, George Noremac, Peter Golden, Gus Guerrero, and George Cartwright, had signified their intentions of competing. It had been hoped to secure the entry of James Albert, but he declined, saying that he was not interested in engaging in another big race unless his record should be beaten.

In spite of the fact that a storm raged outside, a large crowd filled Madison Square Garden on November 26, 1888, when the six-day runners responded to the starter's signal. The Marquis of Queensbury was among the spectators and pugilists Jake Kilrain and Charley Mitchell were serving as judges.

George Littlewood, the odds-on favorite to take first prize, moved into the lead soon after the exhibitionists had used up their strength in spurts around the track in their brief moments of glory at the head of the pack. For twenty hours Littlewood led, piling up a total of 119 miles in that time. The pace was not as fast as it might have been. Something was obviously wrong with Littlewood. He began to take rests frequently. He was passed by Moore and fell back into third position, as he was passed by Cartwright. Throughout the second day he stuck to the sawdust most of the time, but he walked along at a slow pace. During this period he fell back into eighth place and 25 miles behind the leader. It was reported that he was suffering from an upset stomach.

Gradually his condition improved and he began to run. After 33 hours he was back in sixth place; then moved up into fifth position, only to fall back again in 12 hours. After 53 hours, he moved back into 5th spot again, then in 3

hours pulled into 4th place, still far behind the leader. He remained in this position briefly, moving up to 3rd, which place he held until after 76 hours he moved into second place, six miles behind the leader, Dan Herty. After 100 hours, George Littlewood was once again back in the lead in the race and going strong. Dan Herty was also strong, so Littlewood had to put the pressure on to maintain his lead. Gradually on Friday he began to pull away from Herty and at one time led him by 20 miles. He went on to win in a new record of 623 miles, 1320 yards. Herty followed with 605 miles, thus joining Hazael, Fitzgerald, Rowell, Littlewood, and Albert in the select circle of those who had exceeded 600 miles in six days. Covering more than 525 miles and following in order were Moore, Cartwright, Noremac, Hart, Howarth, Conner, and Golden.

James Albert, present among the spectators, came onto the track when Littlewood had exceeded his mark, to congratulate the plucky Englishman. He ran the last lap with Littlewood, one holding aloft the Stars and Stripes and one a new broom, symbolic of a new rec-

An unusual six-day contest was the race on bicycles fitted for rowing. Jacob Gaudaur, the champion sculler, won first prize.

THE PRIZE OF VICTORY.

THE GREAT RECEPTION TENDERED TO THE VICTOR OF THE SIX-DAY WALKING MATCH BY THE CITIZENS OF LONG ISLAND CITY.

I—The Procession From the Ferry. II—Rowell Drinks with Fitzgerald. III—Saluting the Victor. IV—Patrick Fitzgerald. V—Happy Jack Smith, Fitzgerald's Trainer.

ord. The spectators cheered enthusiastically. When Littlewood ended his long journey, many individuals and organizations presented him handsome floral tributes.

Littlewood in setting the record of 623¾ miles established a record which would long survive him; and it still exists as the "best on record." This was the last of the major six day races, although yet another was held in the Garden in May of 1889.

Billed as the final six-day tourney, the race attracted none of the head-liners. James Albert had gone to San Francisco for a race; and Littlewood was back in England. Only the faithful old veteran "wobblers," Dan Herty, George Noremac, Peter Hegelman, George Cartwright, and Peter Golden, responded along with a number of lesser lights. Dan Herty in covering 560 miles won and collected a purse of only $789. James Albert won his six-day race in San Francisco, beating Gus Guerrero in an unimpressive affair.

Following the final "six-day race," the old "wobblers" took to the road again. Pittsburgh, Bangor, Waterbury, San Francisco, Detroit, Saginaw, and other cities and towns found the tired old peds walking circles for purses that grew smaller and smaller. In February 1889, Frank Hart won a six-day race in San Francisco with 525 miles. His companions in the contest were Moore, Howarth, Guerrero, Campana, and Vint.

For some strange reason the ladies were still enjoying some measure of popularity on the circuit. Bertie Lawrence led Mae Howard and Nora Evans in a 60-hour race in Pittsburgh. In a full six-day race at Baltimore in May, Madame Tobias won with 311 miles, followed closely by Bella Kilbury with 308. In the same month Nora Evans won a six-day race at Washington, beating Madame Tobias and Bella Kilbury. The people of Washington must have liked the lady "peds," for they were back there a month later with Madame Tobias winning this one with 346 miles.

No longer a craze, the six-day contests persisted into the '90's with George Noremac and Frank Hart still hanging on. Hart billed himself as "the winner of more six-day races than any man in the world." The troup moved into Saginaw, Michigan, in January 1890 for a 75-hour race at the local roller skating rink. They had just finished a race in Detroit and were planning to return to that city for another race soon after this one. Attendance was light throughout most of the race. Since the admission price was only twenty-five cents, there was little to divide among the contestants at the end of the race. George Noremac won with 275 miles, 5 miles ahead of Frank Hart.

Before this race, efforts had been made to persuade Anton Strokel, the Saginaw pedestrian, to enter the race but he declined, saying that he was not in condition. Later he confided to a reporter that he had left the sawdust arena because of his honesty. He said that he had refused to enter into any scheme to defraud the public. Strokel, after his last victory in the race in Philadelphia, had returned to Saginaw with not only the purse but also a wife. He had purchased a grocery store and had settled down.

It is difficult to understand what fascination the spectators found in the spectacle of the six-day contest. There were runners moving around the track in various stages of exhaustion. The only thing that would indicate that it was a contest was the scoreboard. The records set by these contestants seem incredible and are likely to remain uncontested forever.

Professional running in the 1880's was by no means limited to the long distance contests. In the New England States heel-and-toe walking contests enjoyed popularity over a long period of years. George Hosmer, the professional sculler, during the winter months was a good gate attraction in walking races, particularly in Massachusetts, where he made his home. Ed Holske and T. Harry Armstrong, both of whom had competed as amateurs for the Harlem A.C., developed quite a rivalry as professional walkers. Holske also competed frequently against Dennis Driscoll of Boston.

Most professional contests were on a local level and were not very lucrative affairs. In a twenty mile race held at Mechanics Hall in Worcester, Massachusetts, the sponsor had only twenty-five dollars left to divide among the contestants and had to be protected by the police. Sometimes the athletes performed with variety shows or vaudeville acts at opera houses and theatres.

From the amateur ranks came a number of professional runners. H. M. Johnson had been a sprinter for the Williamsburg A.C. when he decided to turn pro. He entered the Fourth of July handicap races at Echo Park in Philadelphia in 1883. Since he was entering the race as an amateur, he was given a head start, which he did not really need, since he went on to win

~~~~~~~~~~~~~~~~~~~~~~~~~~~

While still in his teens in the 1880's Steve Farrell won the amateur championship of Connecticut in the quarter and half-mile distances. He was soon enlisted as a member of a professional team to compete in "hose-racing," a lucrative aspect of athletic competition. Much of the fire-fighting equipment of that day was hand-drawn, thus the competition had a practical consideration. The team pulled a two-wheeled hose cart a specified distance, unwound the hose, coupled it to a hydrant, and attached the nozzle. The team of Steve Farrell, "Pooch" Donovan, "Piper" Donavan, Keene Fitzpatrick, and Mike Murphy was virtually unbeatable. Farrell and his team-mates, following their retirement from competition, became club and college coaches, serving well into the twentieth century.

~~~~~~~~~~~~~~~~~~~~~~~~~~~

by a larger margin than had been allowed him. Immediately, suspicions were voiced that he was a "ringer." Some thought that he was from England, others said Chicago, and somebody was certain that he was a pro from the West Coast. Since there was a good deal of money riding on the outcome of the race, the sponsor withheld the purse until certain identity of Johnson could be made. Johnson swore before

In the last of the major six-day races at Madison Square Garden, Englishman George Littlewood covered 623¾ miles in 142 hours to establish a new record, which still stands today as "the best on record."

[Copyrighted Photo by GILBERT & BACON, Philadelphia]

GEORGE LITTLEWOOD.

125

a magistrate that he was in fact a former amateur pedestrian with the Williamsburg A.C. and that he was presently a fireman with the Ackerman Hose Company of Richburg, New York. After sufficient investigation, the sponsor, convinced of the veracity of Johnson's testimony, awarded him the purse. Three years later at Cleveland, Ohio, Johnson was timed in 9⅘ seconds for the 100-yard dash, the best time on record. He also deposited his name in the record books for 50 yards, 130, and 150 yards.

H. M. Johnson achieved the ultimate honor

~~~~~~~~~~~~~~~~~~~~~~~~~~~~~~~~~~

Professional running was not without its hazards. According to an item in the *National Police Gazette* of December 25, 1880, Cazad, a noted runner from Montana, had arranged for a match race of eighty yards with a Denver man whom he knew he could beat. He persuaded a friend to back him to the tune of $18,000. At the same time he had made arrangements with his opponent to lose the race by feigning illness at the forty-yard mark. When the runner pulled up short midway through the race, his angry backer put a bullet through him.

~~~~~~~~~~~~~~~~~~~~~~~~~~~~~~~~~~

in professional sprinting by winning a race in the Sheffield Handicaps in England. These races, amounting to the world's championship in professional sprinting, attracted large crowds and vigorous betting. Other Americans to win at Sheffield during the last quarter of the century were sprinters named McIvor, G. H. Smith, Collins, and Donovan. McIvor claimed both Canada and the United States as his residence.

Philadelphia during the 1880's was the scene of a number of contests between sprinters. Just as in England the Sheffield Handicaps attracted professional sprinters from all over,

Stephen Farrell, Connecticut amateur champion, left the amateur ranks to become one of the last professional runners. He retired from athletic competition to become track coach at the University of Michigan.

126

Philadelphia became the American center for sprinters. The races held at Scattergood's Lamb Tavern track brought runners from Canada and throughout the United States to vie for championships and purses. According to one reporter, these meets were not always the acme of sportsmanship. He wrote, "The spectators numbered about three thousand, and behaved in a very unruly and disorderly manner, breaking down fences, etc., and in many ways interfering with the contestants."

There were a number of self-styled champions who roamed about the country seeking races with local runners. From Guelph, Ontario, came Tisdale, "the Canadian champion." A young man from Saginaw, Michigan, one George Wallis, had beaten Tisdale in a 100-yard

To add excitement and interest to running races, handicap meets in which contestants were given head starts over the top runners were frequently held.

race at Tilsonburg, Ontario, not far from Detroit. Now Tisdale had arranged for a race with Wallis in his own home town, where the latter had built up quite a local reputation. He had vanquished the best that all of the surrounding towns had to offer. The race was scheduled for the East Saginaw Driving Park with stakes of $100 a side for a distance of 120 yards. The race generated much attention and was the chief subject of speculation in the local saloons where the odds were established and the bets were made.

On the day of the race Tisdale easily outdistanced Wallis to win the purse and whatever bets he and his confederates had made on it. A few voiced suspicions that Wallis had been permitted to win the race at Tilsonburg in order to set him up for a killing at Saginaw.

The reigning runner among the pro's at five and ten miles was William Steele, who had started his career in Scotland. Since William

127

Cummings dominated the scene so decisively in Scotland, Steele came to America for a tour in 1882. After winning a number of races here, he returned to Scotland. Within a year he was back in the United States, ostensibly to stay. He spent most of 1884 in Ohio, winning races from 5 miles to 20.

In Scotland William Cummings was re-writing the record books for distances from one mile to 15; he was undisputable king of professional runners at these distances. When he decided to visit the United States, another Scotsman, George Noremac, arranged a series of races between him and Steele.

In the first race, five miles, held at the Polo Grounds in New York City, Cummings won with ease. They met again at Blessburg, Pennsylvania, in a ten mile race from which Cummings withdrew after having run five miles. So incensed was one losing gambler that he invaded Cummings' dressing room and struck him, shouting, "Take that, you Scotch thief, for selling out."

The general distrust of the professionals coupled with a lack of organization to promote ethics and establish order, spelled the impending demise of the pro's. Toward the end of the 1880's, strenuous efforts were made to form such an organization; but it was too late. The amateur movement had gained so much that it had became the dominant force in track and field. A few pro's would linger on through the century and beyond, some of them would accept jobs as trainers or trackmasters for the amateur clubs, and some of them would move into positions as college coaches.

Amateurism Takes Hold

Amateur athletic clubs had expanded beyond all predictions during the 1870's, and with that expansion came competition which tested the elements of amateurism. It was estimated that there were more than 90 athletic clubs in the Eastern seaboard area in 1880.

The amateur athlete could not accept any monetary awards for athletic contests, could not receive compensation for coaching, officiating, or scoring, and could not receive payment for any occupation related to track and field or any other form of athletics. The definition stopped short of the English concept of an amateur which barred competition to "mechanics, artisans, and laborers," who could not be considered "gentlemen amateurs."

The amateur athletic contests must have generated a whole new industry for the manufacture of medals alone. In its notice of the club's annual spring games, the New York A.C. announced that the medals would be "the most elegant ever given at an athletic meeting" and that they would be on display in the window of Underhill, Slote, & Muchmore's, at 241 Broadway, opposite the City Hall. In addition to these handsome prizes, a valuable silver cup "of handsome and unique design" was to be given to the winner of the mile race provided the winner beat the best amateur record of 4 minutes 37⅗ seconds. The cup had been presented to the club by the clerks and salesmen of Messrs. Tiffany & Company. Other clubs followed the New York A.C. example of displaying medals in the windows of jewelry stores.

The medals and trophies offered in the amateur contests were often works of art. Gold medals were usually offered for first place and cost the clubs from fifteen to twenty dollars for each of them. Much attention was given to design and execution of the medals and trophies.

The offer of the trophy for the mile race in the New York A.C. spring games was sufficient inducement for L. E. Myers of the Manhattan A.C. to move up from the shorter distances to that event. He had little trouble winning, covering the distance in 4 minutes 29½ seconds, far ahead of the second-place finisher, who crossed the line in 5 minutes 3⅜ seconds.

In the championship meeting of the NAAAA held at Mott Haven in the fall of 1880, it was clear that the domination of the games by the New York A.C. was over, as the Manhattan A.C. edged out the Scottish-American A.C. for the team trophy, 54 to 51. The Scotsmen scored most of their points in the field events and the walking races, while the Manhattan A.C., led by the incomparable L. E. Myers, dominated the running events.

Myers won the 100-yard dash, the 220, 440, and the 880, with very little competition from other athletes. He coasted through to a win in the 440 in 52 seconds, far behind his record of 49⅕ seconds. He took the 880 in 2:04⅘, as compared to his best previous time of 1:56¼. Myers' teammate, H. Fredericks won the mile in 4:39⅗. J. S. Voorhees in the running broad jump at 21 feet 4 inches and L. H. Johnson in the two-mile bicycle race were the other Manhattan

A.C. first place winners. The Manhattans also took four seconds and seven thirds.

The names of the Scottish-American A.C. winners indicate that this club had been doing some recruiting. H. H. Moritz won the 120-yard hurdles; W. J. Van Houten won the pole leap; A. W. Adams took the shot put; and E. E. Merrill won both the one-mile and three-mile walking races.

Good weather and the advance publicity attracted a large crowd, producing gate receipts sufficient to pay all expenses with enough left over to help finance the next meeting. Most of the entries came from the metropolitan area; none from Boston or Canada. For the first time an English athlete appeared to compete in the five mile run, but he dropped out early in that race.

A few weeks later the Manhattan A. C. runners took part in the Canadian Amateur Championships with the same winners repeating their earlier performances. L. E. Myers had things pretty easy, winning the 100, 220, 440, and 880. In most of the races he loafed along until near the finish line when in a burst of speed he left all others behind. He was able to win the 880 in 2:21.

The rivalry between the clubs to attract talented athletes began to surface in 1880. At the meeting of the executive committee of the NAAAA in June, 1880, the Scottish-American A. C. brought charges against the Manhattan A.C. for improper recruiting. The executive committee dismissed the charges as unfounded. At a meeting of the committee six months later the same charges were leveled at the Scottish-American A.C. and the Manhattan A.C. by a number of smaller clubs. The committee considered the charges and passed a rule that a contestant must be a member of a club for at least three months before competing in a championship meeting. This was hardly an adequate solution for the complainants.

The Spirit of the Times, which had become the principal spokesman for the amateurs, in defending the reluctance of the executive committee to interfere in such matters, wrote: "Athletic Clubs are like rolling snow-balls, the larger grow faster than the smaller. A young man would rather graduate at Yale or Harvard than at some backwoods college, although the smaller institutions might give him more and better education for less money. In the same way and for the same reasons, a young athlete would rather ornament his name with M.A.C. or S.A.A.C., than A.B.C. or X.Y.C., or any other of the countless alphabetical puzzles, which embellish the programmes of our athletic meetings."

The problem of recruitment was a product of competition and would not only be around for a long time but would grow. *The Spirit of the Times* thought that it was not a matter which could be solved by legislation, but could "only be suppressed by appealing to the honor and manhood of the offending clubs."

The amateur movement in 1880 drew most of its participants from the white collar class. Of those who competed in the 1880 championships, L. E. Myers was a bookkeeper for a drug importing firm; Moritz was also a bookkeeper; Merrill, a jeweler; Clark, a printer; Carrol, a law student; Durand, a clerk; Voorhees, a medical student; Van Houten, a clerk; and Curtis, an editor. Other prominent figures in athletics were Rene La Montagne, a wealthy businessman; Daniel Stern, very wealthy liquor wholesaler; W. Craig Wilmer, wholesale dry goods merchant; Dick Morgan, bank teller; Bill Duffy, employee of Tiffany's; Fred Sportas, stock broker; Henry Armstrong, insurance broker; and H. Ficken, architect.

This was in contrast with the occupational backgrounds of many of the professionals who were shoemakers, bricklayers, laborers, plumbers, saloon-keepers, ferry boat operators, porters, and the more menial tasks.

On the West Coast there was still a great deal of interest in professional contests. Six-day races were being sponsored in San Francisco and in Portland, Oregon, and the female six-day artists were particularly popular in San Francisco. Amateurism had gained a foot-hold there, however, and a separate association of amateur clubs with objectives similar to those of the NAAAA had been formed.

The leading amateur athlete of the Pacific Coast was Horace Hawes, R. S. Haley, and J. T.

Belcher. Hawes had won the 100-yard championship and desired to race against Archie McComb, the professional champion of the area to determine who the over-all champion was. As a member of the Olympic Club, he applied to the NAAAA to find out if he could do this without endangering his amateur status. The Easterners were appalled at the Californian's naivete. Then Hawes offered to come East to race any amateur at 100-yards in accordance with the Sheffield rules. The Easterners responded that they had their own rules.

On November 20, 1880, R. S. Haley, Olympic A.C., in winning the 440 at the University of California games at Oakland in 51¾, set new records for 300 yards and 350 yards. He was timed at these points in 32⅝ and 38¼, records which exceeded the times for these distances made by L. E. Myers.

Eastern newspapers, much to the displeasure of the Californians, handled with suspicion announcements of records made by amateurs on the West Coast. In order to dispell these doubts, the Olympic A.C. of San Francisco in February 1881 decided to send its star athletes Haley and Belcher to the championships in New York City, just to show these skeptical Easterners. They began fund-raising meets and other projects to raise money for expenses. To stimulate interest in the trip, Haley at the University of California at Oakland on April 30, ran the 200-yards in 21 seconds, claiming a new record.

The Californians in turn cast aspersions upon L. E. Myers' performances, saying that he always jumped the gun and that the officials never called him on it. When Haley set his 200-yard record, *The Spirit of the Times*, completely unimpressed, stated that Myers must have run that distance faster when he set his 220 record of 22¾ seconds, although he had not been timed at that point.

If the Californians were irked at the Easterners' condescension, the latter in their turn were equally disturbed by the attitude of the English. The amateurs across the sea were not merely condescending, they were positively insulting, poking fun at the Americans and openly laughing at their efforts. With the emergence

Lawrence E. Myers dominated the sprints and middle distances among amateurs from 1879 through 1885 so completely that he deserves to be rated among the greatest of American athletes. He won championship titles at distances from 100 yards to the mile.

131

of L. E. Myers as a star whose records equaled or surpassed those of the English amateurs, the Manhattan Athletic Club decided to send Myers across the Atlantic to compete in the English championships in July of 1881.

Myers competed in races in the New York City area up until within a week of his departure. On May 21, 1881, he sailed for England on the steamer *Britannic*, accompanied by his clubmates H. P. Pike and T. A. McEwen. Arrangements had been made with the London A.C. to make that club his headquarters and to train on their track at Stamford Bridge. He had been made an honorary member of the club. "Both in ability as a runner and character as a gentleman, Mr. Myers is eminently fitted to represent, in England, the amateur athletes of America," commented *The Spirit* upon Myers' sailing.

Eugene E. Merrill, the champion walker, now representing the Union Athletic Club of Boston, also sailed for England to compete in the championships. He, too, would stay at the London A.C.

It took some time for Myers to recover from the voyage in which he had suffered seasickness; but by June 25 both he and Merrill were ready for their first competition on English soil. At Stamford Bridge before 6,000 spectators, Merrill led off with an easy victory in the two mile walk in 14 minutes 32 seconds. It had been raining all the previous day and throughout most of the day of the race, although it subsided during Merrill's race. Myers was somewhat nervous at the start of the quarter mile race in which he was entered against the best runners of the London A.C. The track was heavy and the rain had begun to fall again. Nevertheless, Myers spurted into the lead as the runners entered the back-stretch and at the 300-yard mark he knew that the race was his. He finished 8 yards ahead of W. P. Phillips in 49⅜ seconds for a new English record.

Myers received a handsome silver cup, gold gilt, worth $60 to $70 he estimated, and for breaking the record, a beautiful gold medal worth about $80. "I never received such an ovation in my life," he wrote to friends at the Manhattan A.C., "They cheered me to the echo, and they cheered again. I think about 3,000 of

Ed Merrill, Union Athletic Club of Boston, was American amateur champion in 1881, when he sailed to England, where he won races at one mile, two miles, and three miles.

132

the 6,000 slapped me on the back and said, 'Well run, Myers, well run!' I am quite sure I could be elected Lord Mayor of London, if I was large enough, when the next election takes place."

A London reporter described Myers: "He is certainly a wonder to look at, and I should think he must be a 'rare good *un to go*' also. He stands well inside 5 ft. 8 in., and is a trifle over 112 lbs., measurements which should make him far from formidable; but then he is not made like ordinary men. What there is of him is all quality. He carries no lumber, and for thews and sinews will compare favorably with many a 168 lbs. athlete who thinks his proportions unmatchable." As if in surprise, the reporter added that Myers was "amazingly good-natured and agreeable."

Not all of the English reception was cordial. The *Manchester Guardian* suggested that an investigation should be made of Myers' amateur status. The *Guardian* wondered whether the trip was made for "pecuniary speculation."

Later Myers' friends at the London A.C. confessed to him that they had conceived a plan for defeating him in the 440. Myers wrote to his friends, "They put up a job in both races, and they admit it. In the quarter Baker was to rush me for 220 yards, and then Smith was to rush me into the straight, and Phillips was to finish me. Instead of this I rushed the whole gang and all of them were dead beaten."

A week later at the London A.C. grounds at Stamford Bridge, Merrill again won the walking race, easily defeating his London A.C. rivals at three miles in 22 minutes and ⅘ seconds. Myers won the half-mile in 1:55⅘, another English record, adding another trophy and a "huge gold medal" to his collection.

The third series of races was run at Birmingham under the sponsorship of the Mosely Harriers. Myers lowered the record for the 440 once again, covering the distance in 49 seconds flat. Merrill, entered in the one mile handicap, was not so fortunate. When his competitors were disqualified, Merrill was jostled and treated roughly by a mob of tough characters who had bet on him to lose. They were unable to finish the race and had to postpone the balance of the meeting.

Harry Fredericks, Manhattan Athletic Club, held the American amateur championship in the mile for several years.

133

The Americans were generally treated very well by the English. The newspapers were unanimous in their denunciations of the treatment that Merrill had received at the hands of the toughs.

Myers in a letter to his friends wrote, "When they wish to pay me a compliment, they always say, 'You are a Hanlon.' They think no one can scull except Hanlon." Ned Hanlon, the Canadian pro, had won the world's professional rowing championship on the Thames earlier.

The newspapers were persistent in their expressions of suspicion of professionalism. How could an American amateur defeat an English amateur. Surely he must be a professional, they ventured. Myers wrote, "Several of the papers have taken up the cry of 'Pendragon,' and they call me a professional right and left. There is a fellow named Angie, who is a photographer, and wanted to take my picture to sell; I refused him. He gased for a long time, and I refused him again. He was at an athletic meeting out of town, the other day, and gave it out in the presence of a crowd, that I had asked him what I was going to get out of it, etc., and wound up his remarks by saying, of course, I was a professional, etc."

Twenty thousand spectators turned out at Birmingham on July 16 at Aston Lower Grounds to see the Americans in action against the best that Britain had to offer. It was a very hot day; at Greenwich Observatory, they had recorded a temperature of ninety-seven degrees in the shade.

Here Myers suffered his first defeat on English soil. He ran fourth in a rather slow 100-yard dash. Later he explained to his friends that ordinarily he could have given any one of his rivals in this race a five yard start and beaten them. What had happened, he related, was that the course was down hill by about eighteen inches. This had caused him to misjudge his pace and lose his balance. He soon came back to win the 440 in 48 and ⅖ time; but this could not be considered a record because the ground was uneven.

Merrill was entered in the seven mile walking race, a distance that was somewhat longer than his best distances. On the fourth mile he col-

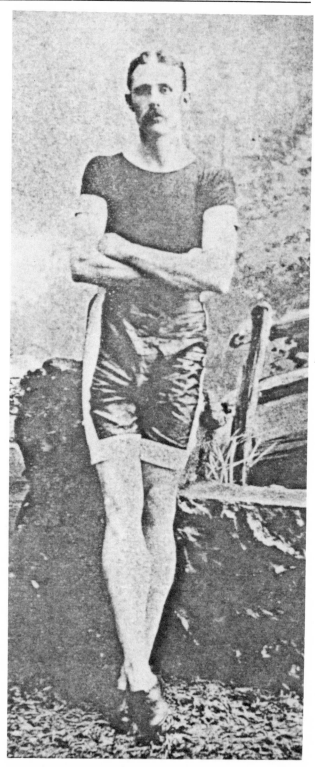

Walter G. George of England reigned supreme as an amateur at distances from one mile to ten. After turning professional, he astounded the sports followers by running the mile in 4:12¾ in 1886.

lopsed from heat exhaustion and was carried from the track.

Merrill soon after the championship meeting sailed for home; but Myers remained for one more meet, at Widnes, in the north country. Here he won both the 440 and the 880 and won an enthusiastic reception from the spectators.

The one disappointment in Myers' trip to England was the fact that he did not race against Walter G. George, the leading amateur distance runner of the Mosely Harriers, who dominated the English amateurs at distances from a half-mile to ten miles. George was ill and unable to compete. However, he expressed his intentions of coming to New York City in September to compete in the American championships.

Two weeks after Myers had departed from England, W. G. George set a new record of 2 minutes 18 seconds for the 1,000-yard run. Shortly after this race he announced that he had canceled his plans to cross the Atlantic to compete in the American and Canadian championships at New York City and Montreal because of an injury to his foot. At the same time it was reported that he was entered in the special handicaps at Birmingham in September. "It is not easy to understand why his injured foot should recover more quickly in England than America," commented *The Spirit of the Times*.

When Myers had left New York for England, G. M. L. Sachs of the Staten Island A.C. had promised to give him a gold and diamond medal costing $500 if he returned undefeated. After Myers first few victories, Sachs was certain that he would earn the medal, so he proceeded to have the medal made. Myers' failure to win the 100-yard race at the English championships deprived him of the chance to earn this remarkable medal. Since the medal had already been made, Sachs offered to award the medal to Myers if he succeeded in breaking the record for 300-yards at the joint games of the New York A.C. and the Manhattan A.C. on September 17. Immediately upon his return from England, Myers started to train for this race. As a tune-up for this race, he engaged in a match race at 100-yards with C. Stetson of Harvard, allowing the Collegian a five yard

start. Although Stetson won by two yards, Myers was clocked unofficially in 9⅘ seconds.

At the track meet on September 17, Myers won the 300-yard run in a record of 31½ seconds, even though he was suffering from a severe chest cold. Belcher, the Californian, finished second, fifteen yards behind. The victory and record won for Myers the elaborate Sachs medal, probably the most valuable prize ever won by an amateur up until that time.

The other Californians did not fare very well. Hawes with a start of 6½ yards won his heat in the 100-yard dash, placed third in the second heat, and failed to place in the final heat. Belcher got off to a bad start in the 120-yard run and failed to place.

A record number of entries signed up for the NAAAA championship meet on September 24 at Mott Haven. Entered were athletes from Boston, Montreal, Baltimore, Pennsylvania, Michigan, and California, in addition to those from the New York City area. There were also two collegians among the entries.

Myers without being pushed easily won the 100-yard dash, the 220, and the 440. Haley, the Californian, was ill and did not compete. But the others failed to live up to the expectations of their sponsors. Belcher was fourth in the 220; and Hawes took the only medal, a bronze medal for third place in the 440, in which he trailed Myers by 17 yards.

H. Fredericks, Manhattan A.C., won the mile in 4:32¾, six seconds better than in his victory in 1880; but still behind Myers' record of 4:29½. The mile race, however, was one of the most improved events on the program. In 1876 it had been won in 4:51½; in 1877, 4:49¾; in 1878, 4:51¼; and 1879, 4:43¾.

From England came the news that W. G. George had failed again in an effort to displace Myers' record for the 880. In a handicap race he had won from scratch but had missed the record by 2¾ seconds. At the same time Myers announced that he was going after George's record for the 1,000-yard run at the American A.C. games.

The American A.C. games were held at Polo Grounds on October 8, 1881. As handicap races, they were expected to provide a good chance for the champion to set a record. Each of the rivals in the race was to be given a head start which in theory would provide the scratch runner, the runner who started from the line, with stiff competition throughout the race. In the 1,000-yard run this did not prove to be the case. Myers had so quickly overtaken his competitors that he was running alone from almost the start. He passed the half-mile post in 1:55⅗ seconds and was still moving at top speed. He kept up the fast pace and crossed the finish line in 2 minutes 13 seconds, shattering W. G. George's record for the distance by five seconds.

Collegiate competition was limited in general to class meets and meets limited to contestants who belonged to the particular college's athletic association. Harvard University, for example, had an association of student athletes who elected their own officers and conducted their own athletic program. Each year the athletic association champions would be decided in a track and field meet. From among these winners, athletes would be selected to compete in the inter-collegiate championships. Inter-collegiate rowing competition had existed for some years between Harvard and Yale, but up until the 1870's there had been few other contests. Baseball by this time had become the undisputed national game and was popular among the collegians as well as the rest of the population. This game tempted the collegiate nines to go beyond the bounds of the campus in search of untested opponents. The newspapers and sporting journals of the period record many baseball games between collegians and outside teams. The outsiders were community teams and even professional nines. The Yale University baseball team regularly played against the Worcester pro's. Football began to find enthusiastic recruits among the collegians in the 1880's, and soon challenges began to fly back and forth between colleges. Within a few years the college administrations would be faced with the problems of control and supervision of sports.

The 1880's witnessed considerable improvement in the performances of college athletes in track and field. At Harvard on June 4, 1881, Evert J. Wendell in the athletic association games won the 100-yard dash in 10 seconds and ran second to his cousin W. H. Goodwin in the quarter mile. Goodwin, a member of the freshman rowing crew, in his first race covered the 440 in 50¾ seconds, fast enough time to beat any amateur, excepting the celebrated L. E. Myers.

In the Inter-Collegiate Athletic Association championships held at Mott Haven in New York City that spring, Wendell won the 100-yard dash in 10¼ seconds; and two days later in the New York A.C. games won the 120 yard dash in 12⅗ seconds. T. Cuyler of Yale University won the inter-collegiate mile in 4:40⅞, creditable time for a collegian but slower than his record of the previous year.

In the fall games at Harvard, Goodwin set a new collegiate record in winning the half-mile in 2:03¾. He now owned the records for both the 440 and the 880; and his teammate Wendell held the college records in the 100 and 220.

The performances of the college athletes began to win the attention of the leading amateur clubs and soon a number of them would be wearing the colors of the New York A.C. and the Manhattan A.C. As a means of attracting more college athletes to the championship meet, the National Association of Amateur Athletes voted in 1882 to hold the title meet in the spring rather than in the fall. It also passed rules which made it possible for collegians to run under club colors without the waiting period required for transfers from club to club. In March 1882 listed among the new members of the New York A.C. were E. J. Wendell and W. H. Goodwin, the Harvard stars.

In the spring games of the Inter-Collegiate Athletic Association on June 3, 1882, Evert Wendell, suffering from an injury, failed to win his events, yielding to Henry Brooks of Yale College, who took the 100-yard dash in 10⅕ seconds and the 220 in a record 22⅝ seconds. Goodwin of Harvard won the 440 in 53 seconds and broke his own 880 record in 2:02⅖. J. F. Jenkins of Columbia won the running long jump with a leap of 21 feet 3 inches and also set a

The inter-collegiate championships, held at the New York A.C. grounds, were well attended by classmates and lady admirers.

NEW YORK ATHLETIC CLUB GROUNDS.

THROWING THE HAMMER.

PUTTING THE SHOT.

THE WALK.

VAE-VICTORIBUS.

THE RUN.

LONG JUMP.

HURDLE RACE.

137

new record in the 120-yard hurdles, 17⅗ seconds. Harvard won the team championship for the third consecutive year.

Two weeks later at the NAAAA championships held at the Polo Grounds, the collegians made their presence felt. Derrickson of Columbia won second in the 100-yard dash. In this race the three finalists, all wearing the colors of the Manhattan Club, loped down the track arm in arm and were vociferously hissed by the spectators. Waldron finished first, followed by Derrickson and Myers. Nobody doubted that Myers could have won if he had desired.

In the 220, Henry Brooks of Yale, who had been shut out in the 100-yard dash, came back to upset the heavy favorite, L. E. Myers, winning in 22⅖ seconds. Myers claimed that he under-rated Brooks and allowed him too much of a lead in the early stages of the race. Brooks, a 6 feet 2¾ inch, 164 pound youth, had been ill before the race.

Myers managed to salvage some glory in winning the 440 in an easy race which he was required to run in only 51⅖ seconds, well behind his own record for the distance. In the 880 Goodwin of Harvard running for the New York A.C. won the gold medal, covering the distance in 1:56⅖, the second fastest half-mile by an amateur. Goodwin said that he had trained for a contest with Myers and was disappointed that the record-holder had chosen not to compete.

J. F. Jenkins of Columbia, wearing the New York A.C. colors, won the running long jump; and another collegian, A. L. Carroll, representing the Staten Island A.C., won the running high jump for the third year in a row.

The performances of Brooks and Goodwin excited considerable interest which led to efforts to bring about a match race between them and L. E. Myers. W. J. Duffy, former mile champion, now a jeweler, offered to put up a handsome silver cup for the winner. Brooks declined, explaining that he had broken training and was soon to leave for his home in San Francisco. Evert Wendell, as president of the Harvard A.A., sent a letter declining in behalf of Goodwin, saying that he, too, had broken training and was in the midst of exams.

Each spring the Manhattan A.C. held a track and field meet for schoolboys, but limited entries to boys from private schools or boys studying under tutors. It was obvious that few Irish boys would be among the contestants. In the 1882 games one Wendell Baker won the 220-yard dash and 440. In September he would be entering Harvard, where his cousin Evert Wendell had distinguished himself as an athlete.

For the poor boys there was little opportunity for purely amateur competition. Sometimes on professional programs there would be races restricted to boys under 18 years of age. In Madison Square Garden in one five mile race at this time out of 23 starters 4 were ejected upon protest from the Society for the Prevention of Cruelty to Children which had complained that the boys were too young for such strenuous exercise. At the conclusion of the race, the purses for first and second places were held up on the complaint that both of the boys were over 18.

Early in the year 1882 there was talk about a race between W. G. George, the English amateur champion, and L. E. Myers, the American. Throughout the year such a meeting became a prominent topic in sporting conversations, stimulated in no small measure by George's assault on the record books in 1882. The English runner succeeded in erasing from the books just about every record from a mile to ten miles. On June 24, 1882, he had set a record for the mile in 4:19⅖. George had expressed an interest in crossing the Atlantic for a race with Myers.

In August William B. Curtis of the New York A.C., who would serve as match-maker, wrote to Walter G. George to inform him that Myers would be ready for a series of races at a half-mile, three-quarters, and one mile, to be run between October 18 and November 15.

Myers had not engaged in such a busy schedule of competition in 1882 as he had in previous years. For one thing, there were far fewer meets in this year as clubs began to lose interest, and also Myers had taken new employment which he said required his time. He had also endured several bouts with malaria.

In preparation for the great match races, Myers won the mile at the Caledonia Club games in 4:35¾, ran second in the 440 handicap at the Manhattan A.C. games, ran an exhibition 880, and won the Canadian Amateur Athletic championships in the 440 and 880. His pre-race performances had not been impressive.

The first race between George and Myers was the 880, a distance in which Myers was the favorite by 3 to 1 odds. Myers had won most of his races over the shorter distances ranging from 100-yards to the 880. His competition at the mile race was infrequent, even though he did hold the American amateur record at that distance. George, on the other hand, preferred the longer distances, often competing in four mile and ten mile races. Myers would have been out of his element at George's best distances; George would have been hopelessly outclassed against Myers in the 100, 220, or 440. The series of races between these two men was a mismatch.

It was a clear, cold day when the runners met for their first contest on November 4 at the Manhattan Polo Grounds. Used for baseball primarily, the Polo Grounds track had been sadly neglected. Efforts had been made to get it into shape for the big races, but it was still soft where new sand or cinders had been laid.

At the starter's pistol George went into the lead followed closely by Myers. For the first 750 yards Myers trailed his opponent, then in a burst of speed went by him to go on to win easily in 1:56⅗, crossing the finish line with his hands held high above his head in jubilation. Myers said that he could have run much faster, 1:53, possibly 1:52; but he had held back, saving himself for the next race.

The next race was George's distance, the mile. It was a bright Indian summer day and 2,500 people were on hand to witness the second race. Many of Myers friends had bet heavily upon him to win, in spite of reports that he had been suffering from a cold since the last race. George again went into the lead and continued to set the pace throughout the race. Myers had planned to stick as closely to George as he could throughout the race, then give it all he had left in the final 220. George read his mind and anticipated this strategy. He pulled ahead coming down the backstretch of the last lap, opening up a lead which Myers would find difficult to make up in the final 220 yards. This proved to be the case as Myers set out to catch George in the final stretch, drawing close to him but falling back exhausted. George won in 4:21⅖, the fastest mile in America, but still two seconds behind his record. Myers finished 18 yards behind in 4:27⅗; but all agreed that his time would have been a full two or three seconds faster if he had not encountered interference from an official who stepped into his path near the finish. He had to stop short to avoid the official, and his friends, thinking he was exhausted, rushed forward to carry him off the track. He struggled free and crossed the line in 4:27⅗, the fastest time for the mile by an American amateur.

Still bothered by his cold, Myers asked for a postponement of the third race. Initially George declined, preferring to claim a forfeit, but he was persuaded finally to accede to Myers' request. They met for the third race in the series on November 30. Although nine inches of snow had to be removed from the track before the runners could start, at post-time everything was in readiness for the race. The three-quarter mile race was a repetition of the mile. George led throughout followed closely by Myers who tried to overtake him in the stretch but failed. George won in a new American record of 3:10½, but two seconds behind his own record. Myers trailed him by six yards.

George then left for a trip through the northeast and Canada. He returned in ten days for a final race at Madison Square Garden, a ten mile handicap. Tom Delaney, the nineteen-year-old youth from the Grammercy A.C. who had won the five mile championship at the NAAAA games with a three minute start over George, won first place without needing the three minutes. George finished third in a disappointing performance. He had not trained in the past ten days, it was reported that he had made the most of night-life during his travels. In the same meet, L. E. Myers easily won the half-mile handicap, starting from scratch.

There had been a marked drop in the interest in athletic meets during the year. The number of meets held had decreased, and in those meets which were held, the entry lists were much smaller than in past years. Furthermore, a number of clubs had withdrawn from the National Association of Amateur Athletes. *The Spirit of the Times* in a long article denounced the association and placed the blame for the decline in interest upon the officers and leaders of the group. *The Spirit* withdrew its support of the NAAAA. Much of the blame placed upon the NAAAA by the editor was that it had deviated from the course which had been set for amateur athletics by the New York A.C. This pioneer organization had been concerned with establishing standards for and encouraging amateur competition. The NAAAA on the other hand had become more concerned with gate receipts than with amateurism. The ruling it had adopted which restricted competition to those athletes who belonged to the member clubs was purely for pecuniary reasons, *The Spirit* insisted. *The Spirit* also denounced the ruling of the executive committee which had permitted athletes to compete in the Caledonia Club games, where professionals also competed. The Caledonians offered expensive prizes of silverware in their amateur contests, which were in effect distorting the conception of amateurism. In other races on the same program, professionals vied for cash purses. Amateurs competing side by side with professionals endangered the amateur movement, *The Spirit* argued. "If a gentleman and a chimneysweep rub against each other, the sweep will be no cleaner, while the gentleman will be dirtier. If you take down the fence, and allow amateurs and professionals to graze in the same field all day, it will be hard work to separate them at night and some will be sure to be driven into the wrong stable," wrote the editor.

The editor was also vexed that the National Association of Amateur Athletes had not become a national organization, but had remained in effect a New York institution. To succeed, such an association would have to become a truly national organization.

Betting which had corrupted the professional sports scene also posed a threat for the amateurs. When the Californians had visited New York City for the championships in 1881 and had returned home after their disappointing performances, they reported to the press on the West Coast that they had been badgered incessantly by members of the Manhattan A.C. to place bets on the outcomes of the races between their men and Myers.

The West Coast newspapers expressed doubts about Myers' amateur standing. According to one writer in the San Francisco *Chronicle*, "A person who is occupied with business cannot train down to such a fine point as to compete with one who devotes himself to running, and to meet such in open field is to discourage amateurs. Myers has no business, and has had none for some time, and is surrounded by people who are ready to make and receive propositions to back their man as any professional backers could possibly be, which injures him and makes the suspicion which I heard expressed openly, that he was somewhat dependent on athletics for a living, possible."

To Dudley A. Sargent, director of the gymnasium at Harvard, professionalism was a horrid monster from which the college athletes had to be protected. Through his efforts Harvard appointed a faculty committee on athletics to have general supervision over all forms of exercise. Up until this time — 1882 — the students had organized and sponsored their own affairs. One of the first rules enacted by Dr. Sargent's committee was a ban against college clubs or associations competing with professionals. Another rule banned any person from assuming the role of trainer or instructor on Harvard College property without authorization in writing from the committee. A number of professional athletes were beginning to find employment as trainers and coaches in both amateur clubs and college athletic associations. Dudley Sargent and his committee wanted to be able to screen these individuals to insure that the students would at all times be under the proper moral influence.

The eighth annual Inter-Collegiate Athletic Association championships were held at the Polo Grounds in New York City on May 26, 1883, before the largest crowd ever seen at such a meet. A large portion of the crowd were ladies who wore the colors of their favored college.

As had become the custom, Harvard dominated the meet, winning 7 firsts and 3 seconds. Princeton and Columbia were next with 2 firsts each and 3 seconds each. W. H. Goodwin of

The New York Athletic Club in addition to its fine building erected at Sixth Avenue and 55th Street in 1885, had a summer club house at Travers Island in Long Island Sound.

Harvard repeated his victories of the year before in the 440 and 880, but because of lack of competition failed to improve upon his record times in these distances. Derickson of Columbia won the 100-yard dash and Brooks of Yale easily won the 220. G. B. Morrison of Harvard ran the mile in 4:38⅜, one second off the record, to win that event. C. H. Kip of Harvard won the shot put and set a new record in the hammer throw. The performances of the collegians were beginning to approach those of the leading amateurs.

A week later the championship meeting of the National Association of Amateur Athletes held at Mott Haven attracted few spectators; and the number of entries was down considerably from the two preceding years. The Manhattan Athletic Club again took team honors with 33 points followed by the New York A.C. with 24 points. Brooks of Yale, a slow starter, was beaten by a scant three inches by Waldron of Manhattan A.C. in the 100-yard dash. He came back, however, to beat L. E. Myers in the 220-yard dash. Again Brooks got off to a slow start but soon overtook Myers and beat him to the tape by one foot in 22⅛ seconds. Myers' only victory was in the 440 which he won in 52⅛ seconds with little opposition. Fredericks of the Manhatton A.C. won the mile in 4:36⅜ for his fourth consecutive championship. F. L. Lambrecht, Pastime A.C., 20 years old, 6 feet tall, and 210 pounds in weight, was a double winner for the third year in a row, taking the hammer throw and setting a record of 43 feet for the shot put.

To many the championship meeting was a great disappointment. In some events the victories were won with little or no opposition. The whole season of track and field athletics proved a disappointment. There were not nearly as many meetings as in previous years, some clubs having given up athletics and having become social clubs. The New York Athletic Club was even undergoing a change. Under its new president, William R. Travers, it was raising funds for an elaborate building and the purchase of an island for an athletic center and boat club. To accomplish these ends it had altered the original objectives of the club and had accepted into membership men of wealth and prestige who would serve as patrons rather than participants. Soon in Boston, Detroit, Chicago, St. Louis, and in other metropolitan centers lavish buildings emblazoned with the title of athletic clubs would be erected. Although they would for a time sponsor teams and athletic events, they would survive mainly as prestigious social clubs.

The amateur stars with the sanction of the executive committee of the NAAAA were competing regularly in Caledonia games and other picnics for valuable prizes of merchandise on the same programs in which professionals were vying for cash prizes. In condemning this situation *The Spirit of the Times* minced no words in writing, "We venture to hazard the prediction that within the next twelve months, the brains of the Executive Committee of the National Association of Amateur Athletes will expand sufficiently to grasp the fundamental fact, that, when our amateur athletic champions can be seen, week after week, on exhibition as sideshows, at professional sports and beer garden picnics, they will thereby cheapen their popularity to such an extent that the public will not flock to see them at games given by their own clubs."

The amateur movement, begun with such dedication for its announced principles, was in danger of disintegrating. This realization was shared by the college officials who were beginning to become concerned over the amount of time and interest which the students were beginning to contribute to sports. The faculty members were concerned that a disproportionate amount of time devoted to sports might interfere with learning which they regarded as the primary purpose of college attendance. At Yale University in the fall of 1883, Walter Camp, a recent alumnus of the University, was engaged to direct athletic sports. His salary of $1,200 was to be paid by the various athletic organizations on the campus.

In his annual report, President Charles Elliott of Harvard University echoed Dr. Sargent's sentiments about the dangers of college ath-

Madison Square Garden in 1890, the scene of many an exciting track and field contest over its long history.

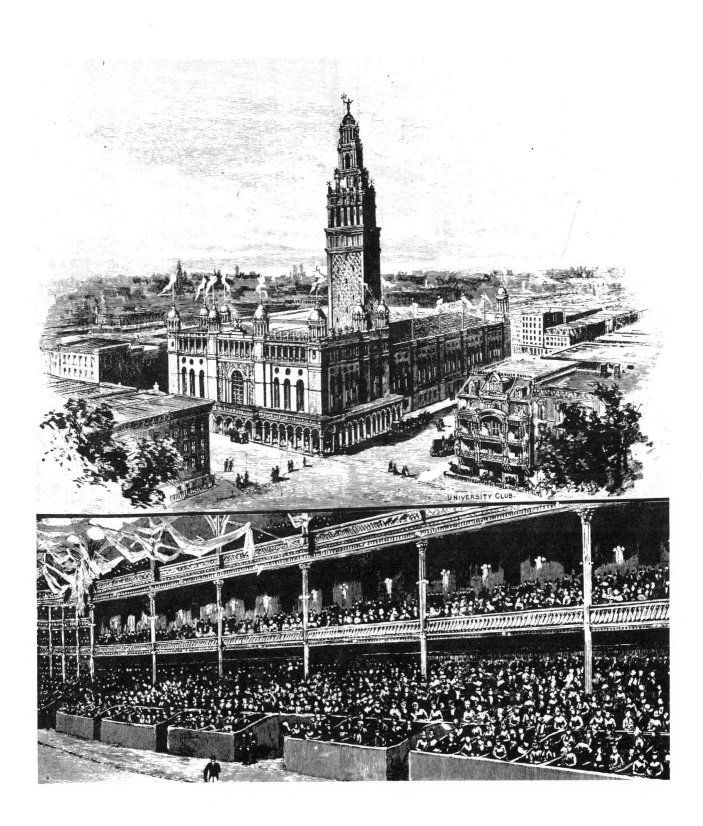

UNIVERSITY CLUB.

letes becoming contaminated by professionalism. He said that the growing interest in intercollegiate competition demanded regulation by agreement between the colleges whose students were participating in contests. Athletic sports, he asserted, "are degrading both to players and spectators if conducted with brutality or in a tricky or jockeying spirit; and they become absurd if some of the competitors employ trainers and play with professionals, while others do not." Harvard, he said, was opposed to hiring trainers and playing with professionals, and the institution was also opposed to competing with those colleges which do so. President Elliott also condemned the colleges which accepted subsidies from hotels and railroads for participation of students in sports events.

The Spirit of the Times, the voice of the simon pure amateur movement, in an editorial endorsed President Elliott's remarks, stating, "If students have any earthly wisdom, they will take warning in time, and at once materially modify both the theory and practice of their conduct of athletic sports; for if radical reforms are not speedily effected, there must ensue a conflict in which it is not hard to prophesy which side will be driven to the wall."

With the amateur movement threatened by disintegration from within its ranks, the influence of the colleges might be the transfusion required to restore the amateurs to their original objectives.

For those who contend that the amateur movement and the college restrictions were barriers to participation for the young men of the lower economic classes, there is little to dispute. The entry fees, club dues, and tuition fees ostensibly eliminated a large number of would-be athletes. However, the desire to win could never be completely obliterated, and this incentive would do much to break down the barriers between classes and offer upward mobility to those on the lower rungs of the social ladder. Athletic clubs through influential members could offer steady employment to promising but impecunious athletes. In time the desire to win would induce the colleges to offer scholarships to young athletes who otherwise would not have had the opportunity to attend college. Wealthy alumni would also offer their assistance with summer employment and other subsidies. Pure amateurism, if it ever actually existed in the United States, enjoyed only a brief life. Throughout its history it has been subject to compromise, and the result has not been bad.

The Pattern Is Set

Of all of the American athletes of the nineteenth century Laurence E. Myers, of the Manhattan A.C., was supreme. He exceeded the performances of both amateurs and professionals, demonstrated an unrivaled versatility, and maintained his supremacy over the athletes of his day for a long period of years. At the distances of from three hundred yards to 1,000 yards, he was invincible in his time. While the records that he set are exceeded by schoolboys today, they are not diminished by this fact. In his day Myers was the outstanding runner in the middle distances and so outranked all others both at home and abroad that he completely dominated the sport. His appearance at a track meet was enough to insure the success of the event and to attract enough spectators to make the affair profitable. He was much in demand, and because he liked to run, he was a frequent participant in meets.

His popularity, his victories, and his frequent appearances in contests led to suspicions of professionalism, which eventually broke into the open with charges being preferred against him. In March 1884 the executive committee of the National Association of Amateur Athletes of America placed notices in the newspapers inviting "all persons holding or having any knowledge or control or any proofs, oral or written, showing, or tending to show, that Mr. L. E. Myers has violated the definition of amateur" to appear before the committee at a meeting to be held at Knickerbocker Cottage.

The charges presented against Myers were that he had been proprietor of a roller skating rink, that he had received pay for serving as a judge in a six-day running race, that he had received a salary for serving as secretary of the Manhattan A.C., that he had been paid for writing a sports column for a newspaper, that he had accepted a twenty dollar gold piece for a prize at a Williamsburg A.C. meet, and that he had deposited some of his trophies as security for a loan.

Myers defended his conduct by maintaining that he had a right to be a proprietor of a skating rink, to serve as secretary of the Manhattan A.C., and to receive compensation for writing a sports column. Nothing in the amateur rules forbade such activities, he insisted. He had served as an official at professional six-day races along with many other amateurs but had discontinued this activity when the association passed a rule against it. As for the twenty dollar gold piece, Myers admitted that he had accepted it but added that it had been accepted with the understanding that he was to exchange it for a prize. He said that in accepting the coin, he was merely acting as a messenger for the club. Before he had taken the coin, he had asked the president of the National Association if it would be permissible. The president advised him to take it and assured him that there would be no trouble. He admitted that he had posted some of his trophies as security for a loan but pointed out that he had redeemed them.

The executive committee dismissed the charges against Myers, declaring that he had not violated the rules of the National Association. *The Spirit of the Times* also defended Myers, but admitted that there were some gray areas in the charges. These, however, were not the fault of Myers, but rather of the Association. The matter should be cleared up by a better definition of amateurism by the Association, *The Spirit* declared.

In June Myers sailed for England accompanied by George Avery, of the Manhattan A.C., and the wealthy patron of the club, Gus M. L. Sachs, who was paying the bill. Teammates Arthur Waldron and Harry Fredericks were also in the party. Frank Murray, Williamsburg A.C., and William Meek, West Side A.C., both amateur walking champions, also sailed for England. The pier of the Cunnard Steamship Company, according to the newspapers, was crowded with ladies and gentlemen, who waved handkerchiefs, threw bouquets, and yelled themselves hoarse, as they jostled each other as they attempted to shake hands or exchange a few words with the departing sports heroes.

In England the American walkers did well, winning most of their contests. Fredericks had trouble in trying to keep up with William Snook, the Mosely Harriers distance ace, and Waldron suffered a knee injury which kept him out of the winning column. Myers, however, was the star. Wherever he competed, large crowds turned out to watch him. "It is decidedly a treat to see the easy way in which he seems to get over the ground. To the on-lookers it did not appear as if he was going at any great pace, and it was wonderful to see the watch at the finish," wrote an English sports columnist.

Everyone commented on Myers' graceful stride. They called him the "gazelle," and marveled at the length of his stride. Although only 5 feet 7½ inches tall, he ran with an 8 feet stride. Throughout the early stages of the race, he seemed to be running without effort, hardly exerting himself, but at the finish he uncorked a burst of speed that would be a credit to any sprinter at a 100 yards.

At Birmingham on July 7, Myers won the half-mile in 1:55⅘ for the best time on record.

Walter George, the English distance champion, was scheduled to run in this race against Myers but withdrew before the meet, much to the disappointment of the crowd.

Throughout his visit Myers continued to dazzle the English sports fans, attracting crowds of 5,000 or more in places where 1,000 had been considered great. Just before Myers' date for sailing home, W. G. George offered to run a series of three races at 1,000, 1,200, and 1,320 yards; but Myers declined. It was too late, he explained.

Myers returned to New York City with a basket full of trophies, ornate silver cups, each one valued in excess of two hundred dollars. The trophies were held at customs to determine whether he should have to pay duty on them. The customs officers were waiting for a decision in another case in which a horse-racing trophy being held for duty was being contested by the owner. The verdict in favor of the horse-owner released Myers' trophies also.

Myers competed in the NAAAA championships in September, winning the 220 in 24¼ seconds and the 440 in 55⅗ seconds, both times the slowest recorded in any championship meet. He also won the 880 in 2:09½, which was the slowest time since 1876. The meet, being held in the fall, prevented the collegians from attending. This robbed the event of much interest, since a tight contest between Myers and Brooks of Yale in the 220 and Myers versus Baker in the 440 had been anticipated with much interest. Three of the leading amateurs, William Meek, Tom Delaney, and Peter Golden, had turned professional before the meet, also depriving the contest of interest. In winning the 440, Myers had scored his sixth championship victory in that event.

Malcolm Ford, of the Brooklyn A.C., the winner of the 100-yard dash in 10⅖ seconds, the slowest time in any championship meet, told friends and reporters that Myers had not entered this event because he was afraid that he would be beaten.

Myers subsequently entered the 100-yard dash at the New York A.C. meet to prove that he was not afraid of being beaten by Ford. Because it was a cold day, Myers remained in the locker room until it was time for the 100-

yard dash. When he came on to the field for his heat, he found that it had already been run. The New York A.C. officials refused to allow him to run in any of the following heats. Ford promptly accused Myers of deliberately missing his heat to avoid running against him. Myers' friends counter-charged that the New York A.C. had conspired against their runner by not sending notice to the locker room in time for Myers to come onto the track for his heat.

The two runners did finally meet on October 25 in a 120-yard handicap race, with Myers winning easily. Ford protested that this had not been a fair trial. Myers' preliminary heat had been an easy one, virtually a walk-over, while his had been a tough one. Myers was fresh for the final heat, and he was fatigued. Ford said that he was through with handicaps but still wanted to demonstrate his supremacy over Myers in a 100-yard scratch race.

Myers responded, saying that it used to be customary for an athlete to make his reputation on the cinder path; now it is being done with lead pencil and paper. "I knew Mr. Ford to be quite an athletic enthusiast, and especially so as to his own performances," Myers declared.

Ford had been going to the newspaper sports writers with diagrams of the 120-yard race, showing them that he would have won if it had been a 100-yard race. To this Myers responded, "I have become disgusted with this 'running on paper,' and will run Ford 100 yards, at our Election Day Games for a medal valued at $50. If he beats me on that occasion, I will have no excuse to offer, or diagrams to present to the various sporting papers around the city."

Election Day, November 8, 1884, was a rainy day; but nonetheless 2,000 spectators showed up to witness the 100-yard race between Myers and Ford. The contest had received much attention in the press. All week long Myers had been laid up with a boil on the inside of his right thigh. He had asked Ford to postpone the race but had received a negative response. The day before the race Myers had the boil lanced and

Malcolm Ford, who won the title of "all-around athlete" among amateurs in the 1880's, was a controversial figure who was suspended for competing with professionals.

spent a sleepless night, bothered by the pain.

The runners were called to the line. They bent together and were off at the pistol shot. Myers got a better start and at 10 yards led by two feet, going on to win in 10½ seconds. On the same program, Henry Hutchens, the English professional, generally acknowledged as "the fastest sprinter in the world," gave an exhibition.

The national championships in 1885 were held at the Manhattan A.C. field on June 13. Brooks of Yale had acceded to his parents' wishes and had withdrawn from athletic competition. Wendell Baker of Harvard was occupied with examinations and could not enter. But missed most of all was "Lon" Myers, who had quietly slipped off to England on his own.

Myers raced at athletic meets throughout England during July and August, attracting large crowds everywhere. At the Alexandra Club games on July 4, more than 8,000 spectators cheered him as he won the 300-yard race and the 440 handicap. "A deafening applause roused the spectators to the highest pitch of enthusiasm," commented one sports writer. On August 1, he wrote to a friend that he was staying in Manchester as the guest of Walter Platt, the publisher of the magazine *Field*. He had won twelve races and had a busy schedule ahead of him. In the English championships he had won both the 440 and 880. Again he failed in his efforts to arrange a series of races with Walter George, who, having established records from one mile to ten miles, had retired from competition. However, everywhere that Myers went, he was greeted with enthusiasm and warm applause. He ended his English tour on August 31 and sailed for home, laden with trophies and medals, after having competed in 35 races.

In the meantime his friends back in New York City had announced that they were planning to hold a benefit meet for Myers at Madison Square Garden on October 17. They explained that Myers, having been raised in affluent surroundings, was indifferent to the value of money and careless in the use of it. His frequent participation in athletic contests had depleted his funds. The testimonial would be held in order to raise money for him. It had

long been the custom to hold benefits for theatrical people and for professional athletes. From time to time the amateur clubs had also sponsored benefits to raise funds for trainers and track masters. A week after Myers' return from England he ran in an exhibition 440 at the Williamsburg A.C. benefit for Jack Masters, the club trackmaster. This type of fund-raising activity for an amateur athlete was something that had not been done before, and there was a serious question about whether Myers could be considered an amateur after it. He had, however, expressed his intention of retiring from athletic competition.

In England, Myers' friend and rival, Walter George, had ended his brief retirement by emerging as a professional to race William Cummings, the reigning professional and record-holder. It may be that Myers had plans for the future which were not fully disclosed to the public.

For Myers there were no rivals in the middle distances either in the United States or in England. He could win with ease at any distance from 300 to 1,000 yards, and could beat most athletes at the shorter distances and the mile. This factor took away much of his interest in racing. From many races he was barred and had to be content with handicap races which required of him a record-breaking effort to win. Few athletes ever reigned so completely over their rivals for so long a period of years.

Myers competed in a few races during the fall of 1885, setting a new mark of 1:55⅘ for the 880 in a handicap race at the Olympic A.C. games. His last race as an amateur was an 880 handicap victory at Madison Square Garden on October 24, 1885, before 2,000 spectators who had gathered there in his honor.

Myers had not declared himself a professional at this stage. There were in circulation rumors about a series of races between Myers and George, but as late as December 26, Myers was still denying that there were any plans for such a meeting, adding that he was unwilling to give up his amateur status. There were questions about his status following the receipt by him of a purse from the benefit. The English, in particular, challenged his status as an amateur. The question would have to be answered.

Myers solved the problem in February 1886, when he accepted a challenge from Walter George for a series of races at 1,000 and 1,160 yards and three-quarters of a mile. He placed a forfeit bond of $250 in the office of *The Spirit of the Times* and agreed to meet George there on February 18 at 10 a.m. to sign the articles of agreement and make the arrangements for the races.

He expressed his regrets at leaving the amateurs and his many friends at the Manhattan A.C. He explained, "Amateur athletic sport has now little or nothing to offer me. I have won prizes and honors enough to satiate any man's ambition. I hold the world's best amateur records at all distances from 250 yards to 1,000 yards; within those limits no amateur will now oppose me, except in a handicap, and I am tired of giving starts so long that I cannot win unless I beat all former records."

He added that he felt that the races between him and George were an obligation that he owed to his country in the face of a challenge from abroad. Furthermore, he said he had an earnest desire to avenge the defeats he suffered in his previous encounters with George.

At the Manhattan A.C. games at Madison Square Garden on February 20, George ran an exhibition mile and Myers displayed his talents by running a 440.

The series of contests between George and Myers was scheduled to start at Madison Square Garden on May 1. Each contestant was required to put up $1,000 for which the runners would contend. There would also be a magnificent trophy emblematic of the championship of the world. The gate receipts would be divided equally.

On May 1, before 3,000 spectators, Myers and George lined up on a newly laid dirt track which measured one-eighth of a mile in circuit. The first race was at the 1,000 yard distance. At the gun the runners took off, with Myers dropping back to trail George. Walter George set the pace throughout most of the race until 160 yards from the finish when Myers speeded

A. B. George was imported from England to run the mile for the Manhattan Athletic Club. He was a brother of Walter George, the mile record-holder.

When Thomas Patrick Conneff won the Irish championship, he was recruited by the Manhattan A.C. Later, when competing under the colors of the New York A.C., he set a new world's amateur record for the mile.

·The·Manhattan·Athletic·Clvb·
·N·Y·C·

150

The Manhattan Athletic Club moved into its elegant club house on Fifth Avenue in November 1886. Two years later the members were making plans for larger quarters, which would be "the largest, handsomest, and best appointed in the United States."

In The Gymnasium.

The Skating Rink...

The Billiard Room.
Café........
Reception Rooms...

The Swimming Tank.

up to pass him and went on to win by 8 yards in 2:23⅜. Most people felt that George was running out of his class against Myers at this distance. The advantage would move to George as the distances lengthened.

In spite of the fact that May 8 was a stormy night, 3,000 people braved the elements to watch the second contest between Myers and George at 1,320 yards, or three-quarters of a mile. The race proved to be a repetition of the earlier contest, with Myers winning at the finish in 3 minutes 15⅜ seconds. This ended the series since Myers had won two of the three races; but Myers agreed to race George at his best distance, the mile, on May 15. They had already rented the Garden and had a schedule of supplementary races with 250 entries. It looked as though Myers was willing to concede one victory to the English champion.

More than 4,000 people crowded into the Garden on the night of May 15. It was a crowd that was rather more than the hall was designed to hold. At the gun George moved into the lead as he had in the past races. The betting was heavily in the English runner's favor. The mile was not only his best distance, but Myers had been ill with a stomach ailment all week and had considered withdrawing from the race. Last minute urgings by his family and friends convinced him that he should at least put in an appearance and make an effort to run. His friends, aware of his illness, placed their money on George to win. George set the pace throughout the race but did not seem to be extending himself. At the finish Myers summoned forth all his reserve and sprinted ahead to win by a yard and a half.

Myers and George divided a net profit of $4,500 for the series. George was returning to England to prepare for another series of races against William Cummings. Myers planned to rest, except for a few exhibitions which he had scheduled. Before departing for home, George sought to explain his defeats by saying that the track was too small and that the curves were too sharp for his long stride. "Bosh!" exclaimed Myers, who stated that his stride was six inches longer than George's. Despite this controversy, Myers was at the pier with a crowd of sports followers to wish George *bon voyage* as he sailed home to England.

On July 1, 1886, Myers saw one of his best amateur records eclipsed, the record for the 440: Wendell Baker, the Harvard sprinter, in a planned attempt for records ran the 100 in 10 seconds flat to tie one record, then ran the 440 in 47¾ seconds on a straight-away. Special care had been taken to insure that the most accurate timing that was available was done so that there could be little question about the records. Myers expressed surprise that his favorite record was beaten so soon after his withdrawal from the amateur ranks. He related that he had been told that the Beacon track where Wendell had made his record was the fastest in the country. In October he would himself travel to Boston to try for a new 440 mark on the Beacon track.

Walter George was doing better in his series with William Cummings in England. Upon returning home, he had gone into serious training to prepare himself for the races and redeem his reputation. On August 23, 1886, at Lillie Bridge track in London, Walter George startled the athletic world by lowering the mile record to 4:12¾ in a close race with Cummings. The old professional record of 4:16½ had been held by Cummings; and George's amateur record was 4:19.

In the fall of 1886, Walter George was back in New York City, where he was visiting his old friends. He was on his way to Australia. The rumor was about that he had stopped in New York City in order to attempt to persuade Myers to go with him to Australia. Soon after George's departure, Myers, accompanied by his old Manhattan A.C. friend, Harry Fredericks, left for Australia. It was also revealed that Harry Hutchens, England's champion among professional sprinters, was also en route to Australia.

Myers arrived in Sidney after a long and tiresome voyage on January 18, 1887. What had promised to be an exciting and lucrative tour proved to be a failure. George left for home after a few races. Myers remained there for 18 months, trying in vain to promote races. When he returned to New York City, his career as a runner was over. He went into horse-racing and worked as a bookmaker for the remainder of his brief life. He died of pneumonia in 1899.

Laurence E. Myers, in spite of the fact that his records have failed to survive, ranks as one of the greatest athletes that the United States has produced. His stellar performances advanced the goals of track athletics and assured the success of the amateur movement. Nobody in the United States has ever maintained such a sustained record of victories in track.

The national championship games were held on the grounds of the Staten Island A.C. on June 26, 1886. Malcolm Ford, of the Brooklyn A.C., no longer having Myers to be concerned about, won the 100, 220, and running long jump. Edward C. Carter, recently imported from England by the New York A.C., won both the mile and five-mile runs.

The all-around championship, comparable to the present-day decathalon, was held at the New York A.C. grounds on September 18. Out of the ten events in the competition, Malcolm Ford, who had since the championship meet in June transferred his allegiance from the Brooklyn A.C. to the New York A.C., won eight first places and one second to capture the all-around title.

Before the year was out, Ford was on trial before the NAAAA on charges of having competed in a professional contest at Hampden Park in Springfield, Massachusetts. Members of the Brooklyn A.C. in preferring the charges produced witnesses who testified that Ford had run second in the 100-yard dash and had won the running high jump. Ford, the witnesses testified, had competed under the name "T. Williams of Baltimore." The prosecution produced witnesses to testify against Ford; and almost as soon, the defense came forth with witnesses to contradict their testimony. There were charges and counter-charges, testimony and recantation. The trial dragged on for days and weeks, attracting as much space in the press as a major crime might. Although the trial started in November, a decision was not reached until the following May. The sub-committee found against Ford and was supported by the executive committee. Ford, still protesting his innocence, announced his retirement from athletics. He submitted his resignation to the New

York A.C., which at first declined to accept it. However, upon Ford's re-submitting his resignation, the club accepted it with regrets and with the assurance that the members did not believe that Ford was guilty of professionalism.

What passed as a trial of an individual for professionalism was in reality the breaking into the open of a long smoldering feud between the New York A.C. and the Manhattan A.C. Both clubs had advanced far beyond the informal organizations devoted only to athletics which they had commenced as. The New York A.C. had moved into an elegant five-story building on the corner of Sixth Avenue and 55th Street. It was more than an athletic club. In addition to a gymnasium, the building included a ballroom, dining halls, billiard rooms, reception rooms, and all of the appurtenances of the most exclusive of social clubs. The membership until 1887 was limited to 2,000 men; and the club was proud of the fact that there was always a list of 600 to 800 waiting to be considered for admission. Most hopefuls even with influential backing would expect to wait about two years. An admission fee of $50 was required and dues were $40 a year. If these costs seem moderate, one need only be reminded that many a laboring man was still working for a dollar a day. These fees were for the social members, not the athletes.

The Manhattan A.C. moved into its elegant club house on Fifth Avenue in November 1886. Two years later the members were making plans for a bigger club house which would be, according to the *New York Times*, "the largest, handsomest, and best appointed in the United States." It appeared as though the club's principal goal was to outdo the New York A.C. in every respect.

The social aspects of the clubs were now fully as important as the athletic activities. They had become status symbols, evidences of social acceptance and prestige.

The bitter feud between the two clubs made the victories on the athletic field of paramount importance. Soon the rosters of these clubs began to list athletes from other clubs, from other cities, from Canada, and even from abroad. The New York A.C. enticed Malcolm Ford from the Brooklyn A.C. W. L. Condon,

who had set a record in the hammer throw while competing for the Baltimore A.C., soon after was wearing the winged foot emblem of the New York A.C. George Gray of the Toronto A.C., a five feet nine, 160-pounder, astonished the sports followers by not only beating all of the big fellows in the shot put at the NAAAA championships but also by setting a new record. A few months later he was wearing the winged foot. Edward C. Carter, after winning the English title in the mile run, crossed the Atlantic to become an insurance broker and a member of the New York A.C.

The competition for the collegians was keen. It looked as though the New York A.C. would get William B. Page, the high jump record-holder from the University of Pennsylvania, but the Manhattan A.C. lured him away and took him on a summer trip to England. When the New York A.C. distance running star Ed Carter was defeated in Dublin in a four-mile race by a 19-year-old youth named Patrick Thomas Conneff, the Irish lad was enlisted by the Manhattan A.C. When A. B. George, the younger brother of the champion, visited New York City to compete in a track meet, he remained as a member of the Manhattan A.C.

With each new recruit there were charges of the violation of the amateur spirit and vehement denials and counter-charges. The Manhattan A.C. denied importing Tommy Conneff and produced a letter from him to Gus M. L. Sachs in which the Irish lad wrote that he was coming to New York City to better himself. The New York A.C. supporters concluded that it was no co-incidence that Conneff was soon employed as a clerk in the Wagner Palace Car Company, whose manager was C. C. Hughes, secretary of the Manhattan A.C.

"Mr. Hughes is such an enthusiastic sportsman that he does not allow business to interfere with sport, in either his own case or that of his clerks, and whenever Conneff wishes to

George Gray, Coldwater, Ontario, who wore the winged foot of the New York A.C., won his first shot put title at the age of 19, when he weighed but 160 pounds. From 1887 through 1896 he won the national championship in the shot every year except 1895, when he did not compete.

attend athletic games in America, Europe, or Australia, Mr. Hughes will give him the necessary leave of absence without loss of pay," wrote a New York A.C. partisan.

Having withdrawn from membership in the National Association of Amateur Athletes of America, the New York A.C. sent a letter to athletic organizations throughout the country inviting them to send delegates to a meeting on October 1, 1887, to discuss the formation of an association to replace the NAAAA. The so-called National Association had failed, they said; it only represented the New York City area. The new association, which the New York A.C. proposed, would be broader in scope, more liberal to clubs at a distance from the city, more far-reaching in its purposes, and more general in its encouragement of amateur athletics than the NAAAA had been.

The meeting attracted delegates from the New York and New Jersey area, Philadelphia, Delaware, Washington, D.C., and Detroit. Letters of support were received from the Pullman A.C. and the Chicago A.A. From this meeting emerged a new organization with W. H. McMillan of the Schuylkill Navy A.C. of Philadelphia as its chairman. A committee was appointed to draft a constitution and by-laws.

The formal organization of the Amateur Athletic Union was completed on January 21, 1888. Mr. McMillan reported that he had taken a trip through the West and had found a large club in Detroit, three large stone clubs in Chicago, three in Milwaukee, two in St. Louis, and clubs in Atchison, Topeka, St. Joseph, and in other cities. Every where he traveled, he reported, club members were anxious that such an organization as the Amateur Athletic Union should be organized.

McMillan was elected president; T. W. Eddy, Detroit A.C., vice-president; and Otto Ruhl, New York A.C., secretary. The secretary was instructed to write to the NAAAA to inform that group that the A.A.U. felt it inexpedient to hold any conference with it.

In March the Amateur Athletic Union published its constitution and by-laws. An amateur was defined as "One who has not entered in an open competition; or for either a stake, public or admission money or entrance fee; or un-

der a fictitious name; or has not competed with or against a professional for any prize or where admission fee is charged; or who has not instructed, pursued, or assisted in the pursuit of athletic exercises as a means of livelihood, or for gain or any emolument; or whose membership in any athletic club of any kind was not brought about or does not continue because of any mutual understanding, express or implied,

Pole vaulting, sometimes called pole jumping, was performed both for height and for distance. Some of the early winning efforts are today exceeded by jumpers without poles.

whereby his becoming or continuing a member of such club would be of any pecuniary benefit to him whatever, direct or indirect, and who shall in other and all respects, conform to the rules and regulations of this organization."

The executive committee of the NAAAA in retaliation attempted to pass a rule that would enable it to expell or discipline a member who joined the A.A.U. The measure failed to gain sufficient support for adoption.

Since the NAAAA was dominated by the Manhattan A.C., and the A.A.U. was essentially the creation of the New York A.C., the conflict between the AAU and the NAAAA became a contest between these two clubs. The newly formed AAU found widespread support, while the NAAAA saw its ranks dwindle away, with its only ally outside of the New York City area being the Missouri A.A.C.

When the AAU announced that it had selected Detroit as the site of the national championships, the NAAAA countered with the announcement that it would hold the western championships at St. Louis under the direction of the Missouri A.A.C. on September 9, 1888, ten days before the AAU meet.

The AAU came back with the adoption of a resolution that any athlete competing in games not held under AAU rules would be barred from competition in any games held under AAU sanction. Specifically named were the NAAAA and Missouri A.A.C. games.

An athlete wrote a letter to *The Spirit of the Times* to ask what would happen to him if he were to complete in the NAAAA championships. He was promptly informed that he would be disqualified from AAU competition. "All members of the Manhattan A.C. who compete October 6 will by that act be practically retired from active athletic sport, as they will not be allowed to enter any games save their own," responded *The Spirit of the Times*. Because this newspaper's managing editor was William B. Curtis, one of the founders of the New York A.C., it served as the voice of the New York A.C. and the AAU.

In order that its athletes might complete in the AAU national championships at Detroit on September 19, the Manhattan A.C. had postponed the dates of the NAAAA title meet. At Detroit, Manhattan A.C. athletes scored 61 points to lead the New York A.C., which had 41 points; but the Manhattan A.C. was not eligible to compete for team honors, since it

---

The tug of war remained as one of the principal events in inter-collegiate athletic meets for many years. In its final refinement it was a most strenuous test of physical strength.

THE TUG OF WAR.

did not hold membership in the AAU. Fred Westing of the Manhattans won both the 100 and 220. Conneff was upset in the mile which was won by George Gibbs of the Toronto A.C. in 4:27⅕; but he came back to outlast Ed Carter of the New York A.C. in the five-mile race in 26:46⅗. George Tracy of the Wanderers A.C. of Halifax, Nova Scotia, won the 880 in 2:02⅕.

The Manhattan A.C. athletes through participation in meets which were not held under AAU rules gradually found themselves out of the competition. Gus Sachs, the wealthy patron of the Manhattan A.C., pleaded for an end to the "athletic war," but to no avail. The conflict only grew more bitter.

The AAU indoor handicap meeting held in Madison Square Garden on January 19, 1889, was called the most successful meet ever held. The attendance was unprecedented; it was a sell-out; 1,500 people had to be turned away.

The "athletic war" raged with such fury that the English newspapers were both puzzled and alarmed. One wrote, "The athletic community of the United States is, as our readers are doubtless aware, torn by a lamentable faction. Two rival organizations dispute the control of amateur athletics with such acrimony that the arguments of their advocates are obscured by their invectives, and it is almost impossible for an outsider to discover whether there be any real question at issue between them."

Another English newspaper commented, "The rivalry between the great clubs of the United States has produced an unhealthy competition which cannot but cast doubt upon the right of certain of their athletes to pass as amateurs. From the charges which they have made against one another in the heat of their strife, it would appear that they are in the habit of seducing away from each other's members by offers of employment; and there is something more than a suspicion that the men who have in the last two or three years left our shores to grace the sports of certain New York clubs have yielded to solicitations of this kind."

The Inter-Collegiate Athletic Association had earlier formed something of an alliance with the NAAAA and had adopted the rules of that

organization for its contests. Early in 1889 the University of Pennsylvania held a program of games under the rules of the ICAA. Since these rules were the same as those of the NAAAA, the AAU declared that all athletes who had competed in the Penn games were henceforth to be barred from AAU competition. In order to forestall further unpleasant episodes of this kind, the ICAA representa-

Luther Cary started his career as a sprinter at Oberlin College in Ohio. When he demonstrated his speed and ability, he was lured away to Princeton University, where he established new records in the dashes.

157

tives met in New York City and voted to withdraw from the NAAAA. The ICAA did not join the AAU. The group decided to remain independent, at least for the time being.

The daily press began to call for an end to the "athletic war" and suggested a compromise. Otto Ruhl, secretary of the AAU, responded that no compromise was necessary. He said that if the Manhattan A.C., or any other clubs, wished to apply for membership in the AAU, "they will be received in the spirit and manner befitting the dignity of the Union." He added that the AAU would be happy to talk with the Manhattan A.C., but not with the NAAAA. The AAU does not recognize any other national body, since it is the national body, he emphatically pointed out.

A. G. Mills, recently elected to the board of governors of the New York A.C., and a member of the board of managers of the AAU, finally was instrumental in bringing an end to the "athletic war." Mills, in writing a business letter to Walton Storm, president of the Manhattan Club, added a personal note to the end of the letter, expressing the hope that the strife would soon end. Storm responded to Mills' postscript with the suggestion that they get together to discuss the matter informally. Out of this discussion developed an armistice which led to peace. The National Association of Amateur Athletes of America was disbanded; and the Manhattan A.C. applied for and was granted membership in the AAU, along with the other four clubs which had tied their fortunes to the Manhattan A.C. The Amateur Athletic Union then granted amnesty to all athletes who had competed in games which were not sanctioned by the Union.

On September 14, 1889, 2,500 people, in spite of bad weather, attended the AAU championships at Travers Island, where the new track and summer home of the New York A.C. had been constructed. This was truly a national meet. A young man named John Owen of the Detroit Athletic Club upset the veteran Westing of the Manhattan A.C. in the 100 and 220. Another Detroit A.C. member, R. A. Ward, who also ran for Hillsdale College in Michigan, won the half-mile title in 2:06⅕. A. B. George won an easy mile in 4:36; and Tommy Con-

C. A. J. Queckberner, 5 feet 8½ inches tall, and 210 pounds in weight, was regarded as the strong man of the New York Athletic Club, winning numerous titles and contests in throwing the 56-pound weight and serving as a member of the tug-of-war team.

W. J. M. Barry, an Irish import, was 6 feet 4 inches in height and weighed 236 pounds. He excelled at throwing the 16-pound hammer and the weights.

neff took the five-mile to help the Manhattan A.C. pile up a total of 46 points for the team title. The New York A.C. finished second with 30 points, barely nosing out the Staten Island A.C. with 29 points. Malcolm Ford, having been re-instated as an amateur before the demise of the NAAAA, was now competing for the Staten Islanders.

The performances of the Detroit and Chicago athletes showed that the objectives of the AAU to promote athletics beyond the bounds of the New York City area were being achieved. The western AAU championships were held at Detroit before 3,000 spectators on June 15, 1889. Much of the credit for the growth and expansion of the AAU belonged to President McMillan, who spent much time on the road promoting the organization. His travels took him to the far West and south to New Orleans.

The expansion of the AAU brought about the need for organizational changes. Originally the Union was an association of clubs; but the number of clubs had increased so greatly by 1890 that the organization was becoming too unwieldy. A change in the constitution in 1890 made the AAU a union of associations rather than clubs. The clubs within a particular area would report to the association there. In turn the association would be represented on the national committees of the AAU. By this time there were flourishing groups from the New England Association of the AAU to the Pacific Coast Association. Even under this system some of the associations became so large that they had to be divided into smaller groups. Athletics were no longer the pastime of the wealthy, exclusive social clubs. Small neighborhood clubs housed in store buildings, barns, and humble quarters were sprouting up all over.

The end of the "athletic war" and the admission of the Manhattan Athletic Club to the AAU did not bring an end to the rivalry between that club and the New York Athletic Club. Both of these clubs competed vigorously to recruit outstanding collegians or club athletes from distant points. They hurled charges and counter charges at each other. *The Spirit of the Times*, which called itself "The American Gentleman's Newspaper," sometimes, nay, often, sounded like a New York A.C. house organ. In its columns one writer penned this barb: "Mr. G. A. Avery is a most enthusiastic seeker after athletic recruits for the Manhattan Athletic Club, and would propose Beelzebub himself if that individual could make records or win championships." In a page-long list in *The Spirit of the Times*, a roster of stars headlined "Lost, Strayed or Stolen Athletes" listed the Manhattan and New York A.C. stars who had been lured away from other clubs.

The Manhattan Athletic Club continued to dominate the track and field scene. At the AAU national championships held at Washington, D.C., in 1890, the Manhattan team scored 78 points to New York's 36; in 1891 at St. Louis, it was Manhattan 69, New York 61; in 1892 at Manhattan Field it was Manhattan 49½, New York, 43.

Shortly after the last meet, a notice was posted in the Manhattan Athletic Club house notifying all athletes that there would no longer be any free rooms, free meals, or free drinks for athletes. The club was in dire financial straits. It had over-extended itself in erecting a $900,000 building. Efforts to bring about a solution to the problems in 1893 failed; and the New York A.C. was left without a serious rival. In the 1893 championships held in conjunction with the Columbian Exposition at Chicago, without the presence of the Manhattan A.C. athletes, the New York A.C. scored 69 points, far ahead of second place Boston A.A., which scored 19 points.

Prior to the organization of the AAU, amateur competition outside of the seaboard states from Maryland to Massachusetts was limited to a few cities in the Midwest and on the Pacific Coast. The Eastern athletes were running the mile in the 4:30's and even lower; those in the hinterlands were running the distance in five minutes plus, and even six minutes on occasion. The Easterners were consistently running the 440 in 50 seconds or less; the others were lucky to break 60 seconds.

With the expansion of interest beyond the eastern metropolitan areas, new stars began to emerge. Within the next few years there would be champions and record-breakers from Detroit, Cleveland, St. Louis, Massachusetts, and Ohio. The goal of the founders of the AAU in

E. C. Carter, amateur long distance champion of England, was lured to America by the New York A.C. and under the club's colors became the long distance champion of the United States.

160

A. A. Jordan started out as a walker, turned to running, then tried the hurdles, at which event he succeeded in winning the national championship.

extending athletic competition to all parts of the country was meeting with success.

For the sophisticated New Yorker, the sports activities of the areas in which amateur competition was just gaining popularity had elements of humor. In commenting on the printed program distributed at the Boston A.A. games in February 1890, *The Spirit of the Times* expressed amusement at the fact that explanations of the events were included. "These points are well known to every schoolboy in New York, and their appearance on a metropolitan programme would be absurd. But the better people of Boston are just now learning to understand and appreciate reputable amateur athletic sport, and Boston Athletic Association will become a university of athletic education," wrote the *Spirit* reporter.

Professional track and field had for many years attracted a large following in the Boston area, particularly among the Irish and the Caledonians, but these meets would not have appealed to the "better people."

When the AAU meet was held in Washington, D.C., in 1890, *The Spirit of the Times* wrote, "The local newspapers have had little experience with athletes and athletics, and some of their statements are comical."

The attitude toward the New Yorkers from the other areas of the country indicated that there was resentment for the superior attitude assumed by the Easterners. When *The Spirit of the Times* reported in critical terms on the AAU meet held in Chicago in 1893, the editor commented, "The residents of Chicago, and the editors who speak for them, are prone to resent any criticism from the East." Resentment of New York's domination also was expressed in Cleveland, St. Louis, and San Francisco. The emergence of champions or contenders from the associations helped to assuage these feelings of resentment.

The sprinters made news in the 1890's. Charles Sherrill of Yale, who competed in the ICAA championships for five consecutive years then closed his career with the New York A.C., introduced the start from a crouching position. Prior to this, sprinters had started from an upright stance, leaning forward. Sherrill had equaled the collegiate records for the 100 and

220. At the Berkeley A.C. games in May 1890, he added his name to the list of those who shared the record of 10 seconds for the 100-yard dash, bringing the total to nine. In the same meet he set a new record for 150-yards, covering the distance in 14⅘ seconds.

Then out of the West there came a whole troup of sprinters. In the Western AAU championships held at Detroit on June 15, 1889, a tall, raw-boned youth, Luther Cary, from Oberlin College, running under the colors of the Chicago A.C., won the 100-yard dash in 10 seconds, the 220 in 22⅕ seconds, and the 440 in 53⅗ seconds. At the national AAU championships in September of the same year, John Owen of the Detroit Athletic Club surprised the Easterners by taking both the 100-yard dash and the 220. In June 1890 still another premier sprinter emerged in the Western AAU meet when Harry Jewett of Notre Dame University and the Detroit A.C. nosed out John Owen in the 100-yard dash; but Owen came back to take both the 220 and the 440.

In October 1890 the AAU national championships were held in Washington, D.C. Luther Cary, now running for Princeton and the Manhattan A.C., was scheduled to run against John Owen in the dashes. At the gun Cary got off to a slow start but soon drew abreast of John Owen. Down the stretch they pounded neck and neck. At the tape Owen lunged forward to win by a scant nine inches in a record-setting 9⅘ seconds, thus becoming the first American amateur to break 10 seconds for the 100.

A week later Luther Cary was timed in 9½ seconds for the 100 in a meet at Princeton. The AAU records committee declined approval of Cary's time, and at the same meeting they placed the stamp of approval on Owen's record. The Manhattan A.C. supporters, indignant at the decision of the AAU committee, accused the members of being prejudiced against Cary. If he had been a New York A.C. runner, the record would have been approved, they claimed.

At the Washington meet, another Detroit A.C. member, F. T. Ducharme, won the 120-yard and 220-yard hurdle races. The Easterners were discovering that there were athletes beyond the Alleghenies.

A year later Luther Cary at the Intercollegiate Athletic Association championships in New York City won the 100 in 10 seconds and set a new amateur record of 21-4/5 seconds in the 220. He followed this with a tour of England, where he won high praise for his speed.

A. S. VOSBURGH, COLUMBIA
Half-Mile, 1.59½

ERNEST S. RAMSDELL, PRINCETON
Running Broad Jump, 22 6

HENRY L. WILLIAMS, YALE
120-yard Hurdle, 15-4/5
World's Record

In the Central AAU games held at Detroit on July 4, 1891, Harry Jewett, the Notre Dame speedster won the 100 in 10 seconds flat and the 220 in 22 seconds. He toed the mark against Luther Cary in the Canadian championships on September 26, running second to the Princeton sprinter by one foot but came back to win by a wide margin in the 220. Cary and Jewett met again in the AAU championships a week later at St. Louis. Cary won both dashes easily. A year later it was Jewett's turn as he beat Cary in the 100 in 10 seconds and won the 220 in 21-4/5 seconds to equal Cary's record.

In the following year, 1893, a young law student from Western Reserve University running for the Cleveland A.C., C. W. Stage, won the 100 and 220 in the AAU championships held at Chicago. Earlier in the year at Cleveland, Stage had been timed in 9-4/5 seconds for the 100-yard dash, but the AAU committee on records, ever skeptical of records achieved beyond the mountains, did not recognize the time.

T. I. Lee, New York A.C. star, was the winner of the national titles in sprinting in 1894, but his reign was brief. A handsome young athlete from Georgetown University had begun to win notice for his extra-ordinary speed. Bernard J. Wefers was soon wearing the winged foot of the New York A.C. and for the next few years would not only dominate the shorter distances but would establish new marks in most of them. In the AAU championships at Manhattan Field in 1895 he won the 100 in 10 seconds and the 220 in 21⅕ seconds. A week later he tied the record for the 100-yard dash, running it in 9⅘ seconds and set a new record in the 220 in 21⅘ secoinds. In 1896 and 1897 he continued to win the 100 and 220 in national competition, being upset only once, in the 220 when he finished second in slow time to J. A. Cofelt of Princeton in the ICAA meet in 1897. He made up for his loss by coming back in the AAU championships to win both sprints and run the winning anchor leg of 440 yards in the mile relay. *Outing* magazine cited him as "the hero of the day," and said that his performance had "never been equaled in actual merit." Re-writing the record book at all of the odd distances up to 300 yards, Wefers became known as "the fastest human in the world." William B. Curtis wrote, "We never before had such a sprinter as B. J. Wefers."

As Bernie Wefers' career drew to an end, two sprinters from the Midwest, J. H. Rush of Grinnell College in Iowa and J. H. Maybury,

E. D. RYDER, YALE
Pole Vault, 10 7½

W. B. WRIGHT, JUN., YALE
Half-Mile, 1.59-1/5

JAMES P. LEE, HARVARD
220-yard Hurdles, 24-4/5
World's Record

University of Wisconsin, became the dominant sprinters. They would soon be replaced by Arthur Duffey, however, who won the 100 at the AAU meet in 1889, and would ere long own the 100-yard record. In 1899 he was running for the East Boston A.A.; but he would soon be en route to Georgetown University to take over Bernie Wefer's mantle of "world's fastest human." His story, however, belongs to another century.

The career of Tommy Conneff, the young Irish lad imported by the Manhattan A.C. in 1888, merits notice. Discovered in Ireland when at the age of nineteen he defeated the New York A.C. ace Ed Carter in the Irish championships, Conneff competed as an amateur for the Manhattan A.C., Holy Cross Lyceum, New York A.C., and Holy Cross College.

For the next few years after his arrival in the United States, Conneff dominated the distance runners, establishing a new American amateur record for the mile at 4:21⅝. At the AAU championships in 1892, it seemed that his career had come to a close, he finished fourth behind George Orton of the Toronto Lacrosse Club, who won the mile in 4:27-4/5. Conneff, fading at the finish, was "a shadow of his former self," according to *The Spirit of the Times*.

When the Manhattan A.C. closed its doors and dismissed its athletes, Conneff ran for the Holy Cross Lyceum A.A., winning a few races, one of which was a record-setting 4:17⅛ mile, then he announced his retirement from running. When the New York A.C. was preparing for its meet with the visiting English team in 1895, Conneff was persuaded to come out of retirement to wear the winged foot. On August 28, 1895, he demonstrated that he was not all done by setting a new world's amateur record for the mile which he won in 4:15-3/5 seconds. At the international meet he won the mile in 4:18½. Every one there thought that he could have run much faster, but he was saving himself for the three-mile which he won in 15:36-1/5. Shortly after this, he turned professional and ran a few races in the United States and England without much success.

A number of Canadian athletes were enticed into competing for the New York A.C. during this period. After George Orton won the AAU title in 1892 while competing for the Toronto Lacrosse Club, he was soon competing as a student for the University of Pennsylvania and wearing the winged foot in non-collegiate competition. Although Orton failed to match Conneff's fast times for the mile, he was consistent

HERBERT MAPES, COLUMBIA
120-yard Hurdles, 16-1/5

C. O. WELLS, AMHERST
Mile Run, 4.29-4/5

GEORGE B. SHATTUCK, AMHERST
Quarter-mile, 49½

in his efforts in winning the AAU mile championships in 1892, 1893, 1894, 1895, 1896, and coming back to close out the century with still another AAU mile title in 1900. His best recorded time for the mile was his inter-collegiate record of 4:23⅘. In 1897 he dropped out of the mile but won the steeplechase. Henceforth this was his event which he won regularly, culminating with a victory in it in the 1900 Olympics.

George Gray, Coldwater, Ontario, was only 19 years old when he won his first championship title. Weighing less than 160 pounds and standing five feet nine inches tall, young Gray provided a startling contrast to his opponents in the shot-put who were all tall and weighed 225 to 250 pounds. In spite of the difference in size, Gray was able to humble his opponents by tossing the 16-pound shot 41 feet five and a half inches. Under the colors of the New York A.C. he won the national championship in the shot-put every year from 1887 through 1896, missing only 1895 when he did not compete. However, a month later he won the event at the international match, tossing the iron ball a foot and a half farther than Hickok of Yale had done in winning the AAU title. Hickok was second to Gray on this occasion. Gray had

raised the shot-put record to 47 feet during his tenure as champion.

The 1890's witnessed a succession of champions and record-breakers in nearly all events, Maxie Long in the 440; T. E. Burke, 440; Charles Kilpatrick, 880; Mike Sweeney, high jump; Ray Ewry, standing jumps; Al Kraenzlein, hurdles and running broad jump; and James Mitchell, weight events.

The international competition which highlighted the 1880's amounted to barn-storming tours in which the fleet-footed L. E. Myers was the chief attraction. In 1891 the Manhattan A.C. sent a team of athletes to England. With the exception of Luther Cary, the Americans were vanquished by the English athletes. Luther Cary, however, was highly praised for his speed; and some 20,000 spectators turned out to see him run at Manchester. The traveling Americans managed to salvage some glory by crossing the channel to Paris, where they competed against the French amateurs, winning every event and prizes worth over $600. One athlete wrote home that French amateur athletic sport was in its infancy and their records were far below average performances in America and Britain.

LLOYD COLLIS, COLUMBIA
Mile Walk, 7.01-3/5

GEORGE FEARING, HARVARD
Running High Jump, 6 2¼

E. B. BLOSS, HARVARD
Running Hop, Step, and Jump, 44 11½

With the demise of the Manhattan A.C., the barn-storming tours appeared to be over. This, however, did not mean that international competition was at an end. In 1894 the Yale athletes traveled to England for a dual meet with the Oxford men. Oxford won 5½ first places to Yale's 3½.

It may be that the Oxford-Yale meet stimulated the idea of a dual meet between the London A.C. and the New York A.C. At any rate, the New Yorkers in December 1894 extended a formal invitation to the Londoners to cross the Atlantic in the summer of 1895 to compete for honors. After some exchange of correspondence to settle points of difference, the London A.C. accepted the invitation.

By January 1895, it was apparent that the contest was to be more than just a trial between two clubs. The London A.C. was given permission to strengthen its team by recruiting members from other clubs, and the New York A.C. petitioned the AAU to suspend certain rules in order to permit the club to do likewise. Obviously, the meet was going to be truly an international meet—England vs. United States. Each team was to have two men in each event; only first places would count in the scoring.

Throughout the year the sporting press gave much attention to the meet. The build-up was tremendous, both in this country and abroad. The Britishers thought that the American athletes were highly over-rated and that their records were grossly exaggerated. The Americans in turn were out to show the English that they no longer dominated the sport.

The New York A.C. threw out a net to bring into its club the top athletes of the nation, although most of these were already on the team. Bernie Wefers, the Georgetown University sprinter, who had represented a club from his hometown in Lawrence, Massachusetts, would represent the New Yorkers in the 100 and 220. John V. Crum, of the University of Iowa, who had won the dashes in the ICAA championships in June 1895, was also recruited. Thomas E. Burke, Boston A.A. and Harvard, would run the 440; and Tommy Conneff was brought out of retirement for the mile and three mile runs. Mike Sweeney, who held the world's record in the high jump, was recruited from the Xavier A.A. In all, the New York A.C. added six athletes to its roster of stars. Some of the 18 original New York A.C. stars were also collegians.

The crowd which assembled for the meet at

VICTOR MAPES, COLUMBIA
Running Broad Jump, 22 11¼

R. S. HALE, HARVARD
Mile Walk, 6.59-4/5

J. R. FINLAY, HARVARD
Hammer, 108 5

Manhattan Field on September 21, 1895, was the greatest ever to pay to witness a track meet in the United States. More than 9,000 spectators walked through the turnstiles. Before the day was over, everyone agreed that all had received their money's worth.

The Americans won every one of the 11 events on the program and demonstrated conclusively that the times and distances which had hitherto been reported were not exaggerations. Bernie Wefers won the 100 in the record-equaling time of 9⅘ seconds and set a new world's record of 21⅗ seconds in the 220. The Bostonian Burke won the 440 in 49 seconds. Charles Kilpatrick, the Union College star, won the half-mile in 1:53⅖ for a new world's record. Mike Sweeney bettered his own world record in the high jump, leaping 6 feet 5⅝ inches. Stephen Chase won the 120-yard hurdles in record time, 15⅗ seconds. Conneff won the mile and three

mile races; Elwood Bloss, the broad jump; James Mitchell, the hammer throw; and George Gray, the shot-put. In six of the events the Americans also took second place honors.

It was a spectacular victory for the Americans. For the first time in the history of athletics, the Americans were no longer second to the British.

The English athletes received high praise for their efforts and sportsmanship. "The behavior of the losing team during and after the match might well make any man proud to be an Englishman," commented *The Spirit of the Times*. "The Englishmen competed like men and lost like gentlemen, and their behavior must be considered a magnificent specimen of

The crowds at the inter-collegiate track championships were enthusiastic rooters for their college heroes.

genuine British sportsmanship," wrote the reporter for *Outing* magazine.

The same reaction to defeat was not shown by the English press. Wild accusations of professionalism and unsportsmanlike conduct were hurled at the American athletes. For months after the meet, through to the end of the year, the English sports writers shed bitter tears over the humiliating defeat, accusing the Americans of gross deception in putting professional athletes against their amateurs.

Efforts to arrange a return meeting on English soil failed. In the London sports journal, *Land and Water*, it was reported, "The feelings of the majority of the London A.C. committee are certainly against such a contest until the American amateur is a person who would pass muster under the A.A.C. laws in England, which at present he certainly is not."

Seven thousand spectators gathered at Manhattan Field on October 5, 1895, to watch the Yale University athletes contend with the visiting Cambridge University team. Some of the participants in the meet had taken part in the previous international meet; but on this occasion the British were treated more gently. Yale won six of the nine events on the schedule. The Cambridge winners of the 880 and the mile were afforded some consolation in this meet, since the same runners had been outdistanced while competing for the London A.C. against the New York A.C.

A new aspect of international competition was added in 1896 with the introduction of the Olympic Games, which were held at Athens, Greece, in April. Little notice was paid to the games in the United States. The New York A.C. was either completely unaware of them, or they chose to ignore them. Professor William M. Sloan, the historian, had tried to promote interest in the games but had failed to attract much notice. From the Boston Athletic Association, a small group of athletes were sent. One James B. Connolly, a student at Harvard, requested permission to take time off to go but was denied leave. He decided to go anyway and thus terminated his career at Harvard. From Princeton Robert S. Garrett, captain of the track team, decided to go on his own.

The games were rather informally organized but attracted athletes from England, France, Germany, Denmark, Hungary, Switzerland, and the United States.

In the track and field program the Americans won nine of the twelve events on the program. Tom Burke won the 100-metre dash in 12 seconds and the 400 metres in 54⅕ seconds. Tom Curtis won the 110-metre hurdles; W. T. Hoyt, the pole vault; Ellery Clark, the broad jump and high jump; Robert Garrett, the shot-put and discus throw; and James Connolly, the Harvard truant, won the hop, step and jump.

E. H. Flack, an Australian representing England, won both the 800 and 1,500 metre races. A Greek Shepherd, Spiridon Louis, won the marathon race, a distance of about 25 miles, so named because it was run over the approximate route followed by the legendary Pheiddippides in carrying the news of the victory at Marathon to Athens.

With the introduction of the marathon race in the Olympic Games, a new event was added to athletics. Long distance running as an amateur sport had all but disappeared in the 1890's. Although the record books continued to carry amateur records for distances up to 150 miles, the last American amateur records at such distances were made by one J. Saunders in 1882. The ten mile championship was the longest running race on the AAU schedule until the Boston Athletic Association on April 19, 1897, held the first of its famous marathon races.

Starting from the box mill at Ashland, about twenty-five miles west of Boston, the runners finished the race with a lap around the Burlington Oval. "The weather was fine, the roads dry and loose, and the wind, fresh behind the runners, kept the air well-filled with dust," recorded one reporter. The first winner was J. J. McDermott, Pastime A.C., New York, in 2 hours 55 minutes 10 seconds.

Thus, the Boston Marathon, one of the greatest athletic contests in the world, was born. The present distance of 26 miles 385 yards was not established until 1908, when the Olympic Games were held in London. In order to amuse the royal grandchildren, the start of the race was set for the lawn in front of Windsor Castle. The distance from this point to the finish line

169

in the stadium was exactly 26 miles 385 yards; and that has become the official marathon distance.

After Yale and Harvard had made up after a spat in 1895 and 1896, they joined forces to form a track team for a meet with the combined teams of Oxford and Cambridge. The Americans lost this meet.

When the Olympic Games of 1900 were held in Paris, there was a more enthusiastic response in the United States than the earlier Olympiad had generated. The games were billed as the "International Championships," with little reference to the Olympic title. Indeed, some of the New York A.C. athletes who competed claimed that they were unaware that they were competing in the Olympics. There was no official United States team. Colleges and university athletic associations sent athletes over to compete; and the New York A.C. recruited a team of stars. There were also some individual entries. In all, more than fifty athletes were reported in the American contingent.

Among the New York A.C. athletes was Alvin Kraenzlein, the University of Pennsylvania star, who in the 1899 AAU championships had won five medals, taking firsts in the 120 and 220-yard hurdles and running broad jump and seconds in the 100-yard dash and high jump. In the Paris games he won the 60-metre dash, the 110-metre hurdles, 200-metre hurdles, and

the running broad jump. His University of Pennsylvania teammate, J. W. B. Tewksbury, won the 200-metre dash and the 400-metre hurdles.

Ray Ewry, a tall, lithe engineering graduate of Purdue, transferred his allegiance from the Chicago A.A. to the New York A.C. He won three first place medals, in the standing high jump, the standing broad jump, and the standing hop, step and jump. Ewry would be around for three more Olympics and would win a total of ten gold medals in his specialties.

George Orton, the New York A.C. distance runner, took the 2,500-metre steeplechase; F. W. Jarvis, Princeton, won the 100-metre dash; Maxey Long, New York A.C., the 400 metres; I. K. Baxter, New York A.C., running high jump and pole vault; and Myer Prinstein, Syracuse University, the running hop, step and jump. In the weight events Americans Richard Sheldon won the shot-put and J. J. Flanagan won the hammer throw.

Of the track and field contests only five events went to other countries. Great Britain won the 800 and 1,500 metre runs and the 4,000 metre steeplechase. A Hungarian won the discus throw and a French runner finished first in the marathon. The results might have been even more heavily in favor of the Americans if some of the events had not been held on Sunday. Several American athletes declined to violate the sabbath by competing on that day.

AT THE COLUMBIA ATHLETIC CLUB GROUNDS.

The principal impulse for the expansion of inter-collegiate competition during the 1880's and 1890's was football. By the end of the 80's track and field athletics had been pushed into the background among college sports; yet colleges were providing the stars in track and the opportunities for competition. For a few decades after the turn of the century an expansion in the organization of small athletic clubs would provide an opportunity for competition for non-collegians, but in the main the stars in track and field, with the exception of distance running, would come from the colleges. A writer in *Outing* magazine following the 1900 Olympic Games declared, "Thus it becomes evident that without the support of the colleges, an international athletic meeting would be impossible, or any meeting so styled of such medi-ocre quality as to bring ridicule upon its projectors."

Initially athletic competition in colleges was controlled by students who formed their own associations. Gradually, as the intercollegiate competition expanded, the college and university administrations began to take measures to control the movement by appointing faculty committees to govern sports activities. In this matter of control, Harvard under Dudley Sargent took the lead, making proposals which they expected other institutions to adopt. Often the Harvard sponsored rules met opposition from other colleges, but gradually uniform controls and methods of administration were developed.

Yale University in 1893 adopted eligibility rules which banned from participation in col-

H. L. Mitchell was the Manhattan Athletic Club's leading half-miler following the retirement of L. E. Myers.

H. S. Youngs, Jr., Manhattan Athletic Club, was one of the fastest hurdlers of his time.

lege athletics anybody who had profited "pe-cuniarily" from athletics. The rules also required that an athlete be a candidate for a degree and attend classes at least eight hours per week. No athlete who had represented any other college for four years would be eligible for further participation. Finally, it was required that an athlete maintain a satisfactory academic record. Comparable rules were adopted by other institutions and would ultimately become requirements of the national association.

The Inter-Collegiate Athletic Association championship meet for 17 of its first 22 years was virtually a dual contest between Harvard and Yale. Although Columbia won three championship titles and Princeton one during the early years of the competition, Harvard enjoyed a winning streak of seven titles in succession before yielding to Yale. In all during the first 22 years, Harvard won 11 titles and Yale won 6. Their dominance of the games was finally broken by the University of Pennsylvania in 1897. Emerging in the 1890's as a track and field powerhouse, the University of Pennsylvania during this decade had started the famous program of relays which has enjoyed a long and distinguished history in American sports. Relay racing at this time was an innovation.

In 1897, after Yale and Harvard had made up their differences after the quarrel that had caused the two schools to break off athletic relations, *The Spirit of the Times* noted the declining sports fortunes of the schools in writing, "During their temporary estrangement Yale and Harvard had ample opportunity to learn several valuable truths. They might have discovered that there are in the United States other universities able to keep step with Yale and Harvard in all branches of athletic sport, and that a victory over Yale or Harvard is no longer synonymous with intercollegiate supremacy...."

The ICAA meet was essentially a meet for the athletes of Yale, Harvard, Columbia, Princeton, and Penn. Occasionally an athlete from one of the smaller colleges won an event as when Wells of Amherst set a new record of 4:29-4/5 in winning the mile in 1889. Charles

E. D. Lange, Manhattan Athletic Club, was amateur champion walker at the one-mile distance.

John Owen, Detroit Athletic Club sprinter, took the Easterners by surprise in winning the 100 and 220 at the National A.A.U. championships in 1889. A year later in defending his title, he became the first amateur to break 10 seconds in the 100-yard dash.

173

Kilpatrick of Union College surprised everyone by winning the half-mile in 1894, then went on to set a new world's record in the distance subsequently.

Such intrusions by athletes from other schools were tolerated by the Ivy Leaguers, as long as they were from the East. If they were from the West, it was a different story. When Frank Bonine of the University of Michigan decided to compete in the ICAA games and succeeded in winning the 100-yard dash, Wendell Baker of Harvard ran up to the judges screaming protests that Bonine had jumped the gun. When Bonine returned the following year to compete again, he was charged with being a professional. It had been learned by the Easterners that as a member of a volunteer fire company Bonine had competed with a hose cart team which had won a cash prize. In later years when Bonine was a physician in Niles, Michigan, and beyond the competitive stage, the AAU committee restored his amateur standing.

When John Crum of the University of Iowa came East to compete in the ICAA meet and won the 100 and 220 in record-tying times, his medals were held up until charges of professionalism could be heard. The charges were based upon the allegations that no Eastern athlete knew him personally, that he ran too well for an amateur, and that he had been seen talking to a professional. In his defense, it was pointed out that his father was a banker in Bedford, Iowa. The medals were finally awarded to him.

There is no disputing the fact that the Eastern athletes were in general far ahead of other

F. L. Lambrecht, Pastime A.C., won his first amateur championship in the hammer throw and shot put at the age of seventeen.

W. C. White competed in the sprints for the Manhattan Athletic Club.

174

collegians in their performances and records. While the Easterners were setting records in running and jumping, the mile was being won in 5:15 at the University of Wisconsin, the 220 in 30 seconds, the 440 in 57 seconds, and the 100 in 13 seconds. A fat man's race was also included on the program. In other college meets the mile was run in over 6 minutes; and high jumpers failed to reach the five feet mark.

In other Midwestern meets the three-legged race, sack race, baseball throw, and football kicking were still parts of the program.

William Byrd Page, University of Pennsylvania, set a new record in the high jump and was promptly recruited by the Manhattan A.C., which rewarded him with a summer trip to England.

W. T. Macpherson, champion Australian sprinter, who visited California in 1894, wrote, "My honest opinion of Americans' capabilities as runners is that they cannot do themselves justice. They are brought up to eat too much and too highly—a bill-of-fare as long as a page of foolscap, and all spiced and highly flavored dishes. I feel quite alone eating my tenderloin and my fine cut off a joint. You seldom see milk or egg puddings; it is always pastry. Well, if American runners have been brought up on this food and still eat it, they will not have the necessary grit and energy and strength to sprint home successfully. . . ."

The Spirit of the Times lamented that it was too bad that the Australian had gained his first impression of American amateur athletes in the Far West. If he had ever visited the East, they asserted, he would have found a different story.

Before the decade of the nineties was over, inter-collegiate competition in the West and Midwest had improved considerably. In 1896 the University of California track team traveled east to vanquish the University of Illinois and Princeton in dual meets. The Californians also competed in the Western Inter-Collegiate championships at Chicago, scoring 35 points to second-place Michigan's 17.

Among the competing athletes in the ICAA championships held at the Berkeley Oval on May 26, 1894, were two Negro athletes, one from Harvard and one from Williams College. Their presence was enough to attract notice. *The Spirit of the Times* pointed out that the League of American Wheelmen banned Negroes from membership, commenting, "This would seem to teach that wheelmen are of a finer mould than collegians, but many people believe quite contrary."

Since the amateur movement in its early years was a class movement, the presence of Negroes among the athletes was not to be expected. In professional circles, however, Negroes competed, both as long distance runners and as sprinters.

Interscholastic track and field competition started with the private schools in the 1880's, often under the sponsorship of the private clubs. The Manhattan A.C. conducted an annual meet of this nature for the New York City area boys. In public schools an annual class day of competition among the boys within the schools gradually extended to rivalry with other schools. By the mid-nineties interscholastic competition was general throughout the country.

Outing magazine in May 1900 aired a complaint which would be echoed and re-echoed for many years. The magazine objected to the custom of alumni canvassing the prep schools for promising athletes. This practice had long been condemned by Harvard officials; yet in 1900 the Harvard football manager mailed a circular letter to high schools in an effort to lure athletes to Cambridge. Many an impoverished youth would now gain access to professions which would otherwise have been denied him. There would be competent lawyers, doctors, dentists, and engineers who would look back with fond memories to the running track or playing field which made their careers possible.

Maxwell Long, the Columbia University star, closed out the century by running the 440 in 47 seconds on a straightaway and in 47⅘ around the track. Of Long's 47-second performance, sports writers were unanimous in their judgment as expressed by one of them, "It will be many a day before the performance is equaled—not to say surpassed."

The quality of the performances of the collegians continued to improve throughout the last years of the century. During the 1880's the times and distances in the NAAAA meet exceeded in most cases those of the collegians. At the close of the century the situation was reversed. In the ICAA mile in 1899, Cregan of Princeton captured that event in 4:25⅕. In the AAU meet in 1900, the aging George Orton was able to win the mile with little opposition in 4:42⅖.

Track and field athletics had settled into the pattern which would continue. With the ex-

ception of long distance running, it would be essentially a college sport. At least, the champions and record-breakers would henceforth come from the colleges, with few exceptions.

Imported from Ireland by the Manhattan A.C., Tommy Conneff won many titles as an amateur at distances of from one mile to five. He ended his amateur career in a blaze of glory when he set a world amateur mark of 4:15-3/5.

PICTURE CREDITS

Harper's Weekly: pages 8, 9, 18, 68, 73, 80, 81, 95, 106-7, 131, 137, 141, 143, 147, 149, 150, 151, 154, 155, 156, 157, 158, 159, 160, 161, 162, 163, 164, 165, 166, 167, 169, 170, 171, 172, 174, 175. *National Police Gazette:* pages 65, 66, 69, 104, 105, 108, 109, 110, 112, 113, 114, 117, 118, 119, 121, 123, 125, 132, 133. *New York Clipper:* pages 18, 21, 27, 35, 36, 39, 42, 43, 46, 47, 48, 49, 176. Collection of Paul Mellon: page 31. American Antiquarian Society: pages 15, 102. Old Print Shop: page 55. Historical Society of Michigan: page 173. Rochester Museum and Science Center: page 60. Author's Collection: frontispiece, pages 13, 36, 71, 86, 87, 99, 122, 134.